Titles in The Metropolitan Opera Classics Library
DER ROSENKAVALIER
LA BOHÈME
LA TRAVIATA

La Traviata

The Metropolitan Opera Classics Library

GIUSEPPE VERDI

LIBRETTO BY
FRANCESCO MARIA PIAVE

STORY ADAPTATION BY
MARY McCARTHY

INTRODUCTION BY
GARY SCHMIDGALL

GENERAL EDITOR
ROBERT SUSSMAN STEWART

LITTLE, BROWN AND COMPANY BOSTON TORONTO

FIRST EDITION

"La Traviata" Copyright © 1983 by Mary McCarthy

English translation of *La Traviata* libretto from *Seven Verdi Librettos.* Copyright © 1966 by William Weaver. Reprinted by permission of Doubleday & Company, Inc.

"The Lady of the Camellias" by Alexandre Dumas *fils,* edited by James L. Smith. Copyright © 1976 by J. M. Dent and Sons Ltd. Reprinted by permission.

LIBRARY OF CONGRESS CATALOGING IN PUBLICATION DATA

Giuseppe Verdi, La traviata.

(The Metropolitan Opera classics library)
Discography: p. 194
Contents: Introduction : La traviata, the autobiographical Verdi / by Gary Schmidgall — The music of La traviata / David Hamilton — La traviata / by Mary McCarthy — [etc.]
   1. Verdi, Giuseppe, 1813–1901. Traviata.   2. Operas — Librettos.   I. Schmidgall, Gary, 1945– II. Piave, Francesco Maria, 1810–1876.   III. McCarthy, Mary, 1912–   . Traviata. 1983.   IV. Dumas, Alexandre, 1824–1895. Dame aux camélias (Play). English. 1983.   V. Verdi, Giuseppe, 1813–1901. Traviata. Libretto. English & Italian. 1983.
VI. Title: Traviata.   VII. Series.
ML410.V4G58   1983   782.1'092'4   83-13526
ISBN 0-316-56842-2
ISBN 0-316-56843-0 (pbk.)

MV

Published simultaneously in Canada
by Little, Brown & Company (Canada) Limited

PRINTED IN THE UNITED STATES OF AMERICA

FOREWORD

The Metropolitan Opera Classics Library, which honors the Metropolitan's centennial, was born out of the often expressed idea that opera is, at one and the same time, music *and* drama. Those familiar with the managing of opera houses know from hard-won experience that few, if any, operas every earn a permanent place in the repertory if they do not bring "good stories" to their music. Indeed, the majority of our most beloved operas have been inspired by the narratives of either ancient myth or legend, or of novels, or of classical comedies and great tragedies.

Yet the historical fact that opera is, essentially, European in its tradition has meant that, for much of the English-speaking world, the use in opera of these literary treasures in languages other than our own narrows rather than expands their immediacy and their hold over us. We are all aware of having to "read up" on the story of an opera before attending a performance — or, drearier still, of having to sit through three or four acts without ever really knowing who is saying what to whom. Far too often the drama is lost completely, and the whole opera itself becomes clouded over, dusty like a museum piece, truly "foreign."

It is with this in mind that The Metropolitan Opera Classics Library has asked some of the most renowned writers of our time to retell the stories of operas in their own way, to bring the characters and the action to life. This is, of course, in no way to take away from, or diminish, the central role of music in opera; but rather to enrich or enhance it, so that, ultimately, the marriage of music and drama will be fulfilled, and opera will become more clear and more available — to more people.

Making opera more available to more people is not a new task for us here at the Metropolitan Opera. Over forty years ago, we added millions of listeners to our regular audiences when we introduced the Texaco Saturday radio broadcasts. Half a decade ago, even more millions were able to join us when we inaugurated our "Live From the Met" telecasts. Now, as we move into our second century, we hope to find still others — in schools, in libraries, and in the thousands of cities and towns and villages across America wherever books are read and loved. For surely the more opera is understood as literature, the more opera will be appreciated, both in performance and for its undoubtedly glorious music.

ANTHONY A. BLISS
GENERAL MANAGER
METROPOLITAN OPERA

ACKNOWLEDGMENTS

I am grateful to many members of the staff of the Metropolitan Opera for their continued contribution to *The Metropolitan Opera Classics Library*. I must first thank Michael Bronson, Director of the Media Department, for the time and the help he has given.

I would also like to thank Clemente D'Alessio in the Media Department for his support and Sue Breger for her attention to details, too numerous to list here.

Robert Tuggle, Director of the Metropolitan Opera Archives, has again on numerous occasions offered sound, scholarly advice and has provided invaluable assistance with the task of gathering research material and historical illustrations and photographs. Others who have been helpful in the selection of photographs are Nina Keller in the Press and Public Relations Department; James Heffernan, the Metropolitan's Official Photographer; Winnie Klotz, Assistant to the Official Photographer; and Clarie Freimann, Presentations Coordinator of the Education Department at the Metropolitan Opera Guild.

Special thanks must go to Mrs. Dorle Soria for the material she has graciously made available from her private Verdi collection. I am also grateful to Francesca Franchi, Director of the Archives at the Royal Opera House in Covent Garden, for her assistance with archival material. I am indebted to Gerald Fitzgerald, Associate Editor of *Opera News*, for his work on the selection of color photographs. David M. Reuben, Director of the Met's Press and Public Relations Department, has again supported this project in innumerable ways. He has also read the entire manuscript. In addition, Jack Beeson, composer and MacDowell Professor of Music at Columbia University, has read the entire manuscript and has made useful suggestions.

My thanks to Deborah Jurkowitz, assistant editor at Little, Brown and Company, for overseeing the many stages in the preparation and the production of this volume. I must also acknowledge Barry Lippman of Little, Brown and Company for his continuing support of this series and for being a helpful editor.

— R.S.S.

CONTENTS

Oh, mysterious love,
Mysterious, aloof,
The heart's cross and delight.

(ALFREDO, ACT I)

INTRODUCTION

La Traviata

THE AUTOBIOGRAPHICAL VERDI

by

GARY SCHMIDGALL

LA TRAVIATA is the most frequently performed of Verdi's works for the lyric stage. I think it is also the most intriguing — intriguing because the work stands apart in various ways from the composer's twenty-seven other operas. To be sure, *La Traviata* richly displays all of the great Verdian characteristics: abundant melodic invention, admirable artistic economy, and compelling dramatic energy. And yet . . . something about this work makes it a special case. What is this something?

One is at first tempted to explain *La Traviata*'s unique place in the Verdi canon by pointing to the obvious ways it differs from the other operas. It is, for instance, one of those rare Verdian works in which there is no strong political or patriotic element in the plot. It is also the only opera set by Verdi in his own time — "about 1850" — and the only one that takes place entirely indoors. Abramo Basevi in 1859 described the special intimacy that results from this setting in his comment that "with *La Traviata* Verdi brought chamber music on the stage with real success." This work is also one of only two Verdi wrote (*Stiffelio* is the other) that can be said to address contemporary social issues: the explicit ones of being a "kept woman" and "living in sin" and the implicit ones of profligate decadence in the highest classes and the double standard that separates womankind into two categories, the sensual/fallen and the chaste/virginal. Nor does any other Verdi opera focus so powerfully and centrally upon the vocal and theatrical resources of a female character; a *Traviata* performance without a superlative singing actress in the title role is as dismal a prospect as *Hamlet* without a fine prince.

These observations surely contain part of the answer to our question, but I am inclined to think that the most convincing answer lies in yet one more remarkable aspect of the opera: the real-life story of how *La Traviata* came into being is the most colorful, psychologically complex, and autobiographically resonant of the composer's entire career. No Verdi opera, in other words, is based so squarely upon real life — or, more accurately, upon real lives. For the story of the opera is in fact the story of three people — Alphonsine Duplessis, Alexandre Dumas *fils*, Giuseppe Verdi himself — and a remarkable cast of supporting characters. Duplessis was the grand Parisian courtesan on whom the character of Violetta in the opera is ultimately based. The young Dumas fell passionately for her, established a liaison with her, then cut short the affair when she failed to devote herself to him. After her death a short time later, he turned her story into a very popular novel and, in due course, a play. Verdi saw the play while on a visit to Paris in 1852 and within a year had transformed it into *La Traviata*.

This is the simple story, but the reality was more complex, fascinating, sometimes even mysterious. I will undertake to sketch this story here, because we cannot possibly appreciate the full power and pathos of the opera without exploring the actual events and relationships from which it evolved. Seldom in the annals of opera have the realms of personal experience and artistic creation mingled so auspiciously and passionately. The place to begin is at the beginning, with the charismatically beautiful siren who came to be known, after her death, as "the lady of the camellias." First, though, it will be helpful to set out the two real-life and two imaginary *dramatis personae* that figure in the following narrative:

DUMAS	NOVEL/PLAY	OPERA	VERDI
Alexandre Dumas *fils*	Armand Duval	Alfredo Germont	Giuseppe Verdi
Alphonsine Duplessis	Marguerite Gautier	Violetta Valery	Giuseppina Strepponi
Alexandre Dumas *père*	Georges Duval	Giorgio Germont	Antonio Barezzi
Comte de Stackelberg	Duc de Mauriac	Baron Douphol	
Eugène Déjazet	Gaston Rieux	Gastone	
Clémence Prat	Prudence Duvernoy	Flora Bervoix	

*   *   *

So long as great international cities with vast accumulated wealth and a thick "upper crust" continue to exist — one thinks of London, Rome, Rio de Janeiro, New York City, and of course Paris — the story of Alphonsine Duplessis will never become dated. It is the story of the penurious but stunningly beautiful young girl or boy who gravitates to the big city and quickly becomes, for certain services rendered (sometimes mere presence), a part of *de luxe* society — a partaker of fine food, designer fashions, lavish town and country establishments, and . . . ennui. This heady, intoxicating life takes its toll, as life lived in the fast lane tends to do. Pursuing pleasure singlemindedly or being the object of such pursuit is a grueling and dehumanizing pastime and, whether with the aid of the nineteenth century's champagne and absinthe or the twentieth century's amphetamines and cocaine, frequently ends in early retirement from "the scene."

Such was the destiny of Duplessis, who took the name Marie when she arrived in Paris. In 1824 she was born into a Norman peasant family and worked as a seamstress before setting out, while still in her mid-teens, for the glittering capital. Within a short time she became a cynosure of the Parisian demimonde and a woman who could command the most lavish carriage, apartment, toilette, and entourage in return for her company. What was her attraction? The shrewdest description we have of her at the height of her appeal and in her downfall was penned by the bellelettrist Jules Janin for an edition of Dumas's novel version of *La Dame aux camélias*. Indeed, Dumas later praised this description: "Janin has told about Marie Duplessis all that could be told about her." Janin makes clear that a volatile mixture of contradictory traits, in addition to her undoubted beauty, made her captivating: "She was a woman who had an ingenuous look about her but was capable of deceptive gestures, one whose bearing could be both audacious and modest at the same time." As well, she was "a woman of spirit, taste, and good sense." She was well read (Dumas *père*, Cervantes, Scott, Rabelais, Molière, and Lamartine were in her library) and had something of a reputation as a free thinker. She apparently was also musical and could play barcarolles and waltzes with considerable feeling.

But it was in the enjoyment of physical comfort that she excelled: as tuberculosis consumed her life, so she nearly made conspicuous consumption an art form. She surrounded herself with Gobelins carpets, Buhl cabinets, Sèvres porcelain, Petitot enamels, and epicurean paintings by Boucher. "She liked that little, coquettish, graceful, elegant art, where even vice looks intelligent, and innocence appears nude; she liked . . . all that taste and luxury have invented for an effete society." No wonder the idle and moneyed cream of Parisian society were riveted by Duplessis: "She had carried the science of domestic comfort and self-adoration," Janin wrote, "to such a pitch that her linen, her dresses, the most trivial things connected with her with utterly consuming, for it was the dearest and most charming occupation of her life to enhance her own beauty."

Janin remained aloof, a keenly observant bystander to this appalling manifestation of wasted life and money in the palmy days of the early 1840s. But others found Marie's practice of her "science" irresistible — among them a young man precisely her age and the son of a hugely famous novelist and playwright, Alexandre Dumas (1802–1870). The younger Dumas (1824–1895) first saw Duplessis sitting in a box at a crowded Parisian theater and some time later, under similar circumstances, was introduced to her by his friend Eugène Déjazet. His ardent spirits caught flame. He pursued her and, no doubt to the amazement of many, soon succeeded in placing himself among the constellation of her lovers. He approached the affair with the most sanguine and idealistic notion — perfectly fitting for a boy barely twenty years old — of saving Duplessis from her immoral life and making an honest woman of her. He saw her, in the words of the novel, as a "courtesan whom a mere nothing would have turned into the most loving and purest of virgins." Unsurprisingly, the quick and miraculous change did not occur. The style to which Duplessis had become accustomed was far beyond the means of Dumas, and she refused to jeopardize her affluent life by devoting attention solely to him. After a period of humiliated suffering, Dumas finally broke with her in a letter that has since become famous:

My dear Marie,
I am not rich enough to love you as you would wish, and not poor enough to be loved as you would desire. So let us forget — you a name which should be almost indifferent to you, I a happiness that has become impossible for me. There is no need for me to tell you that I am sad, since you know already how much I love you. Adieu then. You have too much heart not to understand why I write you this letter, and too much intelligence not to be able to pardon me for it.

A thousand souvenirs, A.D.

Dumas then departed from Paris, not to return until some time after the death of Duplessis in 1847 at the age of twenty-three.

We should pause over the "tragedy" of the life of Marie Duplessis, even though it is profoundly different from the tragedies that Dumas and Verdi drew from her life. Dumas and Verdi focused their works upon a heroine who is faced with a clear and brutal choice between self-interest (i.e., a continued happy *solitude à deux* in the country with Armand/Alfredo) and the interest of another person (Armand's/Alfredo's "pure" and virginal sister — who cannot marry respectably while her brother is living with a woman out of wedlock). With extraordinary courage, the heroine chooses to sacrifice her own happiness. The tragedy of Marguerite and Violetta is, therefore, a deeply personal one. Their heartrending sacrifice and suffering are the result of conscious choice.

The demise of Duplessis was not so deliberate, and so her fate is more pathetic than tragic. The villain (there is no voice of propriety like the elder Germont's in her story) is society as a whole — "that city of perdition," Paris. Duplessis took no heroic stand; she took rather the line of least resistance and allowed herself to become a mere object, a *machine à plaisir*. "She abandoned herself without resistance," concluded Janin, "to the vortex which was swallowing her up." Her end was set not amid heartbreak and sacrifice but amid ennui and emptiness. In Janin's view Duplessis ended her career as an emotional mannequin: "Ennui was the great misfortune of her life. She had seen so many of her affections shattered, had been compelled by necessity to enter into ephemeral liaisons, to pass from one love to another . . . that she had become quite indifferent to all things."

Without Dumas's invention, in his novel, of a genuine tragic heroine, it is very doubtful that Verdi would have concerned himself with the story of Duplessis. For ennui is a nearly impossible trait to convey musically. Only one opera seems to have been able (some would say *barely* able) to make ennui stageworthy: Debussy's *Pelléas et Mélisande*. Opera thrives on passionate engagement, and the original lady of the camellias appears to have been one of the most brilliantly indifferent figures of her time.

Finally, Duplessis was as fragile as the white china shepherds and shepherdesses that caught her fancy. As Janin so well phrased it: "Alas, she also was a useless ornament, a fancy article, a friv-

olous plaything, broken at the first shock — the brilliant creation
of a moribund society, a bird of passage, a momentary dawn."
Paris treated her death with its usual cruel apathy: "Her death,"
Janin remembered, "produced a certain sensation and was talked
about for three days, which is a long time in this town so full of
refined passions and endless partying." The posthumous revenge
of Duplessis was slight but eloquent: she left the residue of her
estate to a niece in Normandy — on the condition that she never
go to Paris.

*   *   *

THE human events reflected in the pages of *La Traviata* become
even more evident when we turn our attention to the younger Dumas. He returned to Paris in 1847 to find Duplessis dead, her establishment dispersed, and her possessions auctioned away. He
chose to purge his mind of the courtesan and his affair with her
by turning life into art, and before the year was out he had written
the novel *La Dame aux camélias*. It was published in 1848, became
the rage of Paris, and served as the first success in a career that
stretched until his death. By 1849 he had worked out a dramatic
version of the story, though because of difficulties with the censor
it did not receive its premiere until 2 February 1852, at the
Vaudeville Theater.

In his novel Dumas succeeded in encompassing the sad, timeless
tale of Duplessis in a simple, highly focused plot with a tragic
raison d'être. To achieve this he reinvented Duplessis as a convincing heroine and, in a sense, invented his father — the father of his
own fictional alter ego, Armand Duval (the autobiographical reference of the initials was intentional). To understand how — perhaps even why — Dumas created Marguerite Gautier and the elder
Duval, we must consider the novelist's life and personality. And
this is impossible without first making the acquaintance of his as-
tonishing real-life father.

Those who are familiar with the stiff, dour father in Verdi's
opera will not be prepared for the father of Alexandre. Dumas
père was an utter opposite to the grim, proper emissary from Provence, Giorgio Germont. Everything about the faher was larger than
life: his vast girth, his enormous literary output (over three hundred
volumes in his collected works), and his Don Juan–style philan-
dering. The brothers Goncourt captured his style and physique in
a sketch made when *père* was about sixty:

A kind of giant with a negro's hair now turning pepper and salt, the small eye of a hippopotamus, bright, shrewd, and for ever on the watch even when the lids are half closed, and all this in an enormous face the features of which are vaguely hemispherical, like those the caricaturists give when they portray the moon with human characteristics. There is something about him very hard to define, something of a barker at a fair, something of a merchant from the *Arabian Nights*. He is never at a loss for words. . . . And always, always, always he talks about himself, with the vanity of a great child.

Father and son could not have been more dissimilar: the former was gregarious, optimistic, the soul of wit, and a notoriously spendthrift bon vivant. The latter was solitary, pessimistic by nature, reticent, practical, and serious-minded. The author of *The Three Musketeers* once wrote to his son, "When one bears the name of Dumas, one lives on a grand scale; one dines at the Café de Paris, and one never says no to pleasure." He was in effect recommending the Parisian life of Duplessis, Marguerite, and Violetta (who echoes Dumas *père* in her Act I toast: "All is folly in the world that isn't pleasure"). The son never took his father's advice, though they maintained, with occasional lapses, an affectionate relationship. Instead, the son became over the years curiously addicted to morality and not a little misogynistic. Remarkably, he came more and more to resemble the ruthless father of *La Dame aux camélias* and *La Traviata*. As André Maurois concludes in his fine biography of the Dumas family, "Dumas *fils* had no liking for women: some he pitied, on others he sat in judgement." Strange transmutation! That the young man infatuated by the reigning courtesan of Paris should become a prudish, moralizing chauvinist in his later years.

Or not strange at all, if we look more closely at life in the Dumas household. An excellent introduction to this fascinating family circle lies in the father's description of how he learned of his son's affair with Duplessis. The event occurred at the Théâtre-Français:

As I was going down one of the passages, the door of a box opened. I felt someone catch hold of my coat-tails. I turned round. It was Alexandre.

"So it's you, is it? Good evening, dear boy."

"Come in here for a moment, father."

"You're not alone."

"All the more reason. Shut your eyes, put your head through the chink in the door. Don't be afraid, nothing unpleasant is going to happen to you."

True enough. Scarcely had I shut my eyes, scarcely had I put my head through the door, than I felt upon my mouth the pressure of two trembling, feverish, burning lips. I opened my eyes. An adorable young woman of twenty, or twenty-two, was alone there with Alexandre, and had just bestowed upon me that far from daughterly greeting. I recognized her from having seen her more than once, from the orchestra. She was Marie Duplessis, the lady of the camellias.

All of the son's best plays were autobiographical, and the father's far-from-fatherly pleasure at this meeting with his son's mistress is a clue to the autobiographical content of the novel. The father views Duplessis with a predatory eye, treating her as just the kind of delicious young thing he himself would have been happy to seduce. And it just might have been in his power: some years after Duplessis died, Dumas *père* produced a daughter thirty-odd years his son's junior! Dumas *père,* in short, led a life of untiring seduction and left a considerable wake of mistresses. At one time he was said to have had ten former conquests on his "payroll."

The life of Dumas *fils,* then, was subject to the whims of an unsinkable womanizer. This was the central fact of his childhood. *Père*'s career as a libertine began with a humble seamstress, but he soon graduated to some of the most famous actresses of the time and eventually even to an opera singer — whose "screeches" he could not bear. (One night the coloratura caught him *in flagrante delicto* in a theater box and upset the performance with her screams!)

What of the mother of Dumas *fils?* The answer reflects interestingly upon his novel: the mother was the humble seamstress who gave *père* his firstborn. Catherine Labay's life was, in the eyes of society, ruined when the father refused to marry her or even acknowledge paternity. At the age of seven, when *père* finally accepted *fils* legally, he was immediately packed off to boarding school — the father hoping to avoid the constant skirmishes between Labay and a new mistress. Labay — who is described by Maurois as "simple, upright, and honest . . . a hard worker, a devout church-goer, and orderly by temperament in all things" —

was always adored by her son, and it must be in part the fate of his mother that gave him his compassion for women — like unwed mothers or (more pertinently) prostitutes — unjustly ostracized by society. Labay rarely ventured near the capital. For her son, she (and the provinces) represented the social proprieties and virtue; his father (and Paris) represented decadence and passion.

The temptation to speculate upon the relevance of all these facts to the novel and the play is irresistible. That the author of *La Dame aux camélias* was for the first seven years of his life an unacknowledged bastard is a fact that should help us unravel the autobiographical connections between Dumas *fils* and his novel. The narrator in the novel asserts that his story "has only one merit, which will perhaps be denied it: that is, that it is true." And it is true — except that, as in a mirror, images are reversed. In the novel the father is called by the son "the most honorable man in the world." Doubtless Dumas *père* took this at face value as a fine compliment (boring though he would have found such a man as Duval *père!*). But this honorable and upright voice of sobriety from the provinces should rather be seen as a projection of the author's *mother*. Georges Duval is a shadow of Catherine Labay. Hers was the voice of "moral" behavior in the son's life. It is therefore touching to note that Dumas *fils* avoided the celebrations after the successful opening performance of his "Camélias" play in order to dine quietly with his mother.

Similarly, I am tempted to suggest that the son's ambivalent attitude toward Marie Duplessis may have, in an unconscious way, reflected his feelings about his father, whose insouciant love life must have generated considerable resentment. Dumas *fils* wrote of his attraction to Duplessis: "This mixture of gaiety, melancholy, simplicity and prostitution, the very malady from which she was suffering, with its resultant nervousness and emotional instability — all these things merely increased my desire to possess her." Except for the vein of melancholy, this description might well apply to Dumas *père* himself. And the ultimate purpose of the son's desire for the possession of Duplessis was hygienic rather than sexual: he had in view the restoration of her health, both physical and moral. This too could have been colored by the son's attitude toward the father. Dumas *père* — like Marguerite Gautier — was incapable of taking care of personal affairs; he squandered great sums of money on trifles; promiscuity was his life too. Armand's

instinct to save Marguerite from the dissipations of Paris and re-
move her to the country perhaps reflected the deep-seated notion
of *fils* that *père* should never have abandoned Labay, gone to Paris,
or failed to be the loving husband and father that he should have
been. The fantasy behind the story is one of the son rescuing the
father and thereby vindicating the mother.

There is of course another side, and that is the son's obvious
love for his father and the excitement of both his personality and
the Parisian culture in which he reveled. The son spoke with feeling of his father's "powerful gaiety of spirit." He generously tele-
graphed his father in Brussels after the success of *La Dame aux
camélias* on the stage: "Great, great success, so great that I felt I
was witnessing the first night of one of your plays." And it should
be added that the instinct to "save" Duplessis/Dumas *père* was at
heart a generous one. Finally, we can make an obvious point: the
son was never able to tear himself away for long from his father's
world or his father's profession, though as he grew older the moral
instincts of his mother held increasing sway.

When there are strong minds on both sides of the generation
gap, sparks will often fly, and parental actions will spur remarkably antithetical reactions. Deeply conservative parents will foster
prodigal children, and (as happened in the Dumas family) vice
versa. But it is not merely the tension between father and son that
gives *La Dame aux camélias* its excitement; it is also the tension
in the author's own mind — the tug and pull between social mores
and self-determination, between familial love and security and
predatory sexual satisfaction, between the cozy, unthreatening Eden
in the country and "that city of perdition." All this we can better
understand now that we have learned something of Catherine Labay and Dumas *père*. All this, too, lies behind the torturing di-
lemma that faces Violetta Valery after her meeting with Giorgio
Germont.

* * *

BEFORE turning attention to Verdi we should pause to consider
the novel and the play in their own right. The former — a relatively short, charming, and stylish work — pleasantly surprised a
French literary world accustomed to the grandiose romances of
Dumas *père*. "Everyone," Janin recalled, "was delighted to say
that the son of Alexandre Dumas, who had barely left school, was

already following with a steady pace in the brilliant footsteps of his father — and that he had his father's vivacity and inward emotion, his vivid, rapid style." Janin, like many others, was captivated by a work "of such vivid interest . . . so truthful, so fresh, and so novel." The subject was indeed not ordinary. Aside from the very recent topical allusions which made it a *roman à clef, La Dame aux camélias* took a strong satiric approach to the sordid "life of dissipation, of balls, of orgies" in Paris. The author had written not only a personal history but a modest social history as well.

The novel is a leisurely and expansive genre, and this allowed Dumas to organize his work in ways that required alteration when he transformed it for the stage. Most obviously, Dumas chose to distance himself from his hero/alter ego, Armand — presumably because with Duplessis now dead he felt himself a bit older and wiser. He achieved this instance by having Armand tell his story in retrospect to a narrator. The narrator in effect takes the novel in dictation. (Interestingly, the technique of having a narrating figure meet a central character who tells the actual story also occurs in the work by Prosper Mérimée that resulted in Bizet's *Carmen* and in the well-known novel of 1731 by the Abbé Prévost, *Manon Lescaut,* now familiar through the operas by Massenet and Puccini.)

Armand and the "author" meet at the auction of Marguerite Gautier's belongings, at which the latter buys her copy of *Manon Lescaut.* Dumas refers many times to *Manon Lescaut,* and it becomes clear that he intended its story (also of love and poverty in the Parisian demimonde) as a continuing literary allusion. Those who know the *Manon* operas and *La Traviata* will be particularly alive to the various parallels in the two stories, for example, the escape of Alfredo and Violetta to the country in which a cozy cottage, a humble garden with flowers, a murmuring brook, and birdsong are imagined.

Dumas makes clever use of Prévost. Before Marguerite leaves for Paris, Armand's eyes fall on a passage in which Manon explains why she is returning to Paris and her old life: "Do you think it possible to be loving on an empty stomach . . . I adore you, you may count on that, but leave me to manage our affairs for a little. Woe to him that falls into my clutches! I am working to make my chevalier rich and happy." Soon Armand finds that *his* mistress has vanished to Paris also. The interplay is telling: Manon — always half mistress and half gold digger — abandons Des Grieux for economic reasons; Marguerite departs out of the pure instinct of self-sacrifice. Literary allusions do not work well in opera, but Verdi and his librettist Francesco Piave were at least able to get a copy of *Manon Lescaut* on stage. Just before Alfredo learns of Violetta's sudden return to Paris and before he meets his father, he "seats himself and opens a book." The book is certainly by Prévost! *

Another part of the novel, understandably, did not survive in the play or the opera. This is the long opening in which the narrator and an almost terminally lovesick Armand become friends. One begins to see why Dumas wished to distance himself from Armand by assuming the guise of a narrator, for he was then apparently capable of looking self-critically at his affair with Duplessis. He does not flinch from making Armand seem awfully stiff, snobbish, sobersided, self-indulgent. And macabre: there is a ghoulish passage (influenced by Poe?) in which the narrator comes with Armand to an exhumation and examination of Gautier's body that the crazed lover demands.

Also missing to some extent in the play and almost completely in the opera is that "vivid, rapid" dialogue Janin admired and much of the harsh representation of Parisian decadence. What finally makes the novel so much more appealing than the play is the presence of a satirical, cynical vinegar that helps to cut the potentially oily sentimentality of the bare plot. Take the cameo character of Prudence Duvernoy, for instance. She is a devastating caricature of the heartless, aging, grasping adventuress with no visible means of support. She knows the way of the world, is an expert on the economics of keeping a mistress, and sees love in the world of Paris as a disagreeable indulgence. "Marguerite is not a saint," she tells Armand, "she likes you, you are very fond of her, let the

---

* At this point in the action of *La Traviata* (Act II, just before "Di Provenza"), we can put the Dumas novel to a second use. We never learn precisely what is in the letter from Violetta to Alfredo that is intended to put an end to their affair. But in the novel Dumas had the space to include a full transcript of this pathetic note:

"By the time you read this letter, Armand, I shall already be the mistress of another man. So all is over between us. Go back to your father, my dear, and to your sister, a pure young girl who knows nothing of all our troubles and who will soon help you forget what you have been made to suffer by the fallen creature they call Marguerite Gautier. You were good enough to love her for a while and it is to you she owes the only happy moments in a life which, she hopes, will not last long now."

rest alone." In the play the character recedes; in the opera — as Flora Bervoix — she almost vanishes.

A similar transmutation occurs in Marguerite/Violetta. In the novel one is quickly struck by how ably Dumas conveyed the sense of a woman who by the force of her personality and wit — as well as her beauty — could wrap Paris around her finger. The heroine of the novel has the chance to display a keen, perceptive intelligence. And she leaves in her path numerous witticisms worthy of Oscar Wilde or Noël Coward. She candidly admits that she has "the bad habit of trying to embarrass people the first time I meet them." When Armand says, with outrageous naïveté, that she should take care of herself, she replies: "If I were to begin to take care of myself, my dear boy, I should die." Armand later writes a petulant letter breaking off their affair (and immediately regrets it); Marguerite comments: "My dear Prudence, your protégé is not polite; one thinks such letters, one does not write them." About her life she has no illusions: "We are sometimes obliged to buy the satisfaction of our souls at the expense of our bodies." And she coins the most succinct and perceptive comment we have on the oldest profession: "We stand first in men's self-esteem, last in their esteem." This heroine with such complete social *and* verbal dexterity also recedes as we move from novel to opera; in *La Traviata* the true dexterity is vocal.

Of course, it is no criticism of *La Traviata* or opera in general to say that the satiric, essentially verbal element of the novel does not reach the stage. The strength of music lies not in conveying linguistically or intellectually complex conceits, but rather in giving life to what Bernard Shaw, in a letter of advice to a librettist, called "the right passional material." For Verdi and his librettist the satiric element of *La Dame aux camélias* could only provide mere background; the right passional material lay in the foreground — in the love of the young man and the courtesan and the great sacrifice she makes for him.

They looked for the *music* in the source. Perhaps they looked to Armand's comment that "a sweet fever thrilled me" and came eventually to create the sweet tenor aria for Alfredo in the second act ("De' miei bollenti spiriti"). Perhaps they considered what we are told about Marguerite's musical tastes — that she played the piano and often "began scraps of music without finishing them," that she often essayed Weber's "Invitation to the Waltz" but always stumbled at "the hard part" with all the sharps. It is amusing to speculate that here might be the invitation Verdi accepted to compose the one work of his career that could be called a "waltz opera."

Dumas's reworking for the stage need only detain us briefly because it is in all important respects similar to the action of *La Traviata* and because, like so many spin-offs into neighboring genres, it is an inferior work of art. Vincent Godefroy spoke for many when he praised the novel for its "fragrant charm" and damned the play as "creak[ing] with labored construction." The play represents a coarsening of the novel's delicate, piquant flavor. It is thus not surprising to find it reprinted recently in a collection of "Victorian melodramas" — in the dubious company of Sedley's *The Drunkard* and Hamblin's *Nick of the Woods*!

But — and this shows how amazingly stage fashions can alter — it was not always thus. The play caused one of the greater theatrical sensations of the nineteenth century (a comment perhaps on how dreary the nineteenth century was in the theater). To contemporary eyes, *La Dame* was revolutionary, nearly on a par with Victor Hugo's notorious *Hernani,* which signaled the fall of the Bastille of literary conservatism to the romantics. *La Dame* was viewed as furthering the revolution in its insistence upon bringing issues of contemporary life on stage, in its blithe rejection of convoluted plotting, and in its approximation of dialogue from "real life." The play was delayed three years by the censors and was produced only after some exertion by the influential father. Those in conservative social quarters obviously recognized it as a volatile theatrical statement.

The poet and novelist Théophile Gautier had set up the war-cry of the romantics at the first performance of *Hernani,* and he was also present to give the Dumas play an enthusiastic reception. His review will, at the least, help us to imagine that the play really was once the center of attention and controversy:

What does the poet the greatest honor is that there is not the least hint of plot, surprise, or complication in the whole of these five acts. As to the *idea* of the play, it is as old as love, and as eternally young. Strictly speaking, it is not an idea at all, but a feeling. The clever must be greatly surprised by this success, which they will completely fail to explain, since it gives the lie to all their theories. . . . Much ability has been needed [by Dumas] to put upon the stage . . . scenes of modern life as it really is, without any hypocritical disguise. The dialogue is rich in vivid touches . . . thrusts and parries which flash and clash with the impact of crossed swords.

There may be some truth in these highly partisan words, but one is forced to look elsewhere to explain why, over the next fifty years or so, the Dumas play was so popular. One explanation recommends itself above all others: the play is an extraordinary vehicle. The role of Marguerite demands from an actress a complete and highly varied emotional palette. The actress must, as Rogers Clark, a recent editor of the play, has summarized, "reflect the changing moods through which the character moves during the five acts of the play; in turn gay and sad, rhapsodic and elegiac, aggressive and timid, cynical and sincere, hopeful and desperate, she must also be able to interpret the various and very different stages of Marguerite's career: the hard-boiled courtesan of Act I must grow into the passionately lyrical lover of acts II and III who must, in her turn, naturally evolve into the pathetic consumption-racked figure of the final acts." The play, then, remained on the boards because it consistently attracted actresses of the first rank — especially the more ambitious ones. Rose Chéri, Aimée Desclée (a favorite of Henry James), Ida Rubinstein, and Sarah Bernhardt were among the many who assumed the role in France. Norma Talmadge, Yvonne Printemps, and Edwige Feuillère were also drawn to it. And of course Greta Garbo made the role famous in the movie *Camille* (the title was taken from the 1856 American version by Matilda Heron, *Camille; or, The fate of a coquette*). One actress, Blanche Dufrêne, was said to have killed herself because she felt she could not do Marguerite justice. But it fell originally to Eugénie Doche to give the premiere performances — which she carried off with great success. "At last," wrote Gautier, "Marie Duplessis has the statue which we asked for her. The poet has taken over the task of the sculptor, and, instead of the body, we have the soul, to which Madame Doche has lent her own charming envelope of flesh. . . ."

*   *   *

GIUSEPPE VERDI attended one of Madame Doche's performances in 1852. It is easy to imagine what pleasure the composer must have experienced at the Vaudeville Theater — and what potential seeds of inspiration were planted there. The play, after all, was praised in the papers for its simplicity, freshness, and naturalness, just the qualities that Verdi for some years had been demanding from his librettists. And it was Verdi who would eventually write, complaining about the oversophistication of Parisian art (and sounding very much like Gautier!): "I believe in *inspiration;* you people believe in *construction.* . . . I strive for *art,* in whatever form it may appear, but never for the *amusement, artifice,* or *system* which you prefer." How Verdi must have exulted in the way *La Dame* upset the Parisian establishment.

Verdi must also have been excited by the daring subject of Dumas's play. A few months later he was casting about for a new libretto and warned a friend, "I don't want any of those ordinary subjects that crop up by the hundred." Such a taste Verdi had often shown before, for instance in his Victor Hugo opera *Ernani* (1844), in an opera about divorce with a Lutheran minister as a central character (*Stiffelio,* 1850), and also in his many operas with strong political themes (*La Battaglia di Legnano, Simon Boccanegra, Don Carlos*). Finally, Verdi must have seen in *La Dame* a work that would require a manageable cast, provide a nearly ready-made scenario, and — given careful casting — offer a tremendous vehicle for a prima donna.

It was apparently not until October 1852 that the sparks took flame. Piave, Verdi's most frequent collaborator (*Ernani, I due Foscari, Macbeth, Il Corsaro, Stiffelio, Rigoletto, Boccanegra, La Forza del destino*), wrote to a friend in November that the composer had shelved a nearly finished libretto in a fit of work on "a new idea." By 1 January 1853 Verdi was willing to disclose his plans for the new opera and express his sense of exhilaration:

For Venice I am doing "La Dame aux camélias" which will probably be called *La Traviata.* A subject for our age. . . . I want plots that are great, beautiful, varied, daring . . . daring to an extreme, new in form and at the same time adapted to composing. Another person would perhaps not have composed it because of the costumes, because of the period, because of a thousand other foolish objections. I did it with particular pleasure. Everybody cried out when I proposed to put a hunchback on the stage. Well, I was overjoyed to compose *Rigoletto,* and it was just the same with *Macbeth,* and so on.

Verdi worked quickly. By the twentieth of February he completed writing the music, and by early March the scoring was done. The premiere was scheduled for March 6 at the Teatro la Fenice in Venice.

The appalling story of this premiere was the kind that left Verdi able to conclude sadly, toward the end of his career: "I know the world in general but the theater in particular, so I am not surprised by any perfidies, great or small, that may be committed there." The performance was doomed. Verdi had originally specified to Piave a heroine who must be "young, have a graceful figure, and sing with passion." But he found himself contractually obliged to accept the laughably unsuitable Fanny Salvini-Donatelli. The baritone, Felice Varesi, was nearing the end of his career and appears to have resented the shape and the demands of the role Verdi wrote for him. The tenor, Ludovico Graziani, was not in good health (and caused a later performance to be canceled). Also disastrous for Verdi was the theater's insistence that the time of the opera be set back to about 1700. After much consternation and argument Verdi caved in. Verdi must have set out for the Venetian premiere with a heavy heart. He took with him a letter from an anonymous Venetian sender promising him "a complete fiasco."

It was a fiasco — as Verdi admitted in letters to various friends. To his secretary Emanuele Muzio he wrote, "*La Traviata* last night was a disaster. Is the fault mine or the singers? Time will tell." To the conductor Angelo Mariani: "I am not upset. Either I am wrong or they are. For my part I do not believe the last word on *Traviata* was spoken last night." As usual, Verdi was right: just over a year later, under more clement artistic conditions and in the same city, the opera triumphed. The last word was Verdi's. On hearing the good news he wrote, "You may as well know that the *Traviata* which is being performed at the Teatro San Benedetto is the same, exactly the same as the one performed last year at the Fenice. . . . Then it was a fiasco; now it has created a furor. Draw your own conclusions!" Verdi had in fact made many relatively minor alterations, but that did not lessen the vindication of his artistic intentions.

The "public" history of the creation of *La Traviata* is well known and tells us something about Verdi the artist and his usual struggles with the conventions and audiences of his time. Curiously, though, this opera is not the best one for showing the essentials of how Verdi, reining his librettists with a very strong hand, went about transforming the literature of his day into music. One reason becomes obvious when we compare the Dumas play with the *Traviata* libretto: they are in their general contours and structure the same. Perhaps the transformation was achieved by Verdi and Piave with less than the usual effort — just some simple pruning. The little *Traviata* correspondence extant may also suggest that (unlike *Aida* for instance) the preparation of the libretto came easily.

.When the artistic struggle with literary material, willful singers, or the demands of venal impresarios is out in the open, we can learn in explicit terms about the principles of Verdi's art. One might point, for example, to *Macbeth,* that great watershed opera in Verdi's artistic development, which came seven years before *Traviata.* With that opera, as I have written elsewhere, the composer finally set down the artistic battle-lines of his own choice, fought tenaciously for them, and, in most important respects, won the day. The interest of *Macbeth* is all the greater, given its estimable literary source. Following *Macbeth* came *Luisa Miller, Rigoletto,* and *Il Trovatore* — works in which Verdi finally relinquished the backward-looking influences of Rossini, Bellini, and Donizetti and settled in his characteristic mold. Then came *Traviata,* the product more of achieved mastery than inner artistic struggle. At about the time of this opera Verdi settled once and for all in rural Busseto; it is tempting to see *Traviata,* too, as a final homecoming of the artist to his true identity.

The story of his actual composition of *Traviata,* then, is not what rivets our attention. More engrossing is the private history lying behind the opera that I have promised to explore. We come now to the last — and surely the most moving — of our biographical excursions. We must consider for a moment Verdi the man. Jules Janin said of the novel and the real story behind it, "The truth being known, the interest of the story was enhanced." Some awareness of certain events in Verdi's life will, I believe, have the same enhancing effect for *La Traviata.*

Consider first where *La Traviata* falls in the arch of Verdi's artistic career. In many respects the career was typical; only the facts that he lived a very long time and was a genius are extraordinary. Born in 1813, he spent his first years in his native town of Le

Roncole. Verdi began his musical studies in this dreary village with the civic organist. When he was twelve he [was com]petent enough to succeed to this position himself. The [years] Verdi spent in the rather larger neighboring town of Busseto studying music as a result of the generous patronage of Antonio Barezzi. Barezzi was a wealthy merchant, devoted music lover, and the president of the town's orchestral society. He took Verdi into his home and subsidized his musical tuition. Verdi made his way in the town's musical life and no doubt suffered his first brushes with the small provincial mind and the volatile musician's world.

It soon became clear that Busseto could offer little to a young man of talent, and, through Barezzi's influence, arrangements were made for Verdi's further education in the nearest metropolis, Milan. From 1833 to 1835 he resided in Milan (under unpleasant and humiliating circumstances that the composer never forgot) and learned as much as pedagogy can afford a composer. From 1835 to 1838 Verdi was back in Busseto, beginning at the bottom of the ladder as *maestro di musica*. He threw himself into marriage — to Barezzi's daughter Margherita — and into the town's highly politicized musical scene.

In a short time, though, Verdi wearied of Busseto, and he escaped back to Milan with his wife in the hope of trying his luck as a composer. His first opera, *Oberto,* appeared in 1839 with modest success, and he then turned to the only comic opera besides *Falstaff* of his entire career, *Un Giorno di regno.* Was ever an *opera buffa* written under sadder circumstances? For its premiere came after he had lost in very short order not only his wife but two small children. And the first (and only) performance proved a cruel disaster. Many years later Verdi wrote bitterly to his publisher of his experience with *Un Giorno di regno:* the "public maltreated the opera of a poor, ill young man, pressed by time, and with his heart torn by a horrible misfortune! All this was known, but the rudeness was without restraint. . . . Oh, if then the public had, not applauded, but borne in silence that opera, I would not have had words enough to thank them!" Verdi never forgave this behavior, and the rest of his life maintained an aloof distance from his public. Its whims and ecstasies, abuse and adoration he accepted with the same nonchalance.

The decade of the 1840s represented Verdi's "salad days" when he made his reputation and began to average about two operas a year. His first resounding success came in 1842 with *Nabucco,* an opera not only musically rich but also possessing a powerful political subtext (the Jewish captivity being associated with the Italian "captivity" by Austria). In the next years many of his works were received with clamorous approval, among them *I Lombardi, Alzira, Ernani,* and *Attila.* The 1840s were years of much travel to oversee productions of his operas, and of ever-sharpening focus in Verdi's musical style, notably in *Luisa Miller* (1849).

In the 1850s Verdi reached his full and characteristic stride with *Rigoletto* (1851) and *Il Trovatore* (1853). He began to amass a considerable fortune and (not coincidentally) also began to compose more and more adamantly upon his own artistic terms. His output also declined drastically: between 1855 and 1871 he wrote only six new operas, and the thirty years after 1871 brought forth only *Otello* and *Falstaff.*

This, then, is the relatively straightforward story of Verdi's career — a story so simple that one begins to wonder why the events of Verdi's life do not loom larger in discussions of his work. Knowledge of the personality and life of Mozart, Beethoven, Berlioz, Wagner, and Britten, for instance, floods with illumination the operas that these men composed. But similar knowledge is not very helpful in Verdi's case. It is instructive that, in casting over the chronology of Verdi's life for significant events, we are forced to grasp at ones that are merely "emblems" of Verdi's creative activity or poignant "symbols" common to many artistic biographies. Here is a sampling of such events worth mentioning:

— 1814: Verdi's mother Luigia hides with her one-year-old son Giuseppe in a bell tower when the invading French pass through the village of Le Roncole. Many have noticed the nice irony that the baby's name was to become, decades later, a war-cry for Italian unification and the expulsion of foreign governors.

— 1820: Verdi assumes the role of prodigy when he substitutes for his own teacher at the civic church organ.

— 1832: Milan's professorial troglodytes rebuff the budding young composer. Here is the old story of conservatism obstructing (temporarily) innovation.

— 1839–1840: Verdi must oversee the premiere of his first opera, *Oberto,* just after his first son dies. Under similarly desperate circumstances, already mentioned, his *Un Giorno di regno* appears. Here is another instance — like Mozart's *Requiem* and

Magic Flute — of the artist rising above personal grief to do his work.

— 1859: "Viva Verdi" is first used as a political slogan: *Vittorio Emanuele Re d'Italia,* the figurehead of the Italian independence movement. The acronym happily reflects the composer's rock-solid humanist and populist principles.

These well-known biographical moments turn up frequently and evocatively in the Verdi literature, even though they do not have much intrinsic "explanatory" value. They are suggestive rather than illuminating. Why is this? Why is Sir Isaiah Berlin able to assert, in his fine essay on "The Naiveté of Verdi," that "Knowledge of basic human emotions is virtually all the extramusical equipment that is needed to understand Verdi's works. . . . The requirements needed to do it justice do not include, as indispensable *sine quibus non,* knowledge of the personal views or attributes of the composer, or the historical circumstances of his life or those of his society"? Time and again, the extraordinary separation of life and art is apparent as one becomes familiar with Verdi and his milieu. An excellent example of this separation is relevant to *La Traviata:* from the end of July to the end of August, 1848, Verdi was in the midst of establishing the great liaison of his life (we shall turn to this liaison shortly). He was cozily rusticated with the woman, and one might have expected Verdi to produce a fine lyric opera from his exhilarating experience, after the manner of Berlioz or Wagner.* But no. Instead of celebrating his newfound love, Verdi chose to celebrate the beginning of the first war of Italian independence, which began with Piedmont's declaration of war on Austria in March 1848. And so, in his love-nest, he began writing one of his most aggressively political operas, *La Battaglia di Legnano.*

We learn nothing of Verdi's private life from *La Battaglia di Legnano,* and that is typical. We come back again to the question: why? Berlin attempts to provide an answer by referring to Friedrich Schiller's famous distinction between "naïve" and "sentimental" artists. "Naïve" artists, according to Schiller, are at one and at ease with their art; Berlin puts Cervantes, Bach, Rubens, Handel, and Haydn in this category. "Sentimental" artists are ill at ease with their art, struggle with it, express and try to complete

---

*He did write for her an art-song, ironically titled "L'abandonnée" ("The Abandoned Woman")!

their identity through their art; Berlin suggests that Byron, Wagner, Flaubert, and Nietzsche fall in this category. The dichotomy is of course a simplification, but it is a convincing one. And, in placing Verdi emphatically among the "naïve" artists, Berlin gives us an explanation for the peculiar irrelevance of Verdi's biography to his art:

Among composers of genius, Verdi is perhaps the last complete, self-fulfilled creator, absorbed in his art; at one with it; seeking to use it for no ulterior purpose, the god wholly concealed by his works . . . suspicious of anyone curious about his inner life, wholly, even grimly, impersonal, drily objective, at one with his music. A man who dissolved everything in his art, with no more personal residue than Shakespeare or Tintoretto.

Eloquent words, but I am convinced that *La Traviata* is the exception that proves the rule. There is a distinct "personal residue" in this opera, and to this personal residue we can now turn.

La Traviata came at a crucial time in Verdi's life. Unlike the novel (written when Dumas was twenty-four), the opera is the work of a mature man of forty — a man who no longer wished to pursue the exhausting regimen of composition and travel that he experienced in his thirties. I think it is possible to hear in *La Traviata*'s lighter, more graceful waltz idiom and in Verdi's simultaneous relinquishment of those propulsive, surging rhythms in his "middle" operas a reflection of change in Verdi. In terms of musical style and working habits *La Traviata* betrays a remarkable relaxation. For reasons that will soon become clear, one can also remark that *La Traviata* is the first full-scale reflection of Verdi's new associations with Paris, a city he first visited in 1847. The ballet, so properly placed in Act II, scene 2 according to Parisian custom, always makes me think so — as, of course, does its very setting and source. What, then, can explain the influence of Paris — that most quintessentially feminine of cities — upon a man who liked to refer to himself as "a peasant from Roncole"? The proper response to that question is, as Parisians will say, *cherchez la femme*.

Her name is Giuseppina Strepponi, and she was a brilliant soprano and a woman of great intelligence. Verdi first heard Strepponi sing in 1839 and first met her in 1841, when she created the bravura role of Abigaille in *Nabucco*. A description of her made in 1840 by Verdi's *Nabucco* librettist, Temistocle Solera, gives us an impressive view of the woman — a view that appears to be borne out by the testimony of her later life:

In the mere five years that she has been exercising her art, with rapid and happy acclaim, and at the fresh age of twenty-four years, she has gloriously covered all of twenty-seven theaters. Vienna, Florence, Venice, Bologna, Rome, Turin, and, last spring, the cultivated Milan, have admired in this young woman the finest gifts of nature, improved by constant study. . . . Endowed with an extremely sensitive spirit, she can win her way, both with singing and expression, into the spectators' hearts. Cultivated and appealing in society, excellent daughter and sister, she has generously taken on the support of her whole family. . . .

Verdi made Strepponi's acquaintance at the most active time of his life, and it may be that his busy-ness was in part his way of sublimating his personal grief. For he had just suffered within the space of two years (mid-1838 to mid-1840) the loss of his wife of four years, a sixteen-month-old daughter, and a fifteen-month-old son. At any rate, the paths of the famous soprano and the constantly traveling composer soon separated, and it was not until 1847, when Verdi made his first trip to Paris, that they met again.

But by 1847 — such is the precarious life of the opera singer — Strepponi's career had come to a sudden end. She was alone in Paris trying to set herself up as a voice teacher, and her personal affairs were in disarray. Soon the composer and the retired singer were living together. The more one learns about the Verdi-Strepponi liaison, the more one recognizes why the role of Violetta — and the opera as a whole — was so feelingly composed.

The Dumas play, in the simplest terms, is about the destruction of a love affair that is outrageous to bourgeois morality. By the time Verdi found himself (perhaps Giuseppina too) sitting in his seat at the Vaudeville Theater in 1852, he would have found much to identify with in the action. In 1848 he was living with Strepponi, and by the summer of that year he had retreated with her to (in the words of the score) "a country house outside of Paris." At Passy, to be exact. The next year Verdi brought her to Busseto for the first time, and in 1851 the two moved into the farmhouse at Sant' Agata that was to become his lifelong country seat. Verdi and Strepponi had saved each other from the prospect of a life of loneliness. It was as if Alfredo and Violetta had never been visited by the elder Germont and had lived happily ever after.*

But there was someone who offered to play the role of the elder Germont to Verdi's Alfredo, someone who offered on behalf of the small-minded and "proper" gentry of Busseto to criticize Verdi for his scandalous living arrangement. Verdi was a man of acutely independent spirit and normally would have laughed off with derision such criticism of his private affairs. But unfortunately the critic happened to be not only the man who was his beloved benefactor as a young music student but also the father of his dead wife, Antonio Barezzi. Verdi — torn between a kind of filial love, gratitude, and indignation — responded with one of the most touching letters from a life filled with marvelous correspondence. This letter is worth quoting at length because the attitude of mind that Verdi attacks here is the attitude personified in the elder Germont — and because Verdi wrote it from Paris on 21 January 1852, just days before he attended *La Dame aux camélias*.

> Dear Father-in-law . . .
> I don't think that you would have written a letter which you knew would only anger me of your own accord. But you live in a neighborhood that has the bad habit of often interfering in other people's affairs and disapproving of everything that does not agree with its view of things. I am not accustomed to interfere in other people's business, unless I am asked to, because I demand that no one interfere in mine. Hence the gossip, the grumbling prattle, the disapproval. This freedom of action, which is respected even in less civilized communities, I claim as my own good right at home. Be the judge yourself, be a strict judge, but cool and dispassionate. What harm is it if I keep apart, if I see fit not to visit titled people? If I manage my property myself, because it is a pleasure and a recreation to me? I repeat, what harm is it? Certainly it hurts no one. . . .
> . . . since we are making revelations, I see no objection to raising the curtain which hides the mysteries hidden within my four walls, to speaking to you about my home life. I have nothing to hide. In my house there lives a free, independent lady who loves seclusion as

---

*Verdi and Strepponi eventually adopted a daughter. When she married, Giuseppina described her in a letter. The description makes her sound fascinatingly like Alfredo's sister in the opera ("Pura siccome un angelo"): "When I saw her walk to the altar, in her white bridal veil, shyly leaning on Verdi's arm, I was profoundly moved. She seemed to me a true symbol of virginity, with a beauty wholly chaste and innocent, full of modesty and virginal grace."

I do, and possesses a fortune which puts her out of the reach of care. Neither she nor I owe any account of our action to anyone. . . . Who knows whether she is my wife or not? And who knows in this special case what our thoughts and reasons are for not making it public? Who knows whether this is good or bad? Why might it not be a good thing? And even if it were bad, who has the right to hurl the ban against us? Indeed, I tell you that in my house she is paid the same or greater respect than I am, and no one is allowed to fail in that regard for any reason whatsoever, and, finally, she has every right to it, as much for her dignity as for her intelligence and her unfailing graciousness to others.

With this long chatter I have meant only to say that I demand my freedom of action, because all people have a right to it and because my whole being rebels against conforming to other people. . . . I swear to you by my honor that I have no intention of hurting you in any way. I have always considered you and still consider you my benefactor. I regard it as an honor. I boast of it! A hearty farewell in old friendship!

There have been few more eloquent arguments for the rights of consenting adults or against society's prying preoccupation with "victimless crimes." Alfredo — so naïve, idealistic, and unbroken to society's reins — could scarcely be expected to stand up to the likes of his father. But Verdi refused to be cowed; he struck back and put the world in its place.* This must help to explain the enormous musical power he invested in the tragedy caused by the elder Germont. He was acutely aware of how wrong Germont is, just as he was sensitive to the threats posed by repressive social convention to a "free, independent lady" like Giuseppina Strepponi . . . or Violetta Valery.

Strepponi, however, was never called upon to make a heroic renunciation like Violetta's. She lived with the composer for fifty years, dying in 1897, a few years before Verdi. In Strepponi, Verdi must have found the great solace and companionship that could assuage his grief for his lost wife and children. Gerald Mendelsohn, a professor of psychology who has written powerfully of Verdi the man, has aptly concluded: "*La Traviata* expresses one

---

* There is a happy ending to the story: Barezzi's misgivings (if indeed they were his own) soon vanished, and he became a beloved fixture in the Verdi household. Strepponi became particularly devoted to him. For unknown reasons, Verdi and Strepponi were formally married on 29 August 1859.

of Verdi's most characteristic themes, the loss and search for wholeness and peace. To know Strepponi and Verdi, then, is to clarify the nature of Violetta's spiritual journey."

But Violetta dies. In fact, she is the only Verdi heroine who does not die a violent death. She succumbs to tuberculosis in the company of her lover and a loving father-figure. This has led Mendelsohn to suggest that there may also be an autobiographical shadow of Verdi's first wife in the heroine of *La Traviata*. There may be in the last act of the opera a distant memory of her death as Antonio Barezzi described it in his diary: "Through a terrible disease there died in my arms at Milan . . . my beloved daughter Margherita in the flower of her years and at the culmination of her good fortune, because married to the excellent youth Giuseppe Verdi." And there may be in the way Violetta sells her jewels in Act II another parallel to Verdi's early married life. Verdi was once ill and unable to pay his rent; he recalled forty years later: "My wife, who saw my agitation, took her few jewels and, I know not how or by what means, got the sum together and brought it to me. I was deeply moved by this proof of her devotion and swore to myself to return everything to her." We can never be certain to what degree Violetta was a fusion — conscious or unconscious — of the two loves of Verdi's life. But it is hard to resist feeling that these women were ultimately responsible for making *La Traviata* the great autobiographical opera from the pen of this most private of artists.

In Verdi's life, then, social morality did not triumph. He and Strepponi lived out — for almost half a century! — the tantalizing dream of the last-act duet, "Parigi, o cara, noi lasceremo." They retired far from the madding crowd of sophisticated urban society to Busseto and their "casa di riposo" — house of repose. But in *La Traviata* society triumphs. In this disparity between real life and art lies the dramatic power and tragedy of Violetta's character. Verdi realized in his own life the Romantic notion that the individual must stubbornly insist upon self-fulfillment on his own terms. But in Violetta's life the heroic act is not one of rising above and rejecting society's demands. Rather, it is the anti-Romantic act of bowing to what she accepts as just punishment for her sinful past.

Violetta's acceptance of her fate on society's terms rather than her own comes in the interview with Alfredo's father in Act II. When he asserts that her domestic life with Alfredo can never receive heaven's blessing, she immediately agrees ("È vero! è vero!"). He then presses his attack with a devastatingly effective appeal to her instinctive generosity and her sense of guilt for her past life. To her the pure young sister of Alfredo clearly deserves happiness more than she. The father asks Violetta to sacrifice her happiness as an act of repentance and become a "consoling angel" ("angiol consolator") to his family. He shrewdly assumes an ecclesiastical posture (how Verdi hated the clergy!), and even asserts that God is speaking through him. Thus, he is able to put Violetta in the position of a sinner acknowledging that she must be punished. The renunciation of Alfredo becomes an act of expiation, and on this basis Violetta very quickly agrees to the challenge. She asks what she must do, and Germont's first suggestion is to tell Alfredo the lie that she does not love him. No expediency is too vile when society makes its impositions!

Nevertheless, Violetta fully accepts Germont's scenario in her final hours. We meet her near death but with the "tranquil soul" of a repentant sinner. In the Finale, "Prendi, quest'è l'immagine," she expresses the hope that Alfredo will find a wife who is pure and virginal — a woman much like his own sister. And she hopes that the couple will remember the person who, by her act of expiation, finally gained a place in heaven. Violetta envisions herself as "a woman among the angels." At the last she takes the role Germont offered her, the role of a consoling angel.

That Violetta bows to the pressures of society as Verdi never did is perhaps the source of the role's tremendous pathos. Verdi invested his full art in this noble and generous woman who is destroyed by a society at once demanding and indifferent. And he succeeded in conveying the sense that such suffering would not occur if society acted more humanely than it does. The test of his success is that we in the audience are so firmly on the heroine's side as the story unfolds. We are with Violetta as she comes to learn that the achievement of happiness and wholeness is not a simple matter of self-determination, that society must be satisfied also. When she is safely near death and therefore neutralized as an antisocial force, the father — experiencing true remorse perhaps — can allow his son to return for a few moments. But for Violetta it is too late. *È tardi!*

A BIBLIOGRAPHICAL NOTE

THE best biography of Alexandre Dumas *fils* (and his illustrious father and grandfather) is André Maurois, *The Titans: A Three-Generation Biography* (New York: Harper & Row, 1957; reprinted by Greenwood Press, Westport, Connecticut, 1971). The most accessible English version of the Dumas novel is the edition, with an introduction by Edmund Gosse, in the Everyman Library. A French edition of the play, with an excellent introduction in English by Rogers Clark, was published in 1972 by Oxford University Press. An English version of the play is included in *Victorian Melodramas* (Totowa, N.J.: Rowman & Littlefield, 1976).

For a good general introduction to Verdi's life and works, the reader may consult the article on Verdi by Andrew Porter in *The New Grove Dictionary of Music and Musicians,* ed. Stanley Sadie (London: Macmillan, 1980), or Frank Walker's *Verdi the Man* (New York: Knopf, 1962). Two useful compilations are William Weaver's *Verdi: A Documentary Study* (London, 1977) and *The Verdi Companion,* edited by William Weaver and Martin Chusid (New York: W.W. Norton, 1979). A good primary selection of Verdi's letters was edited by Franz Werfel and Paul Stefan and translated into English by Edward Downes as *Verdi: The Man in His Letters* (New York: L.B. Fischer, 1942). Charles Osborne has also translated *The Letters of Giuseppe Verdi* (Victor Gollancz, 1971). The standard work on the operas of Verdi is by Julian Budden (three volumes; Oxford University Press, 1973–1981). The reader may also wish to consult Vincent Godefroy's *The Dramatic Genius of Verdi* (two volumes; Victor Gollancz, 1975); the chapter on Verdi in Gary Schmidgall's *Literature as Opera* (Oxford University Press, 1977; Galaxy Paperback, 1981); and Gerald A. Mendelsohn's excellent "Verdi the Man & Verdi the Dramatist," in *19th Century Music,* volume 2, nos. 2 and 3 (1978, 1979), pp. 110–143, 214–230. Isaiah Berlin's essay on "The Naiveté of Verdi" first appeared in *The Hudson Review* in 1968 and can also be found in the Weaver-Chusid volume mentioned above.

THE MUSIC OF
La Traviata

by

DAVID HAMILTON

$\mathcal{J}$HE Prelude to *La Traviata* begins with only sixteen violins playing very softly in a high register. Rather than facing outward, intended to silence the bustle of the audience, this music already assumes our attention, drawing us inward to the specific sound and expressivity of the opera to follow. Those sixteen violins utter two pathetic phrases in slow tempo before more strings join and the music acquires confidence, rising and then fading in a descending phrase. This particular music will not return again until the beginning of the last act, but its fragile, vulnerable character persists as a background to the quite different mood of what comes between.

After a brief pause, the orchestra establishes an accompaniment figure, over which the strings — violins, violas, and cellos, all in their singing upper registers — set forth a broad and memorable melody, in two identical descending phrases and a longer consequent. This is interrupted rather than completed, whereupon the cellos, discreetly doubled by clarinet and bassoon, prepare themselves for a repetition.

Over the repetition, the violins add a rapid dancing counterpoint, as frivolous as the cello theme is fervent. This lingers on even after the cellos twice insist on a conclusion to their melody, and gradually fades in range and volume, to a close as quiet as the Prelude's opening.

What has this Prelude accomplished? For one thing, an intimacy and delicacy of sound has been established, and not only by the initial use of a small string section and the restrained use of winds. Although horns are used with the woodwinds, quietly underlining harmonies or accenting rhythms, we as yet have heard nothing from the other brass (trumpets and trombones) or percussion, held in reserve for more emotionally stressful occasions.

In addition, some contrasts have been propounded: after the sequential contrast of pathetic opening and confident principal melody, there is the simultaneous contrast of that melody and the skittish violin counterpoint, which will recur in the course of the opera's first act. Finally, the principal melody, along with a close relative, will function throughout the opera as a "reminiscence melody," acquiring dramatic associations as the opera proceeds.

The contrast of sincerity and frivolity is most clearly focused in the middle of Act I, when Alfredo tells Violetta of his long-nurtured love ("Un dì felice"). His line begins hesitantly — Verdi marks it to be broken with brief rests, but some tenors with more breath control than perception of character miss the point and phrase right through the rests. On his second reach upward, Alfredo pauses, then resolves his note upward to begin a melody ("Di quell'amor") clearly akin to the singing theme of the Prelude. (See the accompanying example, where the Prelude theme is quoted with the words sung by Violetta in Act II.) The downward course of Alfredo's version is extended by some slight backtracking, and later he follows an independent course, with an apt harmonic coloration on the word "misterioso."

a) Violetta

A— —ma— mi, Al— fre – — do

b) Alfredo

Di quel— l'a— mor, quel – l'a – mor che'è pal – pi – to

To the simple ardor of this plea, Violetta responds with a cascade of coloratura, in the spirit of the Prelude's violin obbligato. When Alfredo again asserts his "misterioso," the brittleness of Violetta's initial flights is muted, but the principal contrast is sustained in the brief cadenza to their duet. (A distant but touching echo of this juxtaposition is sounded in the last act, in the lovers' only other duet, "Parigi, o cara, noi lasceremo." In the second part of that piece, Alfredo's ardent descending phrase is answered by dancing chromatic sixteenth-notes from Violetta, a still more confined transformation of her original wide-ranging floridity.)

Alfredo's music in this duet exemplifies what we might call the typical *Traviata* melody: in triple meter, often with a waltzlike oom-pah-pah accompaniment, moving in small intervals rather than by wide skips. Initially proposed by Alfredo in the boisterous surroundings of Violetta's party, it eventually becomes her prevalent style as well: when she gives in to Germont in Act II, Scene 1 ("Dite alla giovine"), in her lament during the Act II finale ("Alfredo, Alfredo, di questo core"), and in her last-act aria ("Addio del passato"), among other places.

The play of this contrast extends to the end of Act I, but let us first survey the musical shape of Violetta's party, a well-ordered social occasion. Its initial phases are dominated by a fizzy tune set off by a trill, a more vigorous sort of frivolity than the Prelude violins offered. This hearty theme functions as a ritornello, repeatedly giving way to more intimate contrasting episodes: when Gastone introduces Alfredo, a gentler theme is played by an octet of strings, and the same material recurs, in a different key, as background to the table conversation after the guests are seated. Then the principal party theme is used to build up to Alfredo's drinking song, the first set number.

Now a band strikes up behind the scenes, with introductory chords leading to a string of waltz tunes, over which is superimposed the conversation leading to the aforementioned duet of Violetta and Alfredo, for the duration of which the waltzes are suspended. They resume immediately afterward, and when Violetta gives Alfredo the flower, the strings of the pit orchestra add pizzicato downbeats to the stage music for additional impetus. The choral leave-taking of the other guests is introduced and concluded by the party theme from the beginning of the act, rounding off a certain informal symmetry to Violetta's party:

A	B	C	B	A
party music & Brindisi	*waltzes*	*duet*	*waltzes*	*party music*

But this is not the end of the act; Violetta is still on stage, musing on what Alfredo has said about love. This is the occasion for a solo scene, for which there was a well-established pattern in Italian opera of Verdi's time:

(*i*)   an introductory recitative to establish the dramatic and emotional situation;

(*ii*) an aria in a slow or moderate tempo;

(*iii*) an episode in which the situation changes (most characteristically, a messenger brings news or a letter) or a decision is taken;

(*iv*) the cabaletta, a fast and vigorous concluding aria, repeated literally after brief intervening material for chorus or secondary singer.

Violetta's slow aria ("Ah, fors'è lui") begins reflectively in the minor mode, brightening to the major as she recalls Alfredo's description of the love he offers; she repeats exactly his words and his music. (In Verdi's score, this aria has a second stanza, with new words for the minor-mode part, that is almost invariably omitted in performance.) In the intervening episode ("Follie! follie!"), Violetta rejects such a love as impossible for a woman in her position, motivating the cabaletta ("Sempre libera"), marked *allegro brillante,* the adjective exemplified by her trills, scales, and high C.

When she has been once through this piece, instead of the usual ritornello we hear the voice of Alfredo from below Violetta's window, singing his love theme in its original tempo, accompanied by a harp. Touched, Violetta listens but eventually reaffirms her rejection: "Follie!" This effectively justifies the conventional repetition of the cabaletta — at the end of which Alfredo is heard again, more ardently than before (now in Violetta's feverish tempo rather than his own). With further scales and high Cs, she blots out his voice from her mind.

The convention of slow aria followed by fast one, so effective in displaying the various skills of the singer, was much beloved by stars and public alike, but it could not always be turned so ingeniously to apt dramatic ends, particularly when, as in *Traviata,* Verdi was moving toward a more realistic dramaturgy. Certain difficulties in the first scene of Act II result from this convention, for Verdi conceded the standard sequence to both his tenor and baritone (in the former case, at least, only belatedly and probably reluctantly).

There is dramatic justification for Alfredo's cabaletta: after his buoyant aria ("De' miei bollenti spiriti"), Annina reveals Violetta's arrangements for paying their bills, calling for a new attitude — of remorse and resolution to amend his thoughtlessness — from Alfredo. The weakness here is in fact musical, for the cabaletta idiom at Verdi's disposal, with its bounding polonaise-rhythm accompaniments and strenuous vocal accents, does not sit comfortably on the character who has just sung "De' miei bollenti spiriti," no matter how upset. Later, in the gambling scene, outside the stylistic precedents and formal constraints of the cabaletta style, Verdi finds suitable accents for the angry Alfredo ("Ogni suo aver tal femmina").

Unfortunately, it's not easy to omit this cabaletta, and the difficulties tell us something about the music and its style. The most extreme solution, prevalent in many theaters before World War II, was to send Alfredo offstage at the end of "De' miei bollenti spiriti" and skip to the entrance of Violetta. However, this loses, as well as the cabaletta, the crucial exchange with Annina, during which Alfredo — and the audience — is informed about Violetta's financial sacrifice.

But that dialogue ("Annina, donde vieni?") takes place over chugging rhythms and a harmonic buildup of some intensity, designed to prepare the key and the excitement of the cabaletta. The tension therein established cannot simply be left hanging (though I have heard at least one performance that coolly cut from there to Violetta's entrance). The late Tullio Serafin used to throw in a chord that served as a harmonic pivot, but that hardly diffused the tension. Most conductors introduce a rapid descending scale in the violins, which by its brilliance and its direction makes a stab at discharging the accumulated energy.

This, too, leaves a sense that something has *not* happened, even if we do not know what. In recent years, conductors have begun to restore at least one stanza of the tenor's cabaletta. It may be conventional and undistinguished and out of character, but its presence makes the transitions work, the tensions balance out, the proportions fall into place (and perhaps, if performed enough, it may eventually be interpreted more convincingly). Although too insistently, it does usefully foreshadow both the key and the tone of Alfredo's denunciation in the subsequent scene (though by the same token it raises the role's vocal stakes, calling for a more sustained, vigorous attack than anything else in the role, as well as a concluding high C that Verdi didn't write but the public will expect — a note not in the armory of many tenors who have otherwise coped successfully with the remainder of the part).

The baritone's cabaletta ("No, non udrai rimproveri"), following the familiar "Di Provenza il mar" at the end of the scene, is another matter. Musically drab, it is also dramatically otiose, adding little to what Germont has already offered in the way of insufficient solace; nothing about the situation has changed except the tempo. The cut is more easily made than with the tenor piece, by skipping from the dialogue before the cabaletta to Alfredo's discovery of Flora's invitation. Yet even this apparently seamless excision leaves the impression that the act has ended precipitately, and so at least partial restoration of this piece is today not unusual.

Duets in Italian opera could be as formalized as solo arias, but the remarkable duet of Violetta and Germont that occurs between these two problematic arias embeds the conventional requirements in a series of many elements, passing so easily and naturally among recitative, arioso, and more formal melodic patterns that we do not notice. In the first exchanges Violetta dominates, overriding Germont's initial harmonic region with her dignified reply ("Donna son io, signore") in her own key, and then taking the lead into a more expansive lyrical style ("Or amo Alfredo"). Then Germont's more ordered expositions begin to make their effect. First is his cantabile of background narration ("Pura siccome un angelo"), and Violetta's gradual comprehension. To her agitated reply ("Non sapete quale affetto"), he responds with the assertion that Alfredo's passion will inevitably wane when her beauty fades ("Un dì, quando le veneri"). This ends confidently in a key that she immediately turns to minor, with a keening phrase ("Così alla misera") that is all the more poignant for its slight suggestion of Alfredo's familiar love melody.

The sequence of shorter sections, moving to and fro as the emotional pressures shift, now reaches a point of greater formality for Violetta's concession. The quiet center of the duet is her message to Germont's daughter ("Dite all giovine"), with Germont's contrasting reply and the subsequent combination of their voices. After this slow movement comes a cabaletta ("Morrò! la mia memoria"), launched by Violetta after dialogue during which she decides how she will make the break with Alfredo. Instead of the usual freely notated cadenza, this duet closes in tempo, with an *adagio* coda of fragmented reminiscences and phrases of farewell.

The episode that follows is described by Verdi simply as "Scena Violetta." To a mournful clarinet solo, she writes her letter to Alfredo. A series of tension-building passages, not unlike those preceding the tenor cabaletta, mirrors her perturbation and Alfredo's response, finally debouching into her outburst, "Amami, Alfredo." Here the principal melody from the Prelude, more direct and expansive than Alfredo's variant, returns for the only time during the opera. Here, too, the resources of a dramatic soprano are not amiss; a role that encompasses both this powerful farewell and the coloratura of Act I is undoubtedly a great challenge, one rarely met in all its dimensions.

Violetta's party was an orderly and rounded affair. Flora's might also have been, with the cheerful opening ritornello coming back as the guests departed, had Alfredo not appeared and created a scandal. His arrival, followed by Violetta's on the arm of the baron, certainly brings a remarkable change of tone from the previous carefree divertissements of drawing-room gypsies and bullfighters. A nervous figure in violins and clarinets weaves its unsettling way under the surface conversation, thrice punctuated by anguished rising phrases from Violetta ("Ah perchè venni, incauta"). After the second of these phrases, the cellos redouble their subsurface hammering, but eventually the announcement of dinner releases the tension.

From an empty stage, the central finale, the big ensemble traditional in Italian opera, builds with the successive entrances of Violetta, Alfredo, the chorus and subprincipals, and finally Germont, whose dignified pronouncement launches the "Largo concertato." Within a relatively slow basic pulse, Verdi fits, first, Alfredo's choppy, disjunct, almost gabbled asides ("Ah si! che feci!"); a general movement of sympathy, under which the baron is heard warning of revenge; and then, as the orchestra accommodates a gentle waltz beat within the overall pulse, Violetta's solo lament, leading the whole company to a grand climax.

The fragile pathos of the Prelude's opening finally returns at the start of the last act (actually, a semitone higher in pitch, in a key yielding a less bright string tone color). Though often referred to as the "Prelude to Act III," this short orchestral movement bears no such appellation in Verdi's score, and is by no means over at the rise of the curtain; its material recurs throughout the dialogue among Violetta, Annina, and the doctor at the start of the scene. The sound of solo strings will remain a presence during much of the last act, first when playing Alfredo's love theme as Violetta rereads his letter (speaking rather than singing, a standard convention for letter-reading in the Italian tradition). This spell is broken by an ominous chord in the lower register, as Violetta laments, "È tardi!" Her aria, in a minor key that dominates the contrasting major episodes, is imaginatively scored, with the lamenting oboe that seems to fill in when Violetta's breath runs short, and more high solo strings in the last major section ("Ah! della traviata"). (This aria, like "Ah, fors'è lui," has a second verse traditionally omitted; in both cases, the essential point is made the first time, while the major-minor contrasts may be felt to lose their effectiveness upon repetition.)

The duet of reconciliation ("Parigi, o cara") has a well-motivated cabaletta, after Violetta collapses and the doctor is sent for; its expansiveness has often been found excessive, and a once-standard cut (beginning at "Oh Alfredo, il crudo termine!") is now being opened up again. The finale is an ensemble led by Violetta ("Prendi: quest'è l'immagine") over a funeral-march rhythm. For the last time, Alfredo's love theme returns in high solo strings, the delusive momentary revival before Violetta dies; the music, which she had brought into the major by her acceptance of death, now turns to minor again as all join in lamentation.

La Traviata

by
MARY McCARTHY

HE "woman gone astray" of our story is a classic product of her century and of a single country, France — you would not find her in Madrid or London. She is as much a Parisian distillate as perfume is of Grasse. But she is also a universal, an archetype of the misunderstood woman of easy virtue — the Magdalen, Moll Flanders, Dostoevsky's Sonia, Tolstoy's Maslova, Sartre's "Respectful Prostitute." The type perhaps goes back to the temple prostitutes of ancient religions — opposites and counterparts of vestal virgins, tending the sacred flame. Is it in the temple of love that Violetta Valéry, a highly successful cocotte and our special fallen woman, is serving as a votary or somewhere else? The story will show.

In our own century, this Violetta, so alluring to aristocrats, might have been a Coco Chanel, kept by the Duke of Westminster, or the Mlle. Modiste of an opera by Victor Herbert (whence the song "Kiss Me Again"). Or a famous model — there is a continuing relation to fashion. But actually she belongs, historically and in spirit, to the reign (1830–1848) of Louis Philippe, the so-called citizen king. The kept woman, of course, was not invented during those years; the mistresses of French kings over several centuries had been acting as "role models" for young women of luxurious tastes and accommodating habits, and they did not even have to be beautiful to catch the royal eye — look at the portraits. Nor was it necessary to be vicious — think of Madame de Maintenon.

The kept woman, or high-class courtesan (the same as "court lady," originally), was well known to readers of romances long before Violetta's time. Indeed a key book that may well have guided her footsteps was *Manon Lescaut* (1731) by the Abbé Prévost, about a well-born youth, the Chevalier des Grieux, ruined by the bewitching girl of fatally acquisitive propensities he undertakes to keep. Much later, this story became an opera, in fact, two, but Violetta can have known only the novel. She identified herself, very likely, with Manon (higher up than she, to start with, on the social scale), though this would have been a guilty identification; her sympathies, since she is a young woman of heart, must have gone to the Chevalier des Grieux.

The difference in birth between her and Manon is significant. It contributes to making her a girl of her time. She never says where she comes from or how she got where she is. All we know is that she is completely alone in the world, without parents or relations; she must have envied the fictional Manon her army-officer brother, even though he is a bad lot. She might have been a flower-seller, a theater-usher, or a seamstress with a smart dressmaker when she attracted the notice of her first "protector." Her good heart seems to testify to simple origins (though the equation is not always correct); most women of her kind at the time — like Chanel, later — came from poor farms and villages. Violetta reads; she is literate. This is a tribute to the conquests of the French Revolution, thanks to which primary and even secondary education became more than middle-class privileges. Despite her education, Violetta has retained a certain innocence, the mark perhaps of her origins, and even in her dissipations there is something high-minded, abstract, almost principled.

She is not, strictly speaking, a demi-mondaine; that implied somebody half in good society and half out of it. Violetta is not a well-nurtured girl who has made a misstep (had an illegitimate child, say) and thus *fallen* into vice; she is not déclassée (a term designating once upon a time a married woman no longer received socially and the title of a movie of my girlhood starring Corinne Griffith); nor is she exactly a demi-rep (an eighteenth-century term for a person of dubious reputation), though she may come closer to that. She differs from a Greek hetaera in that she is part of a social revolution in which those from below have been rising to the top. She is a ripple on the surface first unsettled by the French Revolution fifty or so years before; when we come to know her, it is around 1845, the apogee of her delicate ethereal type.

By the eighteen forties, France has undergone the Terror, the rise and fall of Napoleon, the Bourbon restoration, the insurrectionary "July days" ending with the installation of the Orléanist branch of the Bourbon family in the form of the moderate, pear-shaped Louis Philippe. It can be said that under that relatively easygoing monarch the French Revolution finally "took," like a vaccination: as with a vaccination, the body politic experienced a mild form of the dread disease of social leveling or equality — slight, feverish symptoms which, it was hoped, would insure against a recurrence of the real, virulent thing. By and large, that hope was not mistaken. Although Louis Philippe was overthrown in 1848, by the uprising that inspired the Communist Manifesto ("A specter is haunting Europe"), his reign nevertheless had been the heyday of mild, reformist progress. Once the '48 revolution was bloodily put down, Napoleon's nephew, Louis Bonaparte, calling himself the Emperor Napoleon III, inaugurated a permissive, coarsely acquisitive society well characterized by Emile Zola in novels picturing real-estate speculation, meat-packing, art, prostitution, alcoholism, coal mines, and the new department-store business.

If Zola was the inspired chronicler of the corrupt Second Empire with its vulgar, driving businessmen and their debased clotheshorses, the *poules de luxe,* it was Balzac and Victor Hugo who described the ebullient and still sometimes generous ruling class of newcomers and former aristocrats of Louis Philippe's time. This is evident in the treatment of the kept-woman figures of Balzac, so often tenderhearted, but also in Victor Hugo's touching picture of Fantine (*Les Misérables*), the orphaned grisette from "M. sur M." who goes wrong with the leader of a gay band of Sorbonne students, themselves provincials, and thus becomes the mother of Cosette. Sweet unworldly Fantine, tubercular, eventually reduced to streetwalking, is wholly altruistic, sacrificing her beautiful hair and her very teeth for her child, and even Balzac's courtesans, who know their way around, far from demanding a luxurious scale of living for *themselves,* are bent on maintaining their poor young lovers in style. Their ideal is to be kept by an old, indulgent (or preoccupied) man who visits once or twice a week and has the further privilege of escorting his cocotte to the theater, where he will be seen by the *beau monde* with her charms on his arm: when her Pantalon returns her to the love-nest he pays for, she is able to serve a delectable after-theater supper to the young genius she adores.

Some such ideal arrangement appears to be in the mind of Violetta Valéry in the early stages of the relation with *her* young man

from the country, Alfredo Germont. She is a long way from the
destitute Fantine, and yet there is an uncanny resemblance, even
to the tuberculosis: "There but for the grace of God," Violetta
might well have murmured to herself, had she read Fantine's history in one of the books she is fond of.

It is to a smallish intimate supper in her flat near the Opéra that
Alfredo has been brought by a friend somewhat better born than
himself — Gaston, the Viscount of Letorières. Alfredo has been
yearning to meet the famous cocotte, at present kept by a Baron
Douphol. He is shy and feels the honor of being taken to one of
her occasions. The young blades are dressed in evening clothes,
and the women, when they begin to appear on the arms of the
gentlemen escorting them, have the air of society ladies in low-cut
silks and velvets, flounces and ribbons — it is the age of the crin-
oline — carrying fans and with jewels in their hair. Only a certain freedom of manners will reveal them to be high-class tarts.

Violetta has been ill. When we first see her, that evening in her
drawing room, she is sitting on a sofa with her doctor — Grenvil — and some friends, as a party of other friends arrives late,
having lingered playing cards at the house of a woman named
Flora. Another fashionable demi-rep, we can surmise, watching her
come in, preening, with the Marquis d'Obigny, a young man who
is now keeping her. "We've all been at Flora's," they chorus, to
excuse themselves. "Flora!" cries Violetta, rising to greet her and
her train. The flower names of these women — before Violetta's
launching there had been a Camille, so called for her white and
red camellias, and a Marguérite (Daisy) — give a whiff of the fashions of the period.

An immense table is laid for the supper to come, with cold fowl
and game, pâtés of little birds, galantines, chaud-froids, lobsters,
Russian salads, hams from York and Prague. Champagne is being
served by liveried footmen; later there will be sherbets, pineapples,
and Italian ices. It is an August night (hence no oysters). Other
servants are bringing platters, richly decorated, and wine bottles
in iced coolers of highly polished silver. Everyone drinks, even the
doctor. To us, the gaiety — clinking of glasses, raised voices, fa-
miliarity of manners — may be slightly reminiscent of some "wild
party" of the twenties or a Hollywood soirée of silent-film days,
when the Mary Pickfords and Gloria Swansons were the style
leaders (and often kept women) of an extravagant new class.

In Violetta's suite of reception rooms, one opening into another, the atmosphere is unusually fevered and hectic, even for this milieu. This is a sign, surely, of her disease, like the doctor's presence at her side, an omen, as in the big mirror over the dainty marble fireplace on the left of the principal room, furnished with sofas, *faces-à-faces*, love seats, footstools, small tables and tabourets, rosewood and buhl cabinets full of Sèvres and Meissen. This is a room designed for moments of intimacy and suggestive of a boudoir. The mirror is Violetta's eternal, warning companion, like the mirror in the fairy tale ("Mirror, mirror, on the wall"), a necessity of her profession of kept woman, who must constantly know the truth about the fluctuating bank account constituted by her beauty. As the saying goes, her face is her fortune, or has been up to now, but it is also her misfortune.

Now, as her guests pour in from Flora's (significant that they should be late, indicating that to them one kept woman's house is the same as another's), Violetta promises an evening of riotous pleasure, to the point where Flora and her new "protector" wonder aloud whether the hostess is allowed to stay up late drinking champagne with so much abandon. "I want it," Violetta says with a little air of obstinacy, glancing at the doctor, who says nothing. "I have the habit. The life of pleasure agrees with me. It's the best medicine I know."

At that very moment, at the entry to the drawing room someone appears who will be her fatal drug: Alfredo. He has hardly been presented to her, as a great admirer, when Flora's marquis speaks to him, tapping him on the shoulder, and the two shake hands. He is a young fellow from the provinces, of middle-class background, and most of the others are titled playboys, but in this house equality reigns; he is greeted by his first name — "Alfredo!" "Marquis!" he replies. Meanwhile Violetta's baron has showed his face among the latecomers who had stayed gambling at Flora's. This seems to be Violetta's signal to summon a servant: "Is everything ready?" At the servant's nod, she calls the company to table as champagne still makes the rounds.

Violetta has put herself between Alfredo and his sponsor, the viscount, who tells her in an undertone about the new young man. Opposite are Flora, with her marquis on one side and Violetta's baron — Douphol — on the other. This is the key group; the rest find places where they can. "He's always thinking of you," Gaston says softly to the hostess. "You're not serious?" she answers, laughing. "When you were ill," Gaston persists, "he came running to ask after you every day." "Oh, stop it!" she decrees, but with a touch of archness. "I'm nothing to him." When she tries to ward off flattery, she is half-serious, half a trained coquette. "I'm not fooling," Gaston retorts, looking toward Alfredo, as if to draw him into the exchange. "Is it true, then?" No longer laughing, she turns to Alfredo. "But why? I don't understand." With her look fixed on him, he speaks to her, shyly, for the first time, to confirm what his friend is reporting. "Yes, it's true." He sighs. Sweetly and seriously, she thanks him for his concern. Then, across the table, to the baron: "But you, baron, how is it you didn't do likewise?" "I've known you only a year," says the baron, harshly. "But this one has known me only a few minutes," she points out.

Alfredo, with his seriousness and shyness, is getting on the baron's nerves. He does not like the change the young provincial is effecting in Violetta. Flora notices this, and, sotto voce, out of the corner of her mouth, chides the baron for his manners. *She* finds Alfredo charming, she adds.

Meanwhile, across the table, Gaston is chiding Alfredo, who is *his* responsibility. "Aren't you going to open your mouth?" he inquires. Flora's protector, the marquis, knows Alfredo well enough to put the burden on the hostess. "It's up to you, my lady," he tells Violetta, "to wake the young fellow up." "I'll be Hebe, your cupbearer, and pour you a glass," she announces to the still dumbstruck Alfredo. "And may you be immortal, like her," he answers, gallantly; he is schoolboy enough for a classical allusion to have loosened his tongue. Then the others join their voices to the wish, raising their glasses. This inspires the viscount to try to jolly up the moody baron. Can't he find some verses — a song — to suit the festive occasion? Without a word, the baron refuses. "All right, it's up to you, then," Gaston tells Alfredo. The others loudly second the suggestion. "A drinking song! Let's have a drinking song!" He, too, declines. "I'm not in the proper mood." "But aren't you a master of the art?" teases his friend Gaston. "Would it please *you* if I sang?" Alfredo turns to Violetta, abruptly altering the tone. "Yes," she tells him, simply. That is all he needs. "Yes? In that case I'll sing. I have the song here in my heart." He rises. "Everybody listen!" cries the marquis. "Attention for the singer," they chorus, the baron excepted.

Alfredo, on his feet, sings in praise of wine — a fairly standard paean. As he goes on, however, more and more carried away, he is singing directly to her, and words and music take on, as it were, an undertone of deeper meaning. Through wine, it is love he is hymning — the hotter kisses that lie at the bottom of the cup. "Love . . . love . . . love" — the word repeats itself like an incantation, as though he were compelled. At one moment, intoxicated by the song, he has pointed straight to Violetta, and now, as his young voice ceases, she, too, rises to her feet as if compelled also, and sings her own paean. Not to wine nor to love but simply to pleasure. Anything but pleasure is folly. The flower of love is born and dies in a day. Take it, joy in it. Seize the alluring occasion, revel in every pleasure, laugh and make merry till dawn.

It is her creed she is pronouncing, of feverish enjoyment, without distinction between sensuous delight and sensual pleasure, a creed, at bottom, of forgetfulness. She has addressed herself to the whole like-minded company and, when she has finished, all but Alfredo join in. Then, in quite another voice, she speaks to Alfredo: "Life is jubilation." Is it an apology for herself or an instruction to him? "Do you hear me, life is having fun," she seems to be telling him, ignoring everyone else. And he replies in the same tone, as though they were alone in a room: "For those who haven't yet loved." This is a mild reprimand or gentle correction. Each of these young people — for all her amorous history, she is not yet twenty-three — is playing teacher. Surrounded by her guests, by a veritable chorus of inane worldlings, they are all by themselves in a schoolroom, as it were, each reciting a lesson, solo. "Don't tell it to somebody who isn't in the know." (To somebody, she is admitting, who has never loved.) "It's my destiny," he says grandly, as if embracing the fate of loving. It is a kind of quarrel — their first falling-out, based on assertions and counter-assertions of principle. Then the mindless chorus breaks in, supporting her side of the argument ("Wine, jesting, and song, All the night long"), but without her desperate dependence on pleasure as oblivion.

At this appropriate moment a band strikes up in the next room. The guests show surprise. "Wouldn't a dance be nice now?" inquires Violetta, who of course has planned it. There is a cry of general delight ("What a lovely thought!"), and Violetta, once more the hostess, leads the way to the center door. "Let's go in, then."

She urges them ahead, to the ballroom. "Oh, my!" She has turned deathly white. "What's the matter?" the choir of guests tunes up. "Nothing, nothing," she replies. "What in the world *is* it?" other voices exclaim, some almost irritable. "Let's go," she repeats. "Oh, God!" She takes a step or two and is obliged to sit down. "Again!" they all cry out. "You're in pain," says Alfredo. "Heavens, what is it?" the others chime. "Just a trembling that comes over me." She makes a gesture toward the inner room, where the band is still playing a waltz. "Please! Do go in! I'll be with you soon." "As you wish," they tell her. And amazingly all of them, except the mute, motionless Alfredo, pass into the next room, drawn by the music like children by a Pied Piper of Hamelin. They leave the drawing room (as Violetta thinks) empty. She goes up to the great mirror over the fireplace — her truth-teller. "Oh, how pale I am." She looks at herself a long time; then a warning instinct makes her turn, and she becomes aware of Alfredo, behind her. "You here?"

He timidly approaches her. "Has your indisposition passed off?" "I'm better," she says curtly. The reserve of her tone tells him that she is trying to put him off, and almost angrily he bursts out. "This way of life will kill you." He moves a little closer so that he can study her still pallid face. "You must take care of your health." "And how am I to do that?" she teases, opposing her experienced lightness to his youthful solemnity. He ignores the levity, and his answer is like a vow. "If you were mine, I'd take *such* care of you. I'd be the faithful guardian of every one of your precious days."

Violetta is startled. "What are you saying? Am I in someone's charge, perhaps?" "No," he replies promptly, flaring up as though a fire in him had suddenly been fanned. "That is because no one in all this world loves you." "No one?" she rallies him. "No one but me." "Is that so?" she gives a trill of laughter, deciding to be amused by him. "Oh, yes, I'd forgotten that grand passion of yours." He is hurt. "You laugh. Is there a heart in your bosom?" "A heart? Well, yes, maybe. And what do you want with it?" He shakes his head sorrowfully. "Ah, if you had one, you couldn't jest."

Up to this point, the dialogue between them in the deserted room has been earnest preaching on his side and on hers a light, practiced fencing, a quasi-professional scoring of points. In other words, she has been firmly treating the interlude as a flirtation, disturbed only by the gravity of his insistent reference to her health, more appropriate to a doctor than to a suitor. But gradually something somber in his tone or the burning expression of his eyes catches her deeper attention, and for the first time she responds with a seriousness matching his.

"Do you mean it?" "I'm not deceiving you," he answers, with the same knightly earnestness. "Is it a long time that you've loved me?" she wonders, curiously, having never felt the sentiment herself. That question is all Alfredo needs. He knows the answer by heart. It is why he is here this evening, having persuaded his friend Gaston to bring him. In the next room the band music stops as if to listen to his declaration. And he begins by taking her question literally; his is a literal nature. "Oh, yes, for a year," he tells her; the true son of a burgher, he counts. But then a simple poetry that is also in his character starts to tug at the earthbound prose in him; he goes up as if in a bright balloon, recalling the first day he saw her — ethereal, a bolt from the blue. Since that day he has loved her, in secret, with a tremulous love throbbing in him like the heartbeat of the entire universe — a mysterious sovereign love, so very mysterious, a torment and a delight.

The rapture of this extravagant declaration takes Violetta aback; she recoils from the fiery furnace of the young man's ardor. If what he says is true, she tells him, he had better leave her alone. Friendship is all she can offer him. He must understand her position. "I don't know how to love. I can't sustain such heroic emotions. I am telling you frankly, in all candor, you must look for another kind of woman. It won't be hard for you to find her, and then you'll forget me." He is paying no attention, continuing to talk raptly of a mysterious, sovereign power, when the band in the next room strikes up more loudly and at the same moment his friend the viscount appears in the doorway as though blown in by a gust of sound. "What's going on here?" "Nothing," Violetta tells him quickly. "We're talking nonsense." "Ah ha!" the viscount exclaims, seeing how the land lies and starting to beat a retreat. "Fine! Stay there!" And he hurriedly withdraws.

But the mood has been dispelled by the intrusion of the world. Violetta once more has the ascendancy over her intemperate suitor. He must make a pact with her, she enjoins him: no more talk of love. He agrees and promptly turns to go. But she detains him. Somewhat surprised or even hurt, she draws a flower from the bosom of her dress. "Take it." "Why?" "Why, to bring it back to me," she says with a little laugh. This catches him midway in his departure and makes him whirl about. "When?" "When it has faded," she replies, on a note of self-evidence. She is amused with him again: evidently there is a language of flowers unfamiliar to the inexperienced youth. We are reminded of the story of Camille, another kept woman, and her red and white camellias. But Alfredo, though ignorant of that history, has finally understood. "Good heavens! You mean tomorrow?" "Well, then, tomorrow," she tells him, indulgently, though that is sooner, apparently, than she meant.

"I am happy," he declares, taking the flower in a transport of bliss. She smiles on him tenderly. "Do you still say you love me?" If she asks, she must want him to repeat it, contrary to the "pact" she has just imposed. "Oh, how much!" he declares, bringing his hand to his heart. Once again, he starts to go. "You're leaving?" she exclaims, wistful all at once. "I'm leaving." During this lingering exchange, it is as if Violetta has grown childish, and he has become a man. "Good-bye," "Good-bye," they tell each other softly. For a last time he returns and kisses her hand.

No sooner have they separated than the band of others bursts in, ready to take their leave and totally forgetful, it emerges, of their hostess's indisposition only an hour or so before. Not a single inquiry from her seeming "best friends," the very ones who were wondering at the outset whether champagne and a late night might not do her harm. Inside, the musicians have stopped, but the parting guests, volleying out their thanks and their dreadful *joie de vivre*, are making enough noise for a whole military band. "Time to go home," "The dawn is breaking," "Thank you, thank you, dear lady, for a marvelous time," "It's the height of the season, everyone's giving parties, so we must get rested up."

This burst of cheerful, unfeeling chatter makes a peculiar contrast with the pitch of intense feeling that Violetta and Alfredo have mounted to when left to themselves. In this very contrast there are premonitions of tragedy. Two beings of extreme sensitivity seem unprotected, like a pair of orphans in an unfeeling world — despite Violetta's sumptuous style of entertainment, they are both babes in the woods. "Life is a tragedy for those who feel" — Violetta, long ago, has learned that lesson and taken measures to ensure herself against love, the most powerful feeling of all. Alfredo, on his side, is less prescient; he finds nothing but joy and ecstasy in his capacity to feel.

What we have just witnessed is a scene of temptation with the sexes reversed: Alfredo, our innocent Adam, is urging a reluctant and fearful Eve to taste with him the delights of something more than mere carnal knowledge — a love-apple that for a girl in her position is poison. It is already evident that she has consumption, that is, something inside her, within her frail chest, that is burning her up. This consumption is allied to the passion that will inevitably devour her, a wasting disease beside which mere dissipation — wine and late hours — is harmless child's play.

Now the beautiful kept woman is alone in her salon. Alfredo has gone off in high spirits and great expectations, not much more sensible than the departing revelers to the struggle she is left to carry on, for self-protection, with herself. The baron has departed and apparently will not return tonight. She thinks aloud. It is strange, strange, she meditates, that those words of his have carved a design in her heart. Would a serious love be a misfortune for her? She cannot answer, never having known one, and there is no one to give her counsel, not even Flora, certainly not the doctor. She can only ask her own confused, ignorant soul. The sensation of being loved while loving (mutual love) is foreign to her experience. But ought she to disdain it for the arid follies of her present life? She paces the room, thinking more and more deeply on the matter.

She asks herself whether Alfredo is not, finally, "the man of her dreams." Didn't he appear to her, as a lonely girl, to paint her soul's prison in vivid, arcane colors? And didn't he in fact, just recently, stand modest guard outside her sickroom and kindle a new fever in her bosom, awakening her to love? She is seeking a supranatural explanation for the novel feeling in her, pretending that she had known him, dreamed him, in an anterior life or that his presence, at the door of her sick chamber, when he came to inquire every day, had been felt by her in the midst of her fever as an "aura" or emanation of love. . . . Sunk in these mystical thoughts, as if in a trance, she is soon like a creature possessed, by this young man or by a kindred spirit speaking his language of mysterious sovereign powers, balms and crosses, torments and delights.

Then she shakes herself out of her reverie. "Follies," she scolds, getting herself in hand. "Madness, vain delirium." Having cast out the love demon, she sighs. "Poor woman, alone, abandoned, in this populous desert they call Paris, what more have I got to hope for? What must I do? Enjoy, enjoy, enjoy. . . . Die on the summits of pleasure." She seems to hear a voice — Alfredo's — in a serenade below the balcony of her open window. Still those heartbeats, crosses, and delights. Her own private music has quite another theme. "Free, forever free, flitting from joy to joy. Let me live for pleasure only. Down the primrose path I fly." This mundane hymn to liberty is raised to a higher plane by the frenzy in it; a fever of commitment redeems the triteness of the pledge this poor young woman, gesturing with a champagne glass, is taking to the principle of enjoyment.

TWO

FIVE months have passed. It is January. Nothing has turned out as a realist might have expected. Violetta has not persisted in her giddy life of pleasure. Instead, she is living in the country near Paris, and with Alfredo. Where is it? Perhaps Auteuil. These kept women, even when they reform, cannot leave Paris far behind. It was the same with Manon Lescaut, before the Revolution. When she and her Chevalier des Grieux decided to play house in the country, living the simple life and saving taxi fares, they removed to Chaillot. (Today both Auteuil with its racetrack and Chaillot have become indistinguishable parts of Paris, but Chaillot got swallowed up earlier.) Violetta has taken a pleasant country house. French doors give on a garden from the ground-floor living room. There is an abundance of chairs and little tables, as well as a writing-desk and a few books — "serious" items that had not been visible in her Parisian dwelling. Another symptom of change is the absence of flunkeys; here one little girl, Annina (Annie), in cap and apron, seems to be doing most of the work. At the back of the room, once again there is a fireplace, rustic this time (built of stone), with a mirror hanging over it and under the mirror a clock of the Empire period.

Alfredo comes into the empty room; when he was last seen, he was in evening clothes, and now he is in hunting dress with a gun on his shoulder, which he lays down. The hunting season must be nearing an end. It is three months since Violetta left Paris — lov-

ers, parties, cards, furniture — to devote herself to creating an idyl
for him. And it has worked. His boiling youthful spirits, under her
serene management, have been tempered to a quiet happiness. He
has changed. Ever since the day she told him "I want to live for
you alone," he has been living in a kind of heaven.

Now Annina comes in, dressed in traveling gear. She has been
to Paris. Alfredo is surprised. "Who sent you?" Clearly, such trips
are unusual. "My mistress," the girl replies. "Why?" he persists,
and Annina tells him: it was to sell the horses and carriages and
whatever else Violetta still had. He is thunderstruck, unable to
believe his ears. "It costs a lot to live alone out here," Annina
informs him. "And you said nothing?" "I was forbidden to."
"Forbidden?" he repeats, still staggered by what she is revealing.
"So how much do we need?" "A thousand," she replies. He has
no visible reaction to the sum of money named — is it a still worse
shock? But he at once tells the little servant to make herself scarce.
He will go to Paris himself. "And you're not to tell your lady
about this conversation. With what I have, I can still repair the
damage. Go, what are you waiting for?"

When the little servant goes out, he apostrophizes himself in
horror. How can he have been so unnoticing? Infamous! Shame-
ful! To live in such delusion! At last the truth has shattered that
rotten dream. There's still time, though, if offended honor will
only be patient, to wash away the shame.

With that thought, he rushes out, bound for Paris. A moment
later, Violetta returns, her own transaction accomplished. She
comes in slowly, in traveling dress, talking to Annie, her little maid,
at the door. In her gloved hand she holds papers — bills of sale,
receipts, and so on. Seeing no one in the room, she calls his name.
"Alfredo!" There is no answer. Then Annina steps forward, to say
that he has left for Paris only a few minutes before. A presentiment
seems to grip Violetta. "Is he coming back?" The maid fails to
hear the trouble in her mistress's voice. "Before sundown," she
says. "He asked me to give you the message." But Violetta is not
wholly reassured. "Strange!" she muses aloud. While she stands
wondering, Joseph, the old manservant, appears. He has a letter
in his hand. "It's for you." As a servant, he is no more stylish than
Annina. "Good," says Violetta, opening the letter with a paper
knife from the writing-desk. "A man of business will be here to
see me soon. Have him come in at once." The servants withdraw.

Now Violetta opens the letter, which proves to be in fact from Flora, who has found out her hiding-place and wants her to come to a dancing-party in Paris that evening. Violetta tosses the letter onto a table and sinks into a chair. She is tired from her journey and all the business she has done. "Well, well! She'll have a long wait for me." Of course she won't go. She yawns. Joseph again appears in the doorway. "There's a gentleman here." "It must be the one I'm expecting," Violetta decides and she motions to the servant to show the caller in.

A handsome old man, stiff as a ruler, enters the room. "Mademoiselle Valéry?" "I am she," Violetta replies curtly, as though sensing a need to assert every bit of her dignity. He makes no move to come near her. "You see before you Alfredo's father," he announces in a deep, austere voice. In her surprise, Violetta utters a cry. "You?" She gestures to him to sit down in a chair opposite her; she had not risen at his entry. "Precisely," replies the elder Germont, taking the seat. "Of the reckless young man you've bewitched and sent rushing to his ruin." Having formally stated this, he leans forward and looks her keenly in the eyes. Violetta, incensed at this language, rises to her feet. "I am a woman, sir, and in her own house. Please allow me to leave you, as much for your sake as for mine." She starts to go out. "What style!" the offended father mutters. He decides to curb his tongue. "However . . ." he continues, in a milder tone. "You have been misled," she tells him but returns to her chair in time to hear him say: "He wants to make you a present of every sou he owns." "Up to now he hasn't dared," retorts Violetta. "I'd refuse." Germont glances around the sitting room. "But all this luxury," he comments.

Violetta has followed his glance. "This is a secret from everyone. Let it not be one from you." Without a further word she hands the unbending old man the papers she has brought back from Paris — papers that speak for themselves. He runs a hurried eye through them. "Good God! What a revelation! You think of stripping yourself of all your possessions — everything you have?" Then an explanation occurs to him. "Ah, because of your past. Why let it accuse you?" He is moved to pity. "That past no longer exists," she announces proudly. "Now I love Alfredo. And God has annulled the past because of my repentance." Germont is more and more struck. "These are noble feelings," he observes. Here is not the kind of wanton he had expected to deal with.

With her acute sensibility, Violetta is immediately aware of the change in his feeling toward her. She leans forward impulsively. "How sweet your words sound to me." Germont ignores this winning speech, intent on his main purpose. "Such feelings demand sacrifices. I am asking one of you." He has stood up. She leaps up herself, affrighted, trembling like a hunted deer. "Ah, no. Be quiet. You'd ask for terrible things. Yes, I foresaw it. I expected you. I was too happy." The old man squares his shoulders and stiffens his bony spine, making himself look even taller. "Alfredo's father demands it in the name of two destinies — the future of his two children." "*Two* children?" She is startled. Seeing her surprise, Germont takes a deep, preparatory breath. Now he can speak to her of the little sister, the daughter God gave him, pure as an angel.

Pure as an angel. But if her truant brother refuses to return to the bosom of the family, then her fiancé — the youth she loves and who loves her in return — will have to back off from his commitment, which had been the joy of both. On the theme of that pure maiden, Germont waxes eloquent. He soars to a pitch of feeling. As he pleads his suit (or the suit of his daughter), the old burgher in his virtuous plain attire curiously recalls the figure of his son in evening dress in the salon of Violetta's apartment holding forth on ethereal rapture, mysterious, sovereign love, and so on. Like father, like son. Violetta listens, transfixed. We are witnessing a seduction scene — nothing less than that.

And, like so many women mesmerized by a seducer, Violetta does not understand at first what Alfredo's father wants of her. "You're not going to turn the roses of love into thorns," he has been pleading, carried away on a fresh rhetorical flight. "You won't withstand my prayers. Your heart will not refuse." "Oh, I understand," she cries, brightening, her next words a clear indication that she does not. "For a little while I shall have to live apart from Alfredo. That will be hard. However . . ." "That's not what I'm asking," he says bluntly.

"Good heavens, what more can you want? I'm offering a great deal." "Not enough, though." "You want me to give him up for good?" "It's necessary." His terse, staccato replies reveal a different, wholly determined man. They come like short pitiless stabs at her tender, quivering heart. At last she understands what this Nemesis wants of her. As comprehension pierces her, she screams.

"Never! No, never!" she shrills, like somebody on the rack. Then she gets hold of herself, her voice drops to a soft pleading tone that begs him pitifully for mercy.

Germont cannot know the love she has burning in her heart. That among the living she has neither friends nor relations. That Alfredo has sworn to her that he will be all of them for her — parents, brother, friends. Nor does her torturer know that she has been stricken by a dread disease, that the end of her days is already in plain sight. And yet he is asking her to give Alfredo up. To such heartless torture, she decidedly prefers death.

Again his attitude changes, to one of respectful sympathy. The resolution of her last few words has showed another side to her, which he must treat with a new deference. The sacrifice will be heavy, he acknowledges. "But still — listen to me calmly — you're beautiful and young. With time —" "Don't go on," she interrupts, as though to spare him useless effort. "I understand you. But for me it's impossible. I can love only him." "Granted," he tells her. "And yet men are inconstant, you know." To this terrible hint, Violetta reacts with a start, as though the idea that Alfredo could be faithless were coming to her for the first time. "Good God!" she cries out. The paterfamilias, confident that he has touched a vulnerable spot, presses on with his insinuations. A day may come, he prophesies, when the pleasures of Venus pall and boredom is quick to follow. . . . What will happen then? "Think!" he bids her. "For you the sweeter affections can never serve as balm, since unions like yours cannot be blessed by heaven." Violetta drops her eyes, again touched to the quick. The fact that Alfredo cannot marry her, which she has accepted with an easy heart, takes on its full, bleak significance in the father's relentless optic: they can never have children, a real home, family life, an assured place in society; when love-making loses its first charm, they will find nothing to occupy them, no binding agent to hold them together. "It's true!" she whispers, excruciated; again the torment he skillfully produces in her is like a physical pain.

"Well, then, abandon that seductive dream." Germont is close to attaining his object; he has only to drive home his points. Vigor and manly confidence now visibly exude from him, like an athlete's sweat. He has shown her enough of the bad and threatening aspects of the future; it is time to point to the rewards in store if she behaves. "Be my family's consoling angel. Violetta" — for the first time he pronounces her name — "think, do think. There's time still, don't you see? Young woman, believe me, God is speaking through a father's voice." It is a privilege he is offering her if she will only understand. Through the sacred character of the family tie (which she has never known, apparently), she will be drawn into the embrace of the *Padre Eterno*, stern but forgiving, like his human simulacrum. Germont, as if bathed himself in holy light, is showing the fallen woman the path to salvation.

But the prevailing erotic undertone, the caressing voice, deeper and more virile than the son's mere tenor, start to make one wonder. Isn't this grave old party the devil? To one more versed in the Gospels than Violetta, this is the familiar temptation in the wilderness, with a perverse Victorian twist. The family is the god to which she and all her sisterhood are required to sacrifice. Indeed, without Violetta and her sisters to "take care of" the coarse lusts of the male, the family as temple of purity could not be enshrined.

Meanwhile, Violetta, writhing on the cross prepared for her, is sadly aware, at last, of her fate. She has been deluded — now she knows it — to suppose that she can rise from ashes and create a new life. There's no hope for a fallen woman. Even if God in His indulgence can forgive her, man will be implacable.

Bitterly weeping, she turns to the parent-extortioner to tell him to tell his daughter, that fair, pure daughter, how a poor wretch, victim of misfortune, had a single ray of happiness and sacrificed it to her. Having done so, the wretch will die. The extraordinary thing is that Violetta, as though to bear out the father's well-worn arguments, is transfigured while speaking by her good (as she thinks) action. Although she weeps bitter tears, her feeling for the fortunate, sheltered maiden has no trace of animus or sarcasm; if there is envy, it is a kind of holy envy, suffused with tender piety. And now Germont, perhaps sincerely, is able to offer consolation to his suffering victim. "Weep, weep," he tells her, "weep, poor woman." Her tears are good for her — a therapy; she must let them flow. And, now that it is over and she has given way, he is able to see — and admit — that it is a supreme sacrifice he is asking of her. In his own breast already he feels the pain of it. "Courage!" he concludes, on a brisker note. "Your noble heart will conquer."

A silence intervenes, as at the conclusion of a rite: *ite, missa est.* Then, like a soldier or a hired assassin, she asks him to give her his orders. "Tell him you don't love him." "He won't believe me."

"Leave." "He'll follow." "Then . . ." Germont is at a loss; he has no experience in these matters. In his stead, Violetta decides what she must do. But first, like a young knight, she needs his blessing. "Embrace me like a daughter," she instructs the old man. "That will make me strong." He puts his arms around her, and for a moment they stand clasped. Then the newly armored woman, the "daughter," speaks. "He'll be delivered to you shortly, but he'll be in a pitiable state." She points to the garden. "Please wait for him there and comfort him." She goes to the writing-desk. "What's in your mind?" he asks, uneasily. She shakes her head. "If you knew, you'd try to stop me."

Germont is more and more impressed and surprised by her. "Generous woman! And what can *I* do for *you*?" Violetta has the answer ready for him — another surprise. Advancing from beside the desk, she takes a few steps in his direction. She has been thinking ahead. "I'll die! When it happens, don't let him curse my memory. If you do feel something for me, at least tell him what I've suffered." "No, generous spirit, live. You must be happy. Heaven will reward you one day for these tears." In a new way they are still at cross-purposes. Her realism and urgency are met by uplifting speeches of a deeply conventional sort. Alfredo's father prefers not to know the truth, which Violetta, for her part, has accepted — almost, in a strange fashion, embraced.

She replies calmly. When she is dead, Alfredo should know of the sacrifice she has made for love of him. He should know that her heart has been his up to her last breath. Germont's answer to this is, of course, the predictable set of clichés. "Your heart's sacrifice will find its reward. You will be proud then of such a noble deed." Violetta is no longer listening. She has heard a sound perhaps from the garden. "Someone's coming! Go!" "Oh, my heart is so grateful," he says, turning to leave. "Go!" she repeats and adds, on reflection: "This may be the last time we'll see each other." Very simply, she turns to him, and they embrace. Each then enjoins the other to be happy — impossible in both cases — and they bid each other farewell. He goes out by a garden window, and she is alone.

"God, give me strength." She sits down at the desk, writes something, then rings the bell. Annina appears. "You wanted me?" "Yes. Deliver this yourself." Annina glances at the folded sheet of paper and is surprised by the name of the addressee. She gives a little shriek. "Quiet," her mistress tells her. "Be off." The girl goes out. Violetta ponders. Now she must write to Alfredo. But what will she tell him? And where will she get the courage? She writes and seals the letter.

Alfredo enters, in city clothes. "What are you doing?" he immediately wants to know. "Nothing," she tells him, hiding the letter. "You were writing!" he exclaims. "Yes, no, no," she answers in confusion. "Why so perturbed? Whom were you writing to?" She faces him. "To you." "Give me that sheet of paper." "No, not now." He is embarrassed by his own brusqueness. "Forgive me. I'm a little upset." She rises. "What has happened?" "My father has arrived." "You've seen him?" "No. He left me a stiff letter. But I'm waiting for him. He'll fall in love with you as soon as he sees you."

She becomes extremely agitated. "He mustn't find me here. Let me leave. . . . You calm him, and then I'll throw myself at his feet." She can barely hold back her tears. "He won't want to separate us any more. We'll be happy. Because you love me. You do, don't you, Alfredo?" "Oh, so much! But you're crying?" "I just felt the need of tears. But now I'm over it. See? I'm smiling at you." She makes an effort. "I'll be there, among those flowers, always near you, always, always near you. Alfredo, love me as much as I love you. Love me, Alfredo. . . . Good-bye." She runs out into the garden.

Strangely enough, Alfredo seems quite undisturbed by this precipitate departure. "That dear heart lives only for my love," he observes, somewhat fatuously. As we have already seen, he is not a noticing young man. He sits down and opens a book (can it be *Manon Lescaut*?) and glances at the clock on the chimney-piece. "It's late. Maybe I shan't see my father today." The old servant, Joseph, comes in. "Madame has left. A carriage was waiting for her and by now it's speeding along the road to Paris. And Annina left even sooner than she did." "I know it," Alfredo tells him. "Calm down." Joseph mutters to himself. "What does it all mean?" After the servant has left the room, Alfredo puts down his book and ponders. Violetta, he decides, has gone off to speed up the disposal of her property. But Annina will prevent it. Through the French windows the father's tall black-clad figure can be seen crossing the garden. "Somebody's in the garden!" Alfredo exclaims. "Hello, who's there?"

A gold-braided messenger appears in a side doorway. "Monsieur Germont?" "I am he," answers Alfredo. The messenger is out of breath. "A lady in a carriage, not far from here, gave me this for you." He hands a letter to Alfredo, pockets a tip, and leaves. Alfredo studies the letter. "From Violetta! Why am I disturbed? Maybe she's asking me to join her. Why, I'm trembling. Oh, Lord, courage!" He unfolds the letter and begins to read. " 'Alfredo, when you get this letter —' Ah!" Turning, with a wild cry, he finds himself face to face with his father, who stands silently waiting as Alfredo falls into his arms. "Oh, Father!" "Oh, my son! Oh, how you're suffering!" He is shocked by the young man's racking sobs, evidently an unfamiliar spectacle for him. To the original surge of pity, parental impatience is a natural sequel. "Oh, dry those tears. Come back to us. Be once more the pride and boast of your father."

The invitation to dry his tears and come home does appear somewhat ill-timed. It's as if Germont were blind to the awful grief he is witnessing, with the willful blindness of old age. While the young man sits unhearing, the old man decides to rally him by singing the praises of their native Provence. The father, like so many Southerners, is a patriot — not to say a booster — of the local air and light. Provence, he seems to be saying, can cure whatever ails anyone.

He invokes the blue sea, the soil, the glittering sun of Alfredo's forefathers. Who could expunge them from the heart of a true-born Provençal? If only Alfredo in his sorrow would remember the joy he once knew under those sparkling skies, the peace that once again can shed its effulgence on a native son! In the course of this reverie laced with exhortation, he has convinced himself that all Alfredo's troubles came from leaving home. And he has treated himself to a bath of sentiment on his own account, the pitiful old sire of a distant son, his white head bowed with shame. He has suffered more than Alfredo can ever know. But if he has found his boy again, if his own power of hope does not falter, if the voice of honor has not been entirely silenced in the errant youth, then God has heard him!

Alfredo, seemingly, has not. Old Germont gives him a shake. "Don't you have any response to a father's affection?" Alfredo shakes himself out of his absorption. "I'm devoured by a thousand furies. Leave me alone." He pushes the old man away. "Leave you here alone?" Alfredo ignores him, speaking to himself with determination. "Revenge!" Germont has no perception of his son's mood or the direction of his thoughts. Characteristically for this story, they are talking at cross-purposes (like Germont with Violetta), each intent on his privately nurtured design. The father supposes that the son is ready to leave with him for the curative blue skies of Provence. "Enough delay. We're leaving. Hurry up." Alfredo remains fixed to his chair, brooding to himself. "It was Douphol," he decides, his fevered brain fixing on his former rival, Violetta's protector of five months before. Germont grows peremptory. "Do you hear me?" he demands. "No!" shouts Alfredo, who at length understands what is being asked of him.

"So it's useless to have found you again, is it, Alfredo?" But from his son's taut face, Germont realizes that he is wrong to antagonize him. "No, Alfredo, you'll hear no reproaches from me. We'll bury the past together. Love has brought me here to find you and love knows how to forgive. Come! Let's surprise your dear ones with the sight of us together. You can't refuse that joy to those you've pained so much. A father and a sister, even now, are hastening to console you." Alfredo is taking no interest. Again he shakes himself, as if to focus his attention. His eye lights on Flora's letter on the table beside him. He reads it. "Ah!" he cries, enlightened. "So she's at the party. I'll fly to avenge the insult." He rushes out, headlong, with his father on his heels. "What are you saying? Stop!" The doors to the garden bang. The love-nest is empty; all the birds have flown.

It is quite another décor that meets our eyes, still that same night. We are at Flora's. A long, richly decorated room is brilliantly lit by crystal chandeliers and bronze candelabra. There is a small refreshment table laid with snowy linen and flowers in silver epergnes. In the middle of the room is a gambling table, holding cards, a roulette wheel, dice. Flora is escorting her first guests into the salon. We recognize the habitués of Violetta's former circle: the doctor, the marquis, and so on. There will be a masquerade this evening, Flora promises; the viscount has got it up. And she has asked Violetta and Alfredo too. Her lover, the marquis, smiles. Hasn't she heard the news? Violetta and Alfredo have separated. Flora and the doctor can hardly believe it. But the marquis is very sure. She will come tonight with the baron; the company will see. The doctor shakes his head, still incredulous. He saw them only the day before, and they seemed so happy.

Just then a distraction occurs: the masquerade. Flora calls for silence, and a band of ladies enters disguised as gypsies. Some are picked out by the guests as members of the familiar select circle. Thus when the "gypsies" begin the game of pretending to tell fortunes, they are able to make use of their intimate knowledge of the private lives of the company — e.g., that Flora's marquis is a rake who gives her countless rivals — without causing too much surprise. Before the artificial storm raised by this intelligence — common knowledge to all, Flora included — new maskers come in: the viscount and his friends disguised as matadors. They put on a frankly amateurish show, reciting parts and singing a Spanish-style chorus of love and bullfighting. But this somewhat perfunctory "theater" soon gives way to the regular business of real life, as masks are removed and everybody either makes for the gambling table or prepares to stroll about, idly flirting.

At this moment Alfredo, having waited perhaps for a lull, chooses to present himself. "You?" they all exclaim, not concealing their astonishment. "Why, yes. It's me, friends." He is alone, manifestly, yet Flora feels that she must ask about Violetta — where is she? Alfredo shrugs. He has no idea. And this casual disclaimer wins him a flurry of applause. They admire his parade of detachment, which leaves them free to pursue their own concerns — the gambling they have promised themselves. He joins the group around the table. His friend Gaston — the viscount — cuts the cards; Alfredo and the other young blades put down stakes. As they do so, Violetta appears, in a low-necked dress, on the arm of the baron — the prediction was right. Flora, as the hostess, hurries up to welcome her. "How delightful that you were able to come." "I could only yield to your very kind invitation." Flora turns to the baron. "So pleased that you, too, were able to accept."

The baron's look lingers on the group at the gaming table. "Germont's here," he murmurs to Violetta. "See him?" "Oh, God, it's true," she whispers to herself. Then, to the baron: "Yes, I see him." "Not a word from you tonight to this Alfredo," the baron warns her in a fierce, sibilant undertone. He is older than the other men and has a deep, disagreeable voice. "Reckless girl, what made you come here?" a frightened Violetta demands of herself. "Oh,

Lord, have pity on me!" Then Flora sweeps her off. "Come, sit next to me. Tell me everything. What's this sudden change I see?" Violetta has no choice but to sit down by her on a sofa; the doctor, as always, hovers near the two women. The marquis, tactful, draws the baron to one side and holds him in conversation.

At the table, the viscount cuts the cards; Alfredo and the other players put down stakes. Some guests are strolling up and down the long room, as though it were their private boulevard, holding the promise of some exciting diversion — a new coupling, a quarrel. Alfredo's light voice can be heard announcing that he has a four. He has won again, marvels his friend Gaston. "Lucky at cards, unlucky in love," Alfredo says dryly. He bets and wins. The onlookers are pressing around the table, making a dense hedge so that Alfredo's play cannot be seen. "He's always the winner," they report. "Oh, I'll win this evening all right," Alfredo declares headily. "I'll take my winnings to the country and be a happy man." "Alone?" The sharp, pertinent question comes from Flora, on the sofa. "No, no," the young man answers, turning to stare at the two women. "With the one who was with me there once and then fled my company."

Eyebrows go up around the room; fans are agitated. "My God," whispers Violetta, stricken to the quick. The viscount nudges Alfredo, pointing to poor Violetta. "Have pity on her," he says. Meanwhile, the baron, detaching himself abruptly from the marquis, pushes up to Alfredo with barely contained fury. "Monsieur!" he says in an insulting tone. But Violetta, rising with determination, interposes in a low voice. "Restrain yourself or I'll leave you." "Were you addressing me, baron?" Alfredo coolly inquires. The baron answers on a note of irony. "You're so very, very lucky that you tempt me to play with you." "Really?" replies Alfredo. "I accept the challenge."

Violetta drops her eyes, unable to bear what she fears is coming. "Oh, dear God, have pity on me. I feel I'm about to die." "A hundred louis!" The baron puts down his stake. "I'll match you!" says Alfredo. They play. Gaston deals cards to Alfredo. "An ace . . . a jack . . . You've won!" "Double it?" says the baron. "Very well, two hundred." Gaston cuts the cards. He deals. "A four . . . a seven." "He's done it again!" the crowd exclaims. "I've won," says Alfredo. "Bravo!" they chime. "Really and truly bravo! Luck's on Alfredo's side." "The baron will foot the bill for that 'month in the country.' That's clear," observes Flora, provocatively. Alfredo lets this pass. He turns to the baron. "Your play."

But now supper is served. A lackey comes in to announce it. "Come along, then!" commands Flora. Obediently, her guests start filing out into the next room. Alfredo is close to the baron as they leave the gaming-table. "If you wish to continue . . ." he suggests, in a low tone. "For the moment we can't," replies the baron, his voice low too. "Later I'll have my revenge." "At any game you like," answers Alfredo. "Let's follow our friends," says the baron. "Later." "At your service, then," Alfredo agrees. The two follow the other guests out through a big set of doors at the back of the apartment. The room stands empty, strewn with discarded masks that the servants have not yet picked up. After a longish interval, Violetta bursts in, breathless.

She has asked Alfredo to follow her and is not sure that he will obey. And even if he comes, will he listen to her? She is afraid that hatred may prove to be stronger than her pleading voice. Alfredo enters. He has obeyed her summons. "You wanted me?" He bows stiffly. "What is it you wish?" Knowing better but unnerved by his manner, she plunges straight to the point. "Leave this place!" She is still breathless. "A danger is hanging over you." Alfredo gives a cynical smile. He has understood, he believes. So she thinks him as vile a creature as that. He is no coward — this much he can show her. That was never in her mind, Violetta protests. "Then what is it you fear?" "I'm in deadly fear of the baron," she confides. Alfredo's answer is chilly. "True," he agrees, "there's bad blood between us that's bound to be fatal to one or the other." If the baron falls by his hand, obviously she'll lose both her lover and her protector at a single blow. Can that be the disaster that terrifies her?

Violetta ignores his sarcasm and replies from the heart. "But if he should be the slayer? That's the sole misfortune that I fear like death." "My death!" he says contemptuously. "Why should that trouble you?" At that she flares up, impatient with his foolishness. He must depart this place at once. To her surprise and relief, he agrees. But then he turns equivocal; he bargains. He will leave but on one condition: that she will swear to follow him wherever he goes. "Ah, no!" she cries out. "Never!" The force of that stuns him. "No, never?" he shouts back. She is angry now herself, an effect of desperation. "Go, unhappy wretch! Forget a name that's infamous to you. Go, leave me at once. I've given my sacred oath to put you out of my life."

In her anger and fear for him (she truly does quake before the baron), she is giving the show away. Hearing herself, she catches her breath: another word of that and she will have gone too far to retract. And of course there is something soft and tender in her that is aching to tell him the truth. "Whom did you swear such an oath to? Tell me. Who could ask it of you?" She first tries an evasive answer, which will be true enough and yet misleading. "Someone who had every right." But the hint does not make him curious. "It was Douphol," he states. In other words, the baron. He has put the lie into her mouth for her. "Yes," she faintly assents, with a supreme effort of her will. But the weakness in her voice only suggests to the young man that she is ashamed of the admission. "You love him, then?" he demands. This lie comes easier. "Well, yes. . . . I love him." For her, the crisis is over. She falls limply back on the sofa.

But for Alfredo it is far from over. He runs furiously to the big central doors and yells into the dining room: "Everybody come here!" In confusion the guests enter from the supper tables; some of the men still have napkins tucked into their evening waistcoats. Behind the guests stand the servants, full of curiosity. "You called us? What do you want?" guests demand. In their bosoms there is evidently a conflict between anticipation of a scandal and desire to finish an exquisite meal in peace. Alfredo draws himself up. He points to Violetta. "You know this woman?" There is something almost biblical in the tableau; he must sense himself as an accusing prophet. She flinches and supports herself by leaning on a table. "Who? Violetta?" They all know her, of course. "But you don't know what she did?" She can half-guess what is coming and tries to stop him. "Be still," she begs, closing her eyes. But the others want to hear. He goes on to recount to the company how this woman they see before them squandered her whole property on him while he, blind, vile, abject, was able to let her do it right down to her last possession. The company listens in silence to this public confession.

"But there's still time!" he begins again, his convulsed voice rising to a shout. "Time to clear my honor of the infamous stain. I call everyone in this room to witness that I have paid her off —

here!" With furious contempt he throws a purse at Violetta's feet.
Coins tumble out onto the carpet as she falls fainting into the arms
of Flora and the doctor.

In his frenzy Alfredo has not noticed the entry of his father, who
has been in time to witness the gesture and hear the last scornful
words. The severe, soberly dressed Germont cuts a path between
the worldlings as they give voice to their shock and horror. They
do not doubt that he has committed an infamous act. He has put
himself beyond the pale. Not only has he struck a death blow at a
sensitive heart but he has dishonored womanhood. This is the sac-
rilege for which he will be banished from society. No door will
open to him again.

His father is in absolute accord. "No man insults a woman
without dishonoring himself," he decrees in deep, measured tones,
constituting himself the spokesman of the social establishment and
the natural judge of his son. The fact that this is not a "respect-
able" gathering and that the insulted and injured party is a profes-
sional woman of pleasure is not felt by anyone as ironical but on
the contrary seems to deepen the crime. "Where is my Alfredo?"
Germont continues inflexibly, running his eyes over the criminal.
"In you I don't find him anymore." In other words, through his
action, the beloved son has vanished as a member of the human
race.

In a curiously parallel reaction, as he comes to his senses, Alfredo before our eyes is driven to *ostracize himself*. He, too, feels
horror at his abominable deed and no longer knows the person
who was capable of it; "mania" is the only word he can find to
characterize the force that propelled him. And, naturally, he believes that he has put himself beyond forgiveness, at least Violetta's, which is suddenly all he cares about.

Simultaneously with his torments of repentance, Violetta is recovering consciousness. As she comes out of her swoon, she is
conscious only of Alfredo, addressing herself to him or, rather, to
the memory of him in feeble, passionate accents. The real young
man, sunk in hopeless remorse, she apparently does not take notice of. Or else he is hidden from her by the throng of sympathiz-
ers that press forward to surround her the moment she sits up.

As she is conscious only of an ideal Alfredo existing as a central
fixture in her unhappy mind, so her only concern is that he should
comprehend how much she has loved him and loves him now. He

does not know the lengths she has gone to prove it, earning his contempt. But one day he will; he will learn of her sacrifice, and she prays God to save him then from bitter remorse.

"Even in death I shall continue to love you." It is another Violetta who weakly sits up in her chair — a pale prophecy of her dying self but already seeing visions and talking, as it were, to a ghost. He does not hear her, and she does not see him, or only indistinctly, like a reflection in the mirror of her thoughts. This is the ultimate case of cross-purposes in this ill-fated story, of a dialogue of the deaf.

Meanwhile Violetta's well-wishers crowding around her chair give the baron the chance he has been waiting for — to address Alfredo unheard by anyone and promise him the duel he asked for by his atrocious insult to a woman. From his point of view, Alfredo, besides being a rival, is an upstart — a little bourgeois from the Midi thrusting his way in — and he intends, with his weapon, to humble his "pride." Pride, though Douphol is too insensitive to guess it, is the last attribute that the wretched Alfredo, banished from his own society by his conscience, is in a position to sport.

At the same time Germont is fighting off a temptation, which is to tell what he knows. He is aware of being the only one in this whole milieu to be able to gauge the full measure of this kept woman's virtue, fidelity, nobility of spirit. But he must be cruel and keep silent. That, he tells himself, is where his duty lies.

In fact, were he to speak out now, the story would be over. Leading a quiet life in the country with her lover by her side, Violetta might even recover her health. Who knows, they might finally brave the conventions and marry. That could lead to children — Violetta is not yet twenty-three — and children could serve to reconcile the family to an accomplished fact. But such a solution is not dreamed of, just as it has entered nobody's mind that the fiancé of that pure and spotless sister might marry the girl anyway, whatever her brother's truancy, if only he loved her as devotedly as the father claimed. No one among these people concerns himself with what one might call practical morality, involving concession and compromise. The ruling principle is sacrifice. For Germont, a skilled missionary of renunciation, it is a lofty program to be carried out by the kept woman mainly and to a lesser degree by Alfredo, who, however, can be expected to suffer less because of serene family influences and the "cure" of Provence. It may actually be that old Germont now sees himself as sacrificing pleasure to duty: it would be pleasant to speak up on Violetta's behalf since she has stirred grateful emotions in him and he is not insensitive to her beauty and charm. But, as head of the family, acting in its best interest, he must reject temptation and bow to duty's command.

Without a word to the deeply injured Violetta, he takes stern leave of the pleasure-den, pulling Alfredo along with him and followed at a discreet distance by the baron, stalking his prey. The remaining guests do their best to comfort Violetta, assuring her that they share her sufferings, that she is among friends, that she must dry her tears now. From this noisy, though well-meaning, consolation, she is rescued by the doctor and by Flora, who lead her into another room, where she can at least be quiet.

THREE

HARDLY a month has passed. It is February now, carnival-time, and Violetta's disease has made its classic "galloping" progress. Her circumstances seem to be reduced; there are no signs of luxury. She is in bed with the bed-curtains half drawn; at the single window closed inside shutters prevent the entry of light. In the fireplace a fire is burning. On the table by the bed are a decanter of water, a glass, bottles of medicine, a thermometer — all the accoutrements of the serious invalid. Across the room there are a dressing-table and a sofa, indicating that she is still able to get up occasionally. A night-light burns on another table. The closed shutters and dim illumination produce a disorienting effect, as though the sickroom were adrift in space. There is no way of knowing where we are or what time it is. In this room there is no clock. Behind the half-drawn curtains Violetta is asleep on the big bed, and in front of the fireplace, in a chair, there is another sleeping figure, apparently a maid — the same one, Annie.

It *is* the same girl. Violetta, waking up, calls her name to ask for some water. The sleepy girl pours her a glass from the carafe. Then Violetta wants to know whether it is morning yet. Nearly seven o'clock, Annina thinks. Violetta orders her to let in some light. Annina opens the shutters and looks out into the street. "Dr. Grenvil," she exclaims. "What a true friend," Violetta murmurs, touched by his calling so early to see after her. She wants to get up to receive him and tells Annina to help her. As soon as she has put her feet down and tries to stand, she falls back on the bed. But then, supported by the maid, she manages to walk slowly toward the sofa. The doctor is in time to give her an arm to lean on.

Again, she is touched by his goodness and tells him so, revealing how alone in life she must be. He takes her pulse. "How are you feeling?" Her body is in pain, she replies honestly, but her soul is at peace. Last night she had a visit from a priest, who brought her some comfort. Religion is a solace for those who suffer — she confides that discovery with an innocent soft smile. Clearly she has never heard before of the consolations of religion. "And how did the night go?" She thinks back. "I slept well." "Take heart, then. Convalescence can't be far off." She gives a half-teasing shake of her head, then lets it fall back wearily on a cushion. "You doctors have the right, don't you, to tell us kindly lies." He presses her thin hand. "Good-bye, till later." "Don't forget me," she begs, sitting up as if in a flurry of alarm.

As Annina is showing him out, she asks him softly how Violetta is. Only a few hours left, he whispers. "That's the way it is with consumptives." Hiding her own disquiet, the girl makes an effort to cheer the patient. "So then, take heart!" Violetta, not deceived, changes the subject. "Isn't today a holiday?" Carnival, Annina tells her (i.e., Mardi Gras); Paris is going wild. This moves Violetta to reflection: amid the general merrymaking, God alone knows how many unfortunates are suffering. It is lonely to be sick or poor on a holiday. She points to a little money chest. "How much have we got left?" Annina unlocks it and counts out some gold coins. "Twenty louis." "Go give ten to the poor." "But that won't leave you much," protests Annina. "Enough to last me," Violetta answers calmly. It is hard to guess whether this sudden profligate gesture springs from the generosity we already know in her character or whether she is using a reliable magic formula to conciliate fortune — women of her profession are superstitious.

"Afterwards, fetch my letters." She dispatches the girl, who seems hesitant to execute the charitable commission. "But what about you?" wonders Annina, turning back at the door. "I won't need anything. But hurry, if you can." As soon as the door has closed, Violetta takes a letter from the bosom of her nightgown, carefully unfolds it, and reads it softly aloud. It is almost a recitation, so well does she know the contents. " 'You kept your promise. The duel took place. The baron was wounded. He's recovering, how-

ever. Alfredo is in foreign lands. I myself have revealed your sacrifice to him. He's coming back to you to beg your forgiveness. I
shall come too — take care of yourself — you deserve a happier
future. Giorgio Germont.' "

"Too late!" she moans in a dead lusterless voice, letting the letter fall. She gets up. "I wait and wait and they never come." She
struggles to the mirror on the dressing-table. "Oh, how changed I
am. Yet the doctor tells me to hope. Ah, with this sickness every
hope is dead!" She hovers before the mirror, peering at images of
the past she seems to see reflected — roses in her cheeks, now
cruelly faded, Alfredo's love. . . . She misses it even now, on the
edge of the grave. What a comfort, what a support it would have
been for her weary soul. . . . She cannot tear herself away from
the mirror. Memories mingle with tears; laments finally yield to
prayers for redemption. But the sudden vision of her earthly tomb,
coldly intervening, is too much for her: no flowers, no mourners,
no cross with her name on it to cover her bones. . . . Will God
not consent to smile on the last desire of "the woman gone astray"
and welcome her to Himself?

She sinks down hopeless on the sofa while outside the window
a wild pagan song is heard. The populace is acclaiming the Fatted
Ox, king and lord of the Carnival, who is being drawn in procession down below in the street with garlands of flowers and vine-
leaves around his neck to the shrilling of pipes and drums. The
piercing sound coming in the window is a hymn of worship to the
ribboned victim. At a thousand altars across the city of Paris, the
guild of aproned butchers awaits his coming with sharpened sacrificial knives. Violetta is not attending. The analogy with herself
as sacrificial victim would not be present to her.

The procession moves off, and Annina hurries into the room.
There is something hesitant in her manner. "Madam . . ." "What's
happened?" "Is it true, madam, that you're feeling better today?"
"Yes, but why?" "You promise to be calm?" Violetta can hardly
fail to guess that some important news is about to be broken to
her. "Yes, yes. What is it you want to tell me?" "I wanted to
prepare you for an unexpected joy — a surprise." "A joy, did you
say?" "Yes, dear madam." Violetta lets out a cry. "Alfredo! You've
seen him!" The girl nods. "He's coming! Oh, make him hurry!"
And, despite her weakness, she is able to rise and post herself in
the doorway. "Alfredo?" In a minute, he is there, still in traveling

clothes, and they fall into each other's arms, exclaiming and marveling, both talking at the same time in a veritable Babel of happiness.

His first distinguishable words are a confession of guilt. He has learned the truth and blames himself for everything. But she will not have that. No explanations or accounting. All she knows or wants to know is that he has come back to her. He takes her hand and presses it to his heart. Its beating will teach her whether or not he loves her. He knows that he will not be able to exist without her anymore. She smiles slightly at this, touched by the characteristic hyperbole. She has made a discovery, she tells him: grief cannot kill. If it could, he would never have found her still alive this morning.

But he has missed the seriousness behind her frail little jest, not observing in his excitement how fearfully changed she is. She must forget grief now, he tells her, and pardon him and his father. "But no, I ask *your* pardon," she answers with great sweetness. "I am the guilty one. But only love could have made me do what I did." She is referring to her resumption of the relation with the baron — a risky subject, one would think. But Alfredo receives it very calmly, which looks like a sign that he has matured.

Together they bury the Douphol interlude. Neither man nor devil, they agree, will ever come between them again. The emphasis they bring to this joint declaration sends a light shiver down the spine. By naming the devil, will they make him appear in their path? And when they speak of him, the Prince of Darkness, what or whom do they mean? It cannot be a mere roué like the Baron Douphol whose advances they must pledge themselves to resist. Douphol is no real danger. Rather, it must be Alfredo's own father — the formidable missionary of middle-class morality, Giorgio Germont. Are these young people alert enough, now that it is too late, to recognize the Father of Lies, smell the whiff of brimstone?

In any case, Alfredo has the remedy for their troubles, which is to leave Paris. Violetta is of the same mind. And this time it will not be to Auteuil they will go, virtually at the city's gates, but to the genuine country. Far from the great world's lures, he will be able to look after her in peace and she to regain her health. Our pity goes out to their ignorance, for we have heard what the doctor said. And in the midst of the plans they are sketching for a smiling future in the classical *rus* (reminiscent of Germont's apostrophe to the purifying sun and sea of Provence), Violetta herself has a *frisson* of foreboding. She halts her joyful lover in the middle of his farewell to Paris. Her voice is unsteady. "No more, please. . . . Alfredo. . . . Let's go to church and give thanks for your return." Moving toward the clothes-cupboard with the intention of dressing for church, she hesitates, sways on her feet. He stares at her, taken aback, observing her, really, for the first time since they left each other a month ago. "You're getting pale!"

She tries to reassure him. "It's nothing. *You* know. I can never stand a sudden access of joy." But even as she offers this half-plausible explanation, she lets herself fall, exhausted, onto a seat. He is terrified. He holds her up and looks into her face with horror. "Good God, Violetta!" "It's my illness. A sinking spell. Now I'm better. See? I'm smiling." That smile, a product of her will, appalls him more than her feebleness. Under his breath, devastated, he laments this last cruel turn of destiny. "It's nothing," she repeats tenderly, still forcing her mechanical smile. "Annina, give me something to put on." "Now?" He is incredulous. "Oh, please, wait." She is determined. "No, I want to go out."

Annina, who understands her mistress, is standing by with a flounced dress. Violetta starts to put it on and then, hindered by her feebleness from getting her arm through a long tight sleeve, throws it on the floor. "Oh, God! I can't do it!" Once more, she falls back onto the seat. Alfredo, still hardly able to believe his eyes, orders Annina to go for the doctor. The mention of that faithful friend somewhat revives Violetta. She sits up straighter. "Tell him," she directs, "that Alfredo has come back to my arms. Tell him that I want to live."

The maid hastens out and, alone with Alfredo, Violetta seems to have regained a little more of her strength. Raising her head, she looks straight at him and utters the truth. "But if you, coming back, can't save me, nobody on earth can." She reflects. "Oh, God, to die so young when I've suffered such a lot already. To die when I'm so close to drying my tears at last." This is said not in a tone of self-commiseration but soberly, with a clear-sighted awareness of the irony of her "narrow escape" from happiness. "But it was a delusion," she goes on, "that credulous hope of mine. It was a waste of effort to fortify my heart to be true. Alfredo, what a rough ending they've reserved for our love."

He does not want to hear this. His torn soul is in no mood for stocktaking. She's his breath and his very heartbeat, he cries out, his dear delight. Her tears call forth his — he cannot tell which are which. But more than ever — she must believe it — he needs her steadfast spirit. For his sake, she must not close her mind to hope. He begs it of her. "Oh, calm yourself, my own, my dear Violetta. Your grief is killing me." What he cannot admit, of course, is that she *is* calm, facing her own extinction. It is he who is agitated. And what he is really begging her is to spare him her death, in other words, not to die.

At that moment, without preparation, when his son's demoralized state has reached a point close to total abjection, Germont enters the sickroom. He is a breath not of fresh air but of authority, and his concern is not with love but with dignity. Standing in the doorway, he speaks Violetta's name, loudly, like a summons. "Ah, Violetta!" Behind him appear Annina and the doctor. "You, sir!" she cries happily, struggling to sit up and arrange her laces and ribbons. "Father!" puts in Alfredo, surprised. He has not been aware of the special relation that has grown up between these two. Wholly intent on each other, Violetta and Germont seem for the moment to forget him. She is oblivious, too, of the doctor, who is taking her pulse. "So you didn't forget me?" she marvels. The father draws himself up. "I am here to keep the promise I gave you. To take you to my heart as a daughter." His stiff form bends down toward her; his deep voice darkens with emotion. "Oh, generous girl." In deference to his father's feeling, Alfredo steps aside. "Alas, you've come too late." The flat words escape her before she can stop herself. "Still, I'm grateful. . . ." She would not wish to take away from his pride in the keeping of the promise. With his assistance, she pulls herself upright and embraces him. As they stand clasped in each other's arms, she catches sight of the doctor. "Do you see this, Grenvil? In the arms of all my dear ones, I'm drawing my last breath."

Startled, Germont releases her, so that he can study her better. Her tone just now with her medical attendant has been gay, almost teasing, but the father does not like what he sees in her over-bright eyes. "What are you saying?" he exclaims. Then he examines her wasted form. "Great Heaven, it's true!" he mutters to himself.

He bows his head, shaken, remembering how he had doubted

her when she had spoken during their last meeting of her failing health. He had taken it for a lie she had invented to put him off. Obviously he had not known this woman at all, despite the god-like part he had played in her unhappy destiny. Or was the part he played diabolical? The thought occurs to him for the first time. Unfortunately she has to die to prove what she really is — a dying woman — and absolve herself of the last of his suspicions. "Do you *see* her, Father?" the son says vehemently. Germont bows to the stinging reproach. He will have a great deal to forgive himself, if he is able.

"Don't torture me, I beg you. No more, please! I'm devoured with remorse already. Every word of hers goes through me like a bolt of lightning. Imprudent old man!" Repentance, as always — is that not its nature? — is too late, just like his arrival in this dingy room in a "popular" neighborhood. He shakes his head. "Only now I see the wrong I did her."

With father and son brooding on either side of her, Violetta is called on to exercise her force of character. The moment is ripe for a universal reconciliation, and she must reconcile these unhappy men, her dear ones, with themselves — their past errors and cruelties — and, more important, with the future. And, wonderfully, she has a plan. From a hiding place at her elbow, she takes a jewel-case that contains a miniature of herself. Unlocking the little casket — unique relic of her worldly past — she turns to Alfredo, her real love, from whom in her simplicity she has let the hideous specter of duty tear her away.

"Come closer, dear Alfredo. Listen, won't you take this? It's the picture of me as I was then, in the good days. It can serve to remind you of her who loved you so." Alfredo still refuses to hear the note of finality, maybe because it speaks to him in that dreamy, dulcet voice, which affects him like a caress. "No, you won't die! Don't tell me that. God cannot have put me here to bear such a torment." But the dulcet voice overrides his protest and grows dreamier still.

It is telling of the life to come, where Violetta sees a vision, of a pure young girl. Is it the little sister for whom she has made the heroic sacrifice? No, it is another maiden, a girl he does not know yet, the girl who will offer him her heart and whom he must marry, because Violetta wishes it. Sister and bride blur as Violetta gazes raptly into the future. This is the ultimate sacrifice, the cruelest and sweetest of all. She has died on the altar of the family and looks down on it from heaven.

"Give her this little image. Tell her that it's a present from one who is praying for her, one who's up above with the angels and prays for her and for you." The fusion is complete. She has made a gift of her life to a young girl "pure as an angel" and now, in reward, she is an angel herself, offering the gift of her image to another chaste spirit. The unchaste one, chastened, is leaning down from heaven dangling a holy eidolon, like the girdle that the Virgin on the day of her Assumption tossed to the Apostle Thomas doubtingly watching her mount.

In an ideal sense, it is all true. Violetta, who was never bad except in the eyes of middle-class morality, has become wholly and visibly "good." This can be a moral fact even if a deception has been practiced on the aspiring soul, even if the new-made angel does not receive a genuine, 24-carat harp, even if it is a shocking case of victimization. In any event, the struggle is over, or nearly so. *Consummatum est*. They gather round her deathbed, Alfredo still begging to be told it is not true, his father repenting, and the doctor and Annie bidding her suffering soul farewell as they see it fly off to join the blessed spirits they believe are "up there." And, for a pseudo-miraculous moment, Violetta herself is brought back to life, rising to her feet with no sign of weakness. All her pains have left her; her former strength, as if by magic, has come back. But only Alfredo is deceived, crying "Violetta!" in an access of joy. It is a phenomenon familiar to medicine — a last flare-up of life. She falls back on the bed. The doctor feels her pulse. She is dead.

The Lady of the Camellias

A DRAMA IN FOUR ACTS
adapted from *La Dame aux camélias*

by ALEXANDRE DUMAS

Giuseppe Verdi.
(Courtesy of Dorle Soria)

Caricature of Francesco Maria Piave,
Verdi's librettist for *La Traviata*.
(Courtesy of Opera News)

Drawing of Giuseppina Strepponi, who became
Verdi's second wife in 1859 after they
had lived together for over a decade.
(Courtesy of Opera News)

Verdi's study at Villa St. Agata.
(Courtesy of Dorle Soria)

Alexandre Dumas *fils*, who wrote *La Dame aux camélias*, the source for Verdi's *La Traviata*.
(Courtesy of Opera News)

Drawing of Marie Duplessis, famous Parisian courtesan. Her real name was Alphonsine Plesis, and her love affair with Dumas was the basis for the story of *La Dame aux camélias*, published as a novel in 1848 and as a play in 1852.

Eleonora Duse as Marguerite Gautier
in *La Dame aux camélias*.
(Courtesy of Opera News)

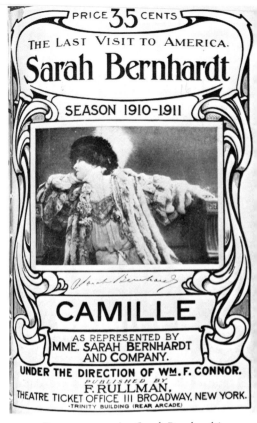

Poster announcing Sarah Bernhardt's
production of *Camille*.
(Courtesy of Opera News)

Greta Garbo as Camille.
(Courtesy of Opera News)

Marcella Sembrich, the first Violetta
at the Metropolitan Opera.

Adelina Patti, one of the early historic Violettas, who sang the
role at Covent Garden in the 1860s.

Nellie Melba, 1896.
(Courtesy of the Robert Tuggle Collection)

Geraldine Farrar, 1908.
(Courtesy of Opera News)

EARLY VIOLETTAS AT THE METROPOLITAN OPERA

Amelita Galli-Curci, 1921.
(Courtesy of the Robert Tuggle Collection)

Lucrezia Bori, 1922.
(Courtesy of the Robert Tuggle Collection)

Rosa Ponselle, 1931.
(Courtesy of the Robert Tuggle Collection)

Claudia Muzio, 1934
(with Tito Schipa as Alfredo).
(Courtesy of the Robert Tuggle Collection)

EARLY VIOLETTAS AT THE METROPOLITAN OPERA

Bidù Sayão, 1937.
(Courtesy of the Archives of the Metropolitan Opera)

Jarmila Novotna, 1940.
(Courtesy of the Archives of the Metropolitan Opera)

Set of Act II, Scene 2, *La Traviata*, Metropolitan Opera, 1966, production
designed by Cecil Beaton, staged by Alfred Lunt.
(Photo: Louis Mélançon. Courtesy of Opera News)

Giuseppe De Luca as Germont, 1915.
(Courtesy of the Robert Tuggle Collection)

Beniamino Gigli as Alfredo, 1921.
(Photo: Alexander Eddy. Courtesy of the Robert Tuggle Collection)

GERMONTS AND ALFREDOS AT THE METROPOLITAN OPERA

Lawrence Tibbett as Germont, 1930.
(Courtesy of the Archives of the Metropolitan Opera)

John Charles Thomas as Germont, 1934.
(Courtesy of the Archives of the Metropolitan Opera)

Leonard Warren as Germont, 1942.
(Photo: Louis Mélançon. Courtesy of the Archives of the Metropolitan Opera)

Jan Peerce as Alfredo, 1941.
(Courtesy of the Archives of the Metropolitan Opera)

GERMONTS AND ALFREDOS AT THE METROPOLITAN OPERA

Robert Merrill as Germont, 1945.
(Photo: Louis Mélançon. Courtesy of the Archives of the Metropolitan Opera)

Richard Tucker as Alfredo, 1945.
(Courtesy of the Archives of the Metropolitan Opera)

Violetta costume sketch by Rolf Gérard, Metropolitan Opera production, 1957, designed by Oliver Smith, directed by Tyrone Guthrie.
(Photo: Louis Mélancon. Courtesy of the Archives of the Metropolitan Opera)

Licia Albanese as Violetta, Metropolitan Opera, 1942.

Dorothy Kirsten, who sang Violetta in the late forties at the Metropolitan Opera.

Victoria de los Angeles as Violetta, Metropolitan Opera, 1957.

Renata Tebaldi as Violetta, Metropolitan Opera, 1957.
(Photo: Louis Mélançon. Courtesy of the Archives of the Metropolitan Opera)

Maria Callas as Violetta, Metropolitan Opera, 1958.
(Photo: Louis Mélançon. Courtesy of the Archives of the Metropolitan Opera)

Anna Moffo as Violetta, Metropolitan Opera, 1959.
(Photo: Louis Mélançon. Courtesy of the Archives of the Metropolitan Opera)

Joan Sutherland as Violetta, Metropolitan Opera, 1963.
(Photo: Louis Mélançon. Courtesy of the Archives of the Metropolitan Opera)

Beverly Sills as Violetta,
Metropolitan Opera, 1976.
(Photo: James Heffernan, Metropolitan Opera)

Ileana Cotrubas as Violetta
and Placido Domingo as Alfredo,
Metropolitan Opera,
current production.
(Photo: James Heffernan, Metropolitan Opera)

[EDITOR'S NOTE: Verdi first saw *La Dame aux camélias,* by Alexandre Dumas *fils,* at the Vaudeville Theater in Paris in 1852. (Dumas's novel of this story, which had the same title, was published in 1847.) He was stirred by it, no doubt by the relation of its moral themes to his own life, and he decided to make it the source for *La Traviata,* which had its premiere, in Venice, one year later. The play first appeared in English in London in 1875, although in a bowdlerized version (Marguerite Gautier's "profession" was glossed over). The text which follows, edited by James L. Smith, and published by J.M. Dent & Sons in *Victorian Melodramas,* restores the original passages which the 1875 version, based on Lacy's four-act translation and Matilda Heron's *Camille,* had omitted. The differences from, and similarities to, *La Traviata,* serve as an illuminating example of the uses of literature in opera.]

La Dame aux camélias was first performed at the Vaudeville Theater, Paris, 2 February 1852

CHARACTERS

ARMAND DUVAL
GEORGES DUVAL, his father
GASTON RIEUX, a beau
SAINT-GAUDENS, an old beau
GUSTAVE, a law student, betrothed to Nichette
ARTHUR DE VARVILLE, Marguerite's admirer
DOCTOR
MESSENGER

MARGUERITE GAUTIER
NICHETTE, a seamstress
PRUDENCE DUVERNOY, a milliner
NANINE, maid to Marguerite
OLYMPE
ARTHUR } ladies of the demi-monde
ANAIS

Guests, Gamblers, Dancers, Servants, etc.

The Second Act is set in a country house near Auteuil. The other acts are set in Paris.

Period: 1848

ACT I

Marguerite's boudoir. A handsome light chamber, elegantly furnished with large mirrors and valuable pictures on the walls, and objects of virtu unobtrusively visible. A fireplace with a fire burning in it; pieces of wood in fire-box by the side of the fire; fender, poker, tongs.

Candelabras by mantel-piece, and over it a large glass. A large window with handsome curtains. A piano and stool, with sheets of music on it. Open door, through which is seen table laid for supper with a dish of birds, china plates, castors, salt-cellar, wine in decanters, wine glasses, champagne glasses, wine-cooler with bottles of champagne wired down, knives, forks and napkins folded on plates. Carpet.

(*De Varville seated in an easy chair at the fire; Nanine discovered arranging the furniture. As the curtain rises, the door-bell is heard.*)

VARVILLE. Someone rang, Nanine.

NANINE. Valentine will open the door.

VARVILLE. 'Tis Marguerite, no doubt.

NANINE. Not yet. 'Tis but ten o'clock, and she said she should not return until half-past ten. (*Nichette speaks without*) Oh, it is Ma'amselle Nichette.

(*Enter Nichette.*)

NICHETTE. (*looking in the door*) Ma'amselle Marguerite not here?

NANINE. No, ma'amselle. You wish to see her?

NICHETTE. Merely to say good evening on my way home.

NANINE. She will not be long.

NICHETTE. Oh, no matter. I shall not stay; Gustave is at the door. Another time, thank you; good evening. (*Exit*)

VARVILLE. Who is that young woman?

NANINE. Ma'amselle Nichette.

VARVILLE. Nichette? That's the name of a cat, not a woman.

NANINE. It is a pet name my mistress gave her. They formerly worked together in the same warehouse.

VARVILLE. Worked?

NANINE. Yes, sir; didn't you know? Oh yes, Ma'amselle Marguerite was an embroideress.

VARVILLE. Indeed?

NANINE. And you really did not know? and yet she makes no secret of the fact.

VARVILLE. This Nichette is rather pretty.

NANINE. And wise!

VARVILLE. But this Monsieur Gustave?

NANINE. What Monsieur Gustave?

VARVILLE. Who was waiting for her below.

NANINE. He is her husband. That is, he is not her husband yet, but he will be, and that is the same thing.

VARVILLE. I understand. She is wise as the world goes, but she has a lover.

NANINE. A very worthy young man who loves her devotedly, and who will marry her and make her a good husband.

VARVILLE. Oh, then Monsieur Gustave is more fortunate than I. (*Rising and coming to Nanine*) Nanine, do you think Marguerite cares any more for me than she used to?

NANINE. Not the least bit in the world!

VARVILLE. But it must be said that she has strange taste, or she never could endure the tedious visits of that old Monsieur de Mauriac; they must be very annoying.

NAINE. Poor old man! It is the only happiness he has, and he regards her as his own child.

VARVILLE. Oh yes, I heard of that very affecting history. Unhappily . . .

NANINE. Unhappily?

VARVILLE. I cannot believe it.

NANINE. Then listen to me, and I will endeavour to convince you. There are many evil things said of Madame, and with truth; but that is the very reason why things that are *not* true should not be said. About two years ago Ma'amselle Marguerite, after a long illness, determined to visit the celebrated waters of Bagnères, to recover, if possible, her health. I accompanied her. Among the invalids at the hotel there was a lovely young girl, the same age as Ma'amselle Marguerite, suffering from the same complaint, and bearing such strong resemblance to her that wherever they went they were called the twin sisters. This young girl was Ma'amselle de Mauriac, daughter of the Duke.

VARVILLE. Ma'amselle de Mauriac died.

NANINE. Yes.

VARVILLE. And the Duke adopted Marguerite as his child, made her his heiress, and introduced her into society, where she was loved and honoured. This was not two years since; and tonight she is at the Opera, the queen of the camellias, fifty thousand francs in debt.

NANINE. Which you have kindly offered to pay. Yes, you are right, Monsieur de Varville. Ma'amselle Marguerite acknowledged to the Duke her true position. He was called away. In his absence her story reached the circle in which she moved. From that moment it was closed against her. She was shunned; and in their cruel sneers they told her to go back to Paris and wear camellias. She did return to Paris, and is gayer now than she ever was before; but no one knows her heart. (*Doorbell rings*) Hush! she is here.

(*Enter Marguerite. She is dressed as for a theatre. Nanine assists her off with her shawl or mantle.*)

MARGUERITE. (*to Nanine*) Order supper! Olympe and Saint-Gaudens will be here; I met them at the Opera. (*Exit Nanine, with mantle. Seeing Varville, who rises and bows*) So, you are here again. (*Sits near fire*)

VARVILLE. It is my destiny ever to hover near you.

MARGUERITE. And it is my destiny to find you ever here on my return. What would you with me now?

VARVILLE. You know the only subject of my heart.

MARGUERITE. Always the same story — how very tedious!

VARVILLE. Is it my fault that I love you?

MARGUERITE. There it is again! My good friend, if I were to listen to every man who tells me he loves me, I would not have time to breakfast. I repeat to you, my good sir, for the hundredth time, I don't like you. Be grateful that as a friend I suffer you to visit here; but speak again of love, and henceforth my doors are closed to you.

VARVILLE. And yet, Marguerite, last year at Bagnères you gave me cause to hope.

MARGUERITE. Yes; but that was a year ago. At Bagnères, a very dull place. I was ill. Things have changed. This is Paris. I am better now.

VARVILLE. Especially since the Duke de Mauriac has fallen in love with you.

MARGUERITE. You are a fool! Will you go?

VARVILLE. (*walking about*) No!

MARGUERITE. Then seat yourself at the piano; 'tis all you are fit for.

VARVILLE. What shall I play?

MARGUERITE. What you will, so that it drowns your voice.

(*Nanine re-enters, while he plays a prelude.*)

NANINE. (*taking up a bouquet of roses and white lilac from table*) I had forgot, Ma'amselle; this bouquet —

VARVILLE. Which I hope you will accept.

MARGUERITE. No! You may keep it, Nanine.

VARVILLE. (*not playing piano*) You will not —

MARGUERITE. Why am I called the Lady of the Camellias?

VARVILLE. Because you never wear any but those flowers.

MARGUERITE. Which means, it is those only that I love. What folly, then, to bring me these. Take them away, their perfume makes me ill.

(*Nanine goes off.*)

VARVILLE. I am unfortunate. Adieu, Marguerite. (*Going*)

MARGUERITE. A moment, Varville. Put some coals on the fire — do something useful before you leave. Ugh, the evening is very chilly. (*Coughs slightly*) Quick, the coals!

(*Re-enter Nanine.*)

NANINE. Madame, here is Ma'amselle Olympe and Monsieur Saint-Gaudens.

(Enter Saint-Gaudens and Olympe.)

MARGUERITE. *(to Olympe)* I thought you would never come.

OLYMPE. 'Tis all the fault of this troublesome Saint-Gaudens.

GAUDENS. Oh, of course! How are you, Varville? You sup with us?

MARGUERITE. No! *(To Varville)* Why are you not gone, sir?

VARVILLE. I am going.

OLYMPE. Prudence is not here.

MARGUERITE. She will arrive presently.

OLYMPE. Of course — if only to borrow a trifle, for she lives by borrowing money, which she never repays.

MARGUERITE. *(laughing)* Oh, wicked! For you know she makes excellent bonnets, which I purchase of her.

OLYMPE. But never wear.

MARGUERITE. Heaven forbid! It is enough that I pay for them. But she is a good creature.

OLYMPE. No doubt — but 'tis a pity she's always so short of money.

MARGUERITE. Do you not think it very cold this evening?   *(Coughs slightly)*

Varville, stir the fire.   *(Varville obeys.)*

(Enter Prudence.)

PRUDENCE. Good evening, everybody! *(Aside to Marguerite)* Armand is coming.

MARGUERITE. Oh, you have seen him?

PRUDENCE. Yes. He does nothing but rave about you.

MARGUERITE. Psha! He has known me scarce a week.

PRUDENCE. Ah, but he has long loved you. You were told how, every day during your late illness, a young gentleman came to make the most anxious enquiries after you?

MARGUERITE. Well?

PRUDENCE. Well — 'twas he.

MARGUERITE. Indeed! 'Twas very kind of him.

PRUDENCE. I am certain that you already love him — a little; and there can be no doubt that he would make you a good husband.

MARGUERITE. Silence, Prudence! What folly.

PRUDENCE. Well, I shall say no more — only, you see, I am somewhat pressed for a little cash, and if it were just now quite convenient to you —

MARGUERITE. Certainly.

PRUDENCE. Thank you.

(*Enter Gaston Rieux.*)

GASTON. (*to Marguerite, ceremoniously*) I most sincerely hope, madame, that you are in perfect health?

PRUDENCE. Yes, yes, we are very well — don't bother. Here is Monsieur Armand Duval.

(*Enter Armand Duval.*)

ARMAND. (*bowing to Marguerite*) Good evening, madame.

PRUDENCE. (*aside to Marguerite*) Take my word for it, he adores you.

MARGUERITE. Prudence!

ARMAND. (*aside to Prudence*) Thanks!

    (*Marguerite gives her hand to Armand, who, bowing, kisses it.*)

GASTON. (*to Saint-Gaudens, who has come up to him*) Still young, my old boy.

GAUDENS. Of course.

GASTON. Still flirting with the fair?

GAUDENS. Yes. There (*pointing to Olympe*) is the object that I at present adore. And poor Varville is not to be permitted to sup with us! Poor fellow, how I pity him!

GASTON. (*approaching Marguerite*) Is not Saint-Gaudens superb? He cannot be more than eighteen.

MARGUERITE. It is only the aged who never grow old. He really is delightful.

GAUDENS. (*to Armand, whom Olympe has introduced to him*) Any relation, sir, may I ask, to Monsieur Duval the Receiver General?

ARMAND. I am his son, sir. Do you know my father?

GAUDENS. Formerly met him at the Baroness de Nersay's; your mother also, a charming and beautiful woman.

ARMAND. Alas, sir, she died three years since.

GAUDENS. Really — I beg pardon for —

ARMAND. Oh, sir, I am ever proud to hear my mother named. The brightest joy, after having experienced a great and pure affection, is that of being permitted to remember it.

GAUDENS. You were an only child, I think?

ARMAND. No, sir. I have a sister.

MARGUERITE. (*calling*) Monsieur Duval!

ARMAND. Madame?   (*Varville hammers at the piano.*)

MARGUERITE. Be quiet, Monsieur Varville.

VARVILLE. You desired me to play.

MARGUERITE. When I was alone with you; but I need no pastime now. Monsieur Duval, I have been told how, two years since, during my long illness, you came each day to my house and —

ARMAND. Oh, madame!

MARGUERITE. You, Varville, did not as much.

VARVILLE. I have known you but a year.

MARGUERITE. And this gentleman but a week! What stupid things you always say.

(*Nanine and Servants bring in the supper table, and place it front; set chairs.*)

PRUDENCE. The table! I am perfectly famished.

VARVILLE. Adieu, Marguerite.

MARGUERITE. Adieu. When shall we again see you?

VARVILLE. When it shall please you, madame.

MARGUERITE. Then, in that case, goodbye for a long time.

                              (*Varville bows and goes off, annoyed.*)

OLYMPE. Goodbye, Varville. Poor fellow!

PRUDENCE. You use that poor man very cruelly.

MARGUERITE. Oh, you have no idea how his pertinacity annoys me.

OLYMPE. You are greatly to be pitied! He is very rich, and I only wish he would pertinaciously annoy me.

GAUDENS. (*to Olympe*) What? Could you have the cruelty to nip my tender affection in the bud? I, who adore you?   (*All sit.*)

MARGUERITE. Now eat, drink, and have no quarrels that cannot be made up again.

OLYMPE. (*to Marguerite*) You complain of Varville's love, and he is young and rich. What would you say if pestered like me by this antiquated youth — as poor as a mouse?   (*All laugh.*)

GAUDENS. You hear how she lacerates my heart! — I'll trouble you for a slice of that fowl.   (*All laugh.*)

PRUDENCE. (*pointing to dish*) What are those white animals?

GASTON. Partridges.

PRUDENCE. (*handing plate*) Send me a few.

OLYMPE. A few partridges! (*All laugh*) I'm sorry, Prudence, that you have no appetite.

GASTON. Marguerite, take wine with Monsieur Duval; he is as melancholy as a drinking song.

MARGUERITE. Come then, Monsieur Armand. To my health!

ALL. (*raising glasses*) To the health of Marguerite!   (*They drink.*)

PRUDENCE. Oh, were I but rich, what parties I would give! But, alas, proverty —. I am just now very much pressed, Saint-Gaudens, and if it were in your power to lend me —   (*All laugh.*)

GAUDENS. Me? I have been myself all the morning trying to borrow. But never mind; I have an uncle, am his heir, and when he dies —

OLYMPE. An uncle at his time of life! Is it likely?

GAUDENS. Nevertheless, it is a fact; I have an uncle —

OLYMPE. Then he must be the Wandering Jew.   (*All laugh.*)

PRUDENCE. These partridges are delicious.

GASTON. Prudence may have a cast-iron digestion.

PRUDENCE. Why, surely there is no law forbidding one to eat.

GASTON. If there were, you would not survive an hour.   (*All laugh.*)

PRUDENCE. Marguerite, will you suffer me to be insulted?

MARGUERITE. For shame, Gaston! You must be treated like a naughty
child, and put in a corner till you know how to behave yourself.

OLYMPE. (*to Gaston*) Yes, go and stand over there.   (*Gaston leaves the
table.*)

GAUDENS. I shouldn't object to that, if you would only kiss me when I
promised to be good.

GASTON. (*at the piano*) This instrument is out of tune.

OLYMPE. Let us have a dance.

GASTON. I can only play one polka.

PRUDENCE. Well, don't play it yet — I have two more partridges to
finish.

(*They laugh.*)

GAUDENS. (*rising*) Yes, yes — away with the table! A polka!

(*They rise. Servants enter, clear the table and carry it out.*)

OLYMPE. But surely I shall not be expected to dance with this young
old gentleman?

MARGUERITE. (*taking Saint-Gaudens' arm*) Oh no, he must be my
partner.

GAUDENS. Ah, you know how to appreciate merit.

OLYMPE. And you, Monsieur Duval, must dance with me.

(*Gaston plays a polka. They dance. Marguerite stops suddenly.*)

GAUDENS. What is the matter?

MARGUERITE. Nothing. A shortness of breath, that —

ARMAND. (*approaching her*) You are ill, madame.

MARGUERITE. I assure you it is nothing; let us proceed.

(*Gaston plays like a madman. Marguerite again tries, and stops.*)

ARMAND. Be quiet, Gaston.

PRUDENCE. Marguerite is ill.

MARGUERITE. (*fighting for breath*) Give me a glass of water.

PRUDENCE. But what is it?

MARGUERITE. Oh, 'tis nothing new to me, and will presently pass away.
Step into the other room, and before you have your cigars lit, I will
be with you.

PRUDENCE. Yes, come along; she prefers to be left alone when these attacks arrive. (*Aside*) I must finish those partridges presently.

ARMAND. (*aside*) Poor girl!   (*He goes out with the others.*)

MARGUERITE. (*alone, trying to recover her breath*) Oh!   (*Looks in the glass*)

How pale I am, oh!   (*Places her hands to her head, and leans her elbows upon the chimney-piece*)

(*Re-enter Armand.*)

ARMAND. (*tenderly*) Well, how do you feel now, madame?

MARGUERITE. Ah, is it you, Monsieur Armand? Better, thank you. Besides, I am accustomed to —

ARMAND. You are destroying yourself. I would I had the right to save you.

MARGUERITE. It is too late. Why, what's the matter?

ARMAND. You have made me ill.

MARGUERITE. Don't be foolish. Pray, go into the next room and enjoy yourself with the others. See, they do not heed me.

ARMAND. The others do not love you as I love you. It is true that I am nothing to you, but if you would allow me, Marguerite, I would guard you like a brother — shield you from this feverish existence, which is bringing you to your grave — surround you with a thousand little cares that will make you in love with life — then, when you are strong and well, I will be as your guiding star, and lead your thoughts to find content in a home more worthy of you.

MARGUERITE. Monsieur Duval, if you would not offend me, let us change this subject.

ARMAND. You have no heart then, Marguerite?

MARGUERITE. A heart? Are you really serious?

ARMAND. Very serious.

MARGUERITE. Prudence did not deceive me, then, when she told me you were sentimental. So, you would take good care of me?

ARMAND. Trust me.

MARGUERITE. For how long?

ARMAND. For ever.

MARGUERITE. How long has this lasted?

ARMAND. For two years.

MARGUERITE. How came it you never told me of this before?

ARMAND. I never knew you until now.

MARGUERITE. You could very easily have made my acquaintance. When I was ill, and you came each day to enquire after me, why did you not ask to see me?

ARMAND. By what right could I have asked?

MARGUERITE. Does one have scruples with a woman like myself?

ARMAND. Yes, too many take a liberty I would not allow another to take in the house of a woman I respected.

MARGUERITE. So you really think you love me?

ARMAND. (seeing her laugh) When you shall give me the right to say so, you will one day learn how well.

MARGUERITE. It were better never told.

ARMAND. And why?

MARGUERITE. Because it can result in but one of two things: first, that I will not believe it; or, believing it, cause you to wish I never had. I am but a sorrowful companion at the best. Always ill, nervous, fretful, sad — or if gay, a gaiety more terrible than tears. Expensive, too; a woman who spends a hundred thousand francs a year — this may do for the dear old Duke, who has plenty of money, but it would not do for you. Now we'll talk sense. Give me your hand. Let us join the others, and I'll light your cigar.

ARMAND. Go, if you will; but allow me to remain.

MARGUERITE. What's the matter?

ARMAND. Your gaiety makes me ill.

MARGUERITE. Shall I prescribe for you?

ARMAND. Speak.

MARGUERITE. Go home and go to bed, if what you say is true. Or love me as a friend; come and see me, we will laugh and chat. But do not overestimate what I am worth, for I am not worth much. You are too young and too sensitive to live in our society. You love too well to be unloved; but love wisely. Find another girl to love, or get married. You see I speak quite frankly.

ARMAND. Marguerite, have you ever been in love?

MARGUERITE. Never, thank God.

ARMAND. Oh, thank you, thank you!

MARGUERITE. What for?

ARMAND. For what you have just told me; nothing could make me happier. If I were to tell you, Marguerite, that I have passed whole nights beneath your windows, that I have cherished for six months a little button which fell from your glove —

MARGUERITE. I would not believe you. I have heard these tales before.

ARMAND. You are right. I know not what I say. I am a fool. Yes, laugh! I deserve it all. Good night!

MARGUERITE. Armand!

ARMAND. Did you call?

MARGUERITE. Let us not part in anger.

ARMAND. Anger! Oh, Marguerite, if you could read my heart!

MARGUERITE. Then let us make it up. Come and see me sometimes —
often. We will speak of this again.

ARMAND. Ah, still you laugh.

MARGUERITE. Speak, Armand; I am not laughing now.

ARMAND. Will you be loved?

MARGUERITE. For how long?

ARMAND. For eternity! Oh, dearest Marguerite, consent then to be
mine. We will live quietly, away from this wild Paris, and the friends
who now are killing you. We will seek amidst the woods and fields,
health and strength for you, and we shall find them. Be my wife! and
if the devotion of a heart as true as ever throbbed within the breast
of man can effect it, you shall live! live in happiness and joy!

MARGUERITE. Madness! Everything forbids my loving you. You have
position, honour, friends — be wise. I have neither. I am young, gay,
reckless, desperate — my name the sport of every tongue in Paris. I
have admirers, lovers, all you will — the first in their vanity, the last
in their esteem. Friends too, like Prudence, whose friendship mounts
to servitude but never to unselfishness. All around destruction, shame,
and falsehood. I should bring ruin on you! Your father —

ARMAND. Oh, trust me, we have naught to fear from him. Let us not
hesitate — we are young — we love each other — who then can have
a right to control our happiness?

MARGUERITE. You would not trifle with me, Armand? Forget not that a
violent emotion would surely kill me. Remember well both who I am
and what I am.

ARMAND. I remember only that you are an angel, and that I adore you.

MARGUERITE. Armand! You are moved; you really do believe in what
you say. Such sincerity merits a reward. Here, take this flower. (*She
gives him a camellia.*) And in the morning, when it has faded, bring it
back to me again.

ARMAND. Yes, dear Marguerite, yes. Oh, how happy you have made
me!

MARGUERITE. Armand, tell me once again you love me.

ARMAND. It's true. I love you.

MARGUERITE. Now, go.

ARMAND. Adieu.

(*He kisses her hand, and goes off, gazing on her as he goes. Laughter
and music heard off.*)

MARGUERITE. (*gazing at the closed door*) He loves me. There is a newfound meaning in those words that never fell upon my ears before.
Oh, what's the use of it? — But why not? Who could have supposed
that a man whom a week since I knew not would today so occupy

my heart and every thought? Can this be love I feel, I who have never felt love? What am I? A creature of fortune! Then let fortune do with me what it will! All the same, there's something tells me I am happier than I have been before. Perhaps 'tis an ill-omen. Oh, we women of the world! We always foresee that we shall be loved, never that we ourselves shall love. Oh, how happy do I now feel! Joy is the best physician, for I am well again, and strong, and —

(*Laughter heard off. Prudence, Olympe, Saint-Gaudens and Gaston Rieux enter tumultuously.*)

GAUDENS. Long live Monsieur and Madame Duval!
OLYMPE. Invite us to the wedding ball.
GAUDENS. Let's practise for it now.
GASTON. Oh, yes; a dance, a dance! Marguerite, play for us.

(*Marguerite plays on piano. Fantastic dance. Gaston has a woman's bonnet on his head. Saint-Gaudens claps a man's hat on Prudence. Loud laughter. Gaston dances with Prudence, who finally faints in his arms. They all run to her.*)

ACT II

A neat drawing-room in a country house near Auteuil. At the back, a fireplace with a plate-glass mirror over the chimney-piece. Doors right and left. French windows opening into the garden. Tables with writing materials and vases of flowers. Chairs, sofas, etc.

(*Nanine, entering with breakfast things, is met by Prudence.*)

PRUDENCE. Where is Marguerite?
NANINE. In the garden with Ma'amselle Nichette and Monsieur Gustave, who have come to spend the day with her.
PRUDENCE. I will join them.

(*Armand enters, meeting Prudence while Nanine goes out.*)

ARMAND. Ah! you here, Prudence! 'Tis well — I wished to speak with you. Two weeks since, you left here in Marguerite's carriage.
PRUDENCE. Exactly.
ARMAND. Since then, neither carriage nor horses have returned. A week since, on leaving, you complained of cold, and Marguerite lent you a cashmere shawl, which I do not think you have returned. Yesterday I saw her place in your hands bracelets and diamonds — to be reset,

she said. Where are the horses, the carriage, the shawl and the diamonds?

PRUDENCE. Must I tell you?

ARMAND. I entreat you.

PRUDENCE. The horses have taken themselves and the carriage back to the man from whom they came, for they were not paid for.

ARMAND. The cashmere shawl?

PRUDENCE. Sold.

ARMAND. The diamonds?

PRUDENCE. Pledged this morning. Perhaps you would like to see the receipts?

ARMAND. Why did you not tell me?

PRUDENCE. Marguerite forbade me.

ARMAND. And why these sales?

PRUDENCE. To obtain money, to be sure. Oh, I suppose you imagine it is quite enough to be in love and live a pastoral and ethereal life away from Paris. Marguerite has studied the reality and, like a good girl, resolved that as she could bring you no fortune, neither would she bring you any debts.

ARMAND. Good Marguerite!

PRUDENCE. Yes, too good Marguerite; for she has not yet done selling. I have now in my pocket a bill of sale on everything she possesses, which was entrusted to me to deliver to her by her man of business.

ARMAND. What sum would be necessary for —

PRUDENCE. Fifty thousand francs, at least.

ARMAND. Obtain a fortnight's grace from the creditors, and I will pay all.

PRUDENCE. You will embroil yourself with your father, and infringe on your future fortune.

ARMAND. I had prepared for this. I knew that Marguerite had creditors, and had written to my lawyer that I wished to dispose of a small estate left me by my mother, and have just received his answer. The deed is quite prepared, and presently I shall return to Paris in order to sign it. In the meantime, pray be careful that Marguerite knows nothing of —

PRUDENCE. But the papers that I bring?

ARMAND. When I am gone, give them to her as if nothing had occurred, for she must be ignorant of our conversation.

PRUDENCE. You may depend on me — and, by the by, Monsieur Armand, I am dreadfully pressed for money just now, and if you could —

ARMAND. Hush! she is here. Silence!

(Marguerite, entering, puts a finger to her lips as a sign to Prudence to be silent.)

ARMAND. *(to Marguerite)* Dear Marguerite! Scold Prudence.

MARGUERITE. Why?

ARMAND. Yesterday I begged her to call at my rooms and bring me any letters that were there, for it is a fortnight since I went to Paris. The first thing she does, is to forget them. So I must leave you for an hour or two. Nichette and Gustave are here to keep you company — so that you will not miss me much.

MARGUERITE. Have you yet written to your father?

ARMAND. No — but I shall this very day do so.

MARGUERITE. Go, then, and hasten your return.

ARMAND. I shall not be absent above an hour.

(Exit Armand, accompanied to the door by Marguerite.)

MARGUERITE. *(returning)* All is arranged?

PRUDENCE. Yes.

MARGUERITE. The papers?

PRUDENCE. Here they are. Your lawyer will come today and settle matters with you; but I must go and breakfast now, for I am dying of hunger. You have, I hope, something substantial in the house?

MARGUERITE. Nanine will attend to you.   *(Exit Prudence.)*

(Enter Nichette and Gustave.)

MARGUERITE. You see? This is how we have been living for the last three months.

NICHETTE. And you are happy?

MARGUERITE. You are right — I am.

NICHETTE. And you are right, Marguerite, when you say that happiness is in the heart. How many times Gustave and I have wished that you would fall in love with someone, and lead a calmer life.

MARGUERITE. Well, you have your wish. I love — and I am happy; but it is your love and happiness I envy.

GUSTAVE. The fact is, we are happy too — are we not, Nichette?

NICHETTE. I believe we are. After all, happiness doesn't cost much. You think you live simply here; what would you say if you could but see where I live — two little rooms on the fifth storey in the Rue Blanche, with windows that overlook some gardens in which nobody ever walks! How can there be people who have gardens that they never walk in?

MARGUERITE. *(giving a hand to each)* Ah, you are worthy creatures, and will be happy — as happy as I am now.

NICHETTE. Marguerite, you cannot guess what Gustave wants me to do — to give up embroidering, and not work any more! He'll be wanting to buy me a carriage one of these days.

GUSTAVE. That may come, perhaps. Then, you will drive out with us, will you not?

MARGUERITE. Yes, Gustave, that I will.

NICHETTE. Oh, we will have such a time? You must know that Gustave has a rich old uncle, who is going to make him heir. . . . But I forgot to tell you — Gustave is a lawyer now, if you please.

MARGUERITE. Indeed! You shall plead my first case.

NICHETTE. Oh, he has pleaded already.

MARGUERITE. Did he win?

GUSTAVE. No. My client was condemned to ten years' hard labour.

NICHETTE. Yes! And I was so glad.

MARGUERITE. Glad? Why so?

NICHETTE. Because the man deserved it.

MARGUERITE. And now that Gustave is a lawyer, Nichette will soon be a bride. Is it not so?

NICHETTE. If he behaves himself.

GUSTAVE. You hear the conditions! Then, Marguerite, may we not hope that you too will be a bride some day?

MARGUERITE. The bride of whom?

NICHETTE. Armand.

MARGUERITE. Armand? That can never be. Armand would marry me tomorrow if I would have it so; but I love him too well to ask of him such a sacrifice. Am I not right, Monsieur Gustave?

GUSTAVE. You are very generous, Marguerite.

MARGUERITE. Not generous, Gustave, but just. There are some things a woman cannot blot out from her past, things for which her husband would have every right to reproach her. I am unworthy to be Armand Duval's wife. Besides, I have a happiness I never dared to hope for; why should I tempt Providence and ask for more?

NICHETTE. Gustave would marry you, if he were in Armand's place. Wouldn't you, Gustave?

GUSTAVE. Perhaps. A woman's maidenhood belongs to her first love, and not to her first lover.

NICHETTE. Unless her first lover is at the same time her first love. There may be examples of this —

GUSTAVE. (clasping her hand) And not far away, either.

NICHETTE. (to Marguerite) Well, provided you're happy, the rest doesn't matter.

MARGUERITE. And how happy I am! To be near the man I love, to hear his voice, to read to him, or hear him read to me? From time to time I can forget the woman I once was, as if she had never been. In a simple white dress, with a great straw hat on my head and a cape over my arm against the freshness of the evening, I take a boat upon the lake with Armand; and as we drift to a halt under the weeping willows on the island, no one, not even I myself, supposes that this pale shadow is Marguerite Gautier. I have spent more money on bouquets than a poor family would need to live on for a year; well, this simple flower which Armand gave me this morning now seems to me enough to scent the air all day. Yes, I am happy. But you do not know all.

NICHETTE. What's the secret?

MARGUERITE. You said just now that I should see your home; perhaps I will.

NICHETTE. But how?

MARGUERITE. Unknown to Armand, I am about to sell all I possess to liquidate my debts. I shall rent a small apartment near to yours, furnish it very simply, and there we will live together, forgetting and forgot. In the summer we will come back to the country, but not in so fine a house as this. Have I not taken the right path towards happiness?

GUSTAVE. And you will reach the goal.

(*Enter Nanine.*)

NANINE. Madame, a gentleman would speak with you.

MARGUERITE. (*to Gustave and Nichette*) Doubtless the lawyer whom I was expecting; he has the arrangement of the sale. If you will walk for a while in the garden, I will rejoin you.   (*Exeunt Gustave and Nichette.*)

Bid him enter.   (*Exit Nanine.*)

(*Monsieur Duval enters, and remains in doorway.*)

DUVAL. Mademoiselle Marguerite Gautier?

MARGUERITE. Yes, monsieur. To whom have I the honour of speaking?

DUVAL. To Monsieur Duval.

MARGUERITE. Monsieur Duval!

DUVAL. Yes, mademoiselle, the father of Armand.

MARGUERITE. (*disturbed*) Armand is not here, sir.

DUVAL. I know it. But it is with you I wish to come to terms. Pray hear me. My son, mademoiselle, is compromised and ruined on your account.

MARGUERITE. You are deceived, sir. Thanks be to God, I am now beyond the reach of scandal, and I accept nothing from your son.

DUVAL. Which means my son is wretch enough to waste with you what you accept from others.

MARGUERITE. Pardon me, sir; but I am a woman and in my own house — two reasons that should plead in my favour for your courtesy. Your tone is not what I should expect from a gentleman I have the honour to see for the first time. I pray you will allow me to retire.

DUVAL. In truth, to hear you speak, it is difficult to believe that such assurance must be assumed. Oh, I was told that you were a dangerous woman!

MARGUERITE. Yes, sir; dangerous to myself, but not to others.

DUVAL. But it is none the less true that you are ruining my son.

MARGUERITE. Sir, I repeat, with all the respect I owe to Armand's father, that you are wrong.

DUVAL. Then what is the meaning of this letter from my lawyer, which apprises me that Armand wishes to resign to you a small estate?

(*Gives her a letter*)

MARGUERITE. I assure you, sir, Armand has done this without my knowledge; for he knows well that if he offered such a gift I would refuse it.

DUVAL. Indeed? You have not always spoken thus.

MARGUERITE. True, sir; but I have not always loved.

DUVAL. And now?

MARGUERITE. I am no longer what I was.

DUVAL. These are very fine words.

MARGUERITE. What can I say to convince you? I know the oaths of women like myself command no faith, but I swear to you by the love I bear your son — the holiest thing that ever filled my heart — I swear that I was ignorant of this transaction.

DUVAL. Yet you must live by some means?

MARGUERITE. You force me, sir, to be explicit. So far from resembling the other associations of my life, my liaison with your son has made me penniless. (*She gives the paper which Prudence had brought her*) I pray you read that paper. It contains a list of all that I possess on earth. When you were announced just now, I thought you were the person to whom I had sold them.

DUVAL. (*reading paper*) A bill of sale of all your furniture, pictures, plate, etc., with which to pay your creditors, the surplus to be returned to you. (*Hands back the paper and regards her with astonishment*) Have I been deceived?

MARGUERITE. You have, sir. I know my past life has been clouded; I have been foolish; but I would give the last drop of my blood to purge away the stain. Oh, despite what others may have told you, I have a heart; believe me, there is some goodness in me. It is Armand's love which has transformed me and saved me from myself.

You are his father, you must be good like him. Let me entreat you, do not speak badly of me to him; he would believe you, for he loves you; and I also love and honour you because you are his father.

DUVAL. Pardon me for the manner in which I introduced myself just now. I was angry with my son for his silence and ingratitude, which I laid at your door. I pray you to excuse me.

MARGUERITE. I can only bless you, sir, for those kind words.

DUVAL. Well, it is in the name of your noblest feelings that I am going to ask of you to give Armand the greatest proof of your love that you could ever give him.

MARGUERITE. Oh, sir, I entreat you, say no more. You are going to ask me something terrible, more terrible than I have ever imagined. My heart foresees it — I was too happy.

DUVAL. It is as a father that I speak to you, Marguerite, a father who comes to ask of you the happiness of both his children.

MARGUERITE. Of both your children?

DUVAL. Yes, Marguerite, of both. I have a daughter, young, beautiful, and pure as an angel. She loves a young man and, like you, has made that love the dream of her life. Marguerite, although your soul is cleansed in Armand's eyes, and mine, the world will always judge you by your past and pitilessly shut its doors against you. The family of my future son-in-law has learned of your relationship with Armand, and refuses to consent to Blanche's marriage unless he gives you up. The future of a young girl who has never done you wrong could be shattered by your touch. Marguerite, in the name of your love, I ask of you the happiness of my child.

MARGUERITE. You are very good, sir, to speak to me so frankly. I understand you, and you are right. I will leave Paris and remain apart from Armand for some time. It will be a sacrifice, I confess, but I will make it for your sake so that you may have nothing with which to reproach me. Besides, the joy of my return will obliterate the misery of separation. You will allow him to write to me sometimes, and when his sister is married —

DUVAL. Thank you, Marguerite; but I am asking something more of you.

MARGUERITE. More? What could I do more?

DUVAL. My child, a temporary absence will not suffice.

MARGUERITE. Ah, you would not have me leave Armand for ever?

DUVAL. You must.

MARGUERITE. Never! Do you not know what it is to love as we do? Do you not know that I have neither parents, friends, nor family? When Armand forgave my faults, he swore to be all these, and I have grafted life and hope on him till they and he are one. Do you not know that I have caught a mortal illness, that I have but few years to live? Renounce Armand! Better that at once you kill me.

DUVAL. Come, come, be calm. You are young and beautiful, and take for a disease the weariness of a disordered life; you will surely live until you reach the age at which 'tis happiness to die. I ask of you an enormous sacrifice, I know, but it is one you are inevitably forced to yield. Listen. You have known Armand for three months, and you love him. But are you certain that this love will last for ever? Have you not perhaps deceived yourself already? And if — too late — you were suddenly to realise you did not love my son, if you were to fall in love with someone else? Forgive me, Marguerite, but your past decides in favour of such doubts.

MARGUERITE. Never, sir; I have never loved and never will as I do now.

DUVAL. So be it! But if you are not deceived, my son may be. At his age, can the heart accept a never-changing contract? Does it not change perpetually in its affections? Nature is very hard to please, because she is so prodigal. It may be that you are both deceived. Do you hear me?

MARGUERITE. Yes, I hear you. Oh, heaven!

DUVAL. You are willing to sacrifice all for my son; but if he should accept this, what sacrifice could he make you in return? He will take the best years of your life, and what will happen later on, when cloying surfeit comes, as come it will? If he is an average man he will leave you, flinging your past in your face and saying he has only done what all the others did. If he is honourable he will marry you or keep you with him; what kind of union would that be which has neither chastity nor religion to commend it to the world's esteem? What career would then be open to him? What honourable ambition could he then pursue? Your union is not the fruit of two innocent affections; it is an earthy, human passion, born of caprice on one side and imagination on the other. What will remain of it when you are old? The first wrinkles on your brow will tear the veil from his eyes, and his fond illusions vanish with your youth.

MARGUERITE. Oh, my dream is shattered!

DUVAL. For three months you have been happy; keep the memory of that time unspotted in your heart, and it will make you strong. One day you will be proud of having saved Armand from a fate which he would all his life regret; and all your life you will have your self-respect. I speak to you as a man who knows the world; I implore you as a father, save my child. Come, Marguerite, prove to me you truly love my son. Have courage.

MARGUERITE. (to herself) Thus, no matter what she does, a fallen woman may never rise again. God, perhaps, will pardon her, but the world remains inflexible! What man would wish to call her 'wife,' what child would wish to call her 'mother'? (*To Duval*) You are right, sir. Everything you tell me I have told myself a thousand times. I must obey. One day will you tell your daughter — for 'tis to her I sacrifice my happiness — will you tell her that there was somewhere a woman who in this world had but one hope, one thought, one dream of joy, and that at the invocation of her name this woman renounced it all, and broke her heart, and died — for I shall die of this, sir, and perhaps then God will forgive me.

DUVAL. (*overcome despite himself*) Poor creature!

MARGUERITE. You pity me, sir, and I think you weep. May heaven thank you for those tears, for they have made me as brave as you could wish. You ask that I should part company with your son, for his good, his honour and his future. What must I do? Command me, I am ready.

DUVAL. Say to my son that you no longer love him.

MARGUERITE. (*smiling sadly*) He would not believe me.

DUVAL. You must leave Paris.

MARGUERITE. He would follow me.

DUVAL. Then —

MARGUERITE. Then trust me, sir; the sacrifice shall be complete. I swear to be victorious over my love, and ere a week be ended your son shall return to you, for a while perhaps to be unhappy, but for ever cured of his love for me; and I swear too that he shall never know what has transpired between us.

DUVAL. Marguerite, you are a noble girl — but I fear —

MARGUERITE. Fear nothing, sir. He will hate me.   (*She rings*)

(*Enter Nanine.*)

Beg Madame Duvernoy to come to me.

NANINE. Yes, madame.   (*Exit Nanine.*)

MARGUERITE. A last favour, sir.

DUVAL. Oh, pray speak, madame.

MARGUERITE. In a few hours Armand will be stricken with the heaviest grief he has yet known, that he perhaps will ever know. He will have need of a heart that loves him; be you then near him. And now, sir, let us part. He may return at any moment; should he see you, all would be lost.

DUVAL. What then are you about to do?

MARGUERITE. Were I to tell you, sir, 'twould be your duty to forbid me.

DUVAL. What can I do, Marguerite, to reward you for your generous devotion to my wishes?

MARGUERITE. You could, when I am dead and Armand heaps curses on

my memory, you could swear to him I loved him well and proved it
fatally. I hear a noise; adieu, sir. We shall never meet again. May you
be happy! (*Monsieur Duval goes out.*) Oh, heaven! Give me strength.
                                    (*She sits at the table and writes a letter.*)

(*Enter Prudence.*)

PRUDENCE. You wish to see me, dear Marguerite?
MARGUERITE. Yes; I have something to entrust to you.
PRUDENCE. What?
MARGUERITE. This letter.
PRUDENCE. To whom?
MARGUERITE. Look! (*Prudence reads the envelope and starts.*) Silence!
    Prepare to leave at once. (*Exit Prudence; Marguerite goes on writing.*)
    Now a letter to Armand. But what can I say? Oh, I shall go mad — I
    cannot do it! Impossible! I shall never have the courage. It is too
    much to ask of poor, weak, human nature.

(*Armand has entered, unobserved.*)

ARMAND. What are you doing there, Marguerite?
MARGUERITE. Armand! Nothing.
ARMAND. Writing?
MARGUERITE. No — yes.
ARMAND. How pale you are! To whom were you writing? Marguerite,
    let me see that letter.
MARGUERITE. This letter is for you, Armand, but in the name of heaven
    ask me not to give it to you now.
ARMAND. A mystery? — But no matter for it now; my father is coming!
MARGUERITE. You have seen him?
ARMAND. No; he left a letter at my rooms, and will be here this
    evening. Someone informed him of my retreat here and my life with
    you; God knows what rumours he has heard. But let him come! He
    will see you, and when he sees you he will love you. If not, what does
    it matter? I am dependent on him, I admit; but if need be, I will work
    and free myself from his bondage.
MARGUERITE. (*aside*) How he loves me! (*To Armand*) But you must not
    incense your father, Armand. He is coming, you say? Then I will
    retire and let him see you first. But I will come back; I will be there,
    by your side. I will fling myself at his feet and implore him not to
    part us.
ARMAND. How strangely you said that, Marguerite! Something is
    wrong. It is not my news which agitates you so. You can scarcely
    stand. This letter —   (*He holds out his hand.*)
MARGUERITE. (*stopping him*) This letter says something which I cannot

say to you; you know, there are such things? It is a proof of the love I bear you, Armand; I swear it. Ask me no more.

ARMAND. Keep the letter, Marguerite; I know all. Prudence told me this morning, and it was that which took me to Paris. I know the sacrifice that you wish to make for me; and while you were considering my happiness, I was not unmindful of yours. Dear Marguerite! How can I ever recompense so much devotion?

MARGUERITE. And now, now that you know all, let me depart.

ARMAND. Depart!

MARGUERITE. Withdraw, I would say. Your father may arrive at any moment. I will be in the garden with Gustave and Nichette; you have only to call, and I will rejoin you. How could I ever leave you? You will calm your father, if he is enraged, and win him to forgive us, will you not? Then we will live together, and love each other as before, and be as happy as we have been for these last three months! And you are happy, are you not? And have nothing to reproach me with? If I have ever caused you any sorrow, forgive me; it was not my fault, for I love you more than all the world. And you — you love me — do you not? When you recall one day the tokens of my love, you would not despise or curse me if —

ARMAND. But why these tears?

MARGUERITE. Sometimes I need to weep a little; now, you see, I am calm. I am going to join Nichette and Gustave. I will be there, always by your side, always ready to rejoin you, always loving you. Look, I am smiling. Adieu — for ever! (*She goes out, blowing him kisses.*)

ARMAND. Dear Marguerite! How she fears the idea of a separation! How she loves me! (*Rings the bell*)

(*Enter Nanine.*)

Nanine, if a gentleman — my father — asks to see me, show him in here at once.

NANINE. Very well, sir. (*Exit Nanine.*)

ARMAND. I am taking fright at nothing. My father will understand. The past is dead. Besides, what a difference between Marguerite and those other women! I met Olympe today, still occupied with empty pleasures. (*Takes letters from his pocket*) Here is an invitation to her ball next week — as if Marguerite and I ever could return to that society! Ah, how time drags when she is not here. Seven o'clock! (*Rings the bell*) My father will not come tonight.

(*Enter Nanine.*)

Ask madame to come in.

NANINE. Madame is not here, sir.

ARMAND. How? Where is she, then?

NANINE. I saw her go down the road. She told me to tell you, sir, that she would return presently.

ARMAND. Did Madame Duvernoy go with her?

NANINE. Madame Duvernoy and the others left a little before madame.

ARMAND. Very well. (*Exit Nanine.*) She could have gone to Paris to see about the sale; happily, Prudence will find the means to prevent her. (*He looks out of the window.*) Is that a shadow I can see in the garden? It must be her. (*He calls*) Marguerite! (*He goes out and calls again*) Marguerite! Marguerite! (*He returns*) No, there is no one there. (*He rings the bell*) Nanine! Nanine! Nanine, I say! No answer. What can this mean? This silence chills me. Why did I let Marguerite go out? She was hiding something from me. She was weeping! Has she deceived me? How could I think it, when she thought to sacrifice all for my sake! Perhaps something has happened to her! Perhaps she is injured! dead! I must find out.

(*He goes towards the garden. A Messenger confronts him at the door.*)

MESSENGER. Monsieur Armand Duval?

ARMAND. Yes.

MESSENGER. Here is a letter for you.

ARMAND. Where from?

MESSENGER. Paris.

ARMAND. Who gave it you?

MESSENGER. A lady.

ARMAND. Why do you come here?

MESSENGER. The garden gate was open. There was no one about. I saw a light, and thought —

ARMAND. Very well. Leave me. (*The Messenger withdraws.*) A letter from Marguerite. Why am I go agitated? Doubtless she is waiting for me somewhere, and writes to me to go and meet her. (*He goes to open the letter*) I'm trembling. Nonsense! This is childish.

(*Monsieur Duval enters unperceived, and stands behind his son.*)

ARMAND. (*reading*) 'Armand, by the time that you receive this letter . . .' (*He utters a cry of fury, turns and sees his father, and flings himself into his arms, sobbing.*) Ah! Father! Father!

ACT III

A splendid reception room in the house of Olympe; gaming table with lighted candles on it, cards, and plenty of loose money. Chairs round. Large chandeliers. Arch, center, opening onto a brilliantly lighted saloon.

(Gaston, Doctor, Prudence, Mademoiselle Arthur and Mademoiselle Anais discovered at the gaming table; two Players seated with their backs to the audience. Servants handing refreshments; music; Guests dance and promenade in the saloon.)

GASTON. *(dealing the cards for baccarat)* Put down your stakes, gentlemen!

ARTHUR. How much is there in the bank?

GASTON. A hundred louis.

ARTHUR. In that case, I shall stake five francs.

GASTON. With the enormous sum of five francs to hazard, no wonder you were anxious to know the amount of the bank!

ARTHUR. I can go in with five francs ready money, or, if you prefer, I can stake ten louis on credit.

GASTON. You are very good but, thank you, no. *(To Doctor)* You are not playing, doctor?

DOCTOR. No.

GASTON *(dealing cards)* Then why are you here?

DOCTOR. *(laughing)* To increase my practice, of course; I'm introducing myself to all the charming ladies.
                    (Laughter and gossip from all round the table)

GASTON. If this is how you play, I'm passing the bank.

PRUDENCE. Stop! I stake ten francs.

GASTON. Where are they?

PRUDENCE. In my pocket.

GASTON. *(laughing)* I would give fifteen francs to see them.

PRUDENCE. *(putting her hand in her pocket)* Bless me! I have forgotten my purse.

GASTON. Well, here's a purser who knows his job. Take these ten francs.

PRUDENCE. Thanks. I shall be certain to return them.   *(Stakes money)*

GASTON. You are certain to do nothing of the kind; and I beg you won't, for the surprise would be too much for me.   *(Giving cards)*
I am nine.   *(He collects in the money)*

PRUDENCE. He always wins. My ten francs gone already!

GASTON. Mine, you mean — returned to their rightful owner.

ARTHUR. That makes fifty louis that I have lost.

ANAIS. A thousand francs! Oh, and she had but two louis in her pocket when she arrived.

ARTHUR. Exactly — I owe the rest.

ANAIS. I pity your creditors. Doctor, cure Arthur of that serious complaint — losing money which she has not got.

DOCTOR. Time is the only remedy for that.

GASTON. Put down your stakes, gentlemen; we are not here to amuse ourselves.

(*Enter Olympe and Saint-Gaudens.*)

OLYMPE. Still gambling?

ARTHUR. Still — and for ever.

OLYMPE. Give me ten louis, Saint-Gaudens, to play with.

GAUDENS. There. Ah, there you are, doctor. I must consult you. Cure me of too much good nature. Sometimes I have fits of giddiness.

DOCTOR. Indeed!

OLYMPE. What did he want?

DOCTOR. He thinks there's something wrong with his head.

OLYMPE. The conceited ass — I have lost. Saint-Gaudens, play for me and try to win.

PRUDENCE. Saint-Gaudens, lend me three louis.   (*He gives them.*)

ANAIS. Saint-Gaudens, go and find me a water-ice.

GAUDENS. Presently.

ANAIS. Then tell us the story about your uncle and the heiress.

GAUDENS. I'm going, I'm going.   (*He goes out.*)

PRUDENCE. (*to Gaston*) Do you remember that story?

GASTON. I should say I do. How Marguerite laughed! How Marguerite laughed! By the by, is she here?

OLYMPE. She has yet to arrive.

GASTON. And Armand?

OLYMPE. Armand is not in Paris. — Then you know not what has happened?

GASTON. What?

PRUDENCE. They have separated.

ANAIS. Fiddlesticks!

PRUDENCE. It is true. Marguerite has left him.

GASTON. But when?

PRUDENCE. A month ago.

ANAIS. She has done well.

GASTON. Why so?

ANAIS. You should always leave a man before he leaves you.

ARTHUR. Come, gentlemen; is there a game in progress, or is there not?

(Re-enter Saint-Gaudens.)

GAUDENS. Anais, here is the water-ice you asked for.

ANAIS. You have been a very long time, my poor old fellow; after all, at your age . . .

GASTON. *(rising)* The bank is broken, gentlemen, and the banker has resigned. Had I been offered five hundred francs to deal the cards for an entire evening I would have refused; and yet here I have been banker for only two hours, and have lost two thousand. Ah! 'tis a delightful occupation. *(Another guest takes over the bank.)*

(Enter Armand.)

PRUDENCE. Hullo! Here's Armand.

GASTON. *(to Armand)* We were but now speaking of you.

ARMAND. And what were you saying?

PRUDENCE. That you were at Tours, and would not be here tonight.

ARMAND. You were mistaken, then.

GASTON. When did you arrive?

ARMAND. An hour since.

PRUDENCE. Have you seen Marguerite?

ARMAND. No.

PRUDENCE. She will be here tonight.

ARMAND. *(coolly)* Indeed? Then perhaps I may see her.

PRUDENCE. Perhaps you may see her! How strangely you talk!

ARMAND. How would you have me talk?

PRUDENCE. Your heart then is cured?

ARMAND. Perfectly.

PRUDENCE. So you no longer think of her?

ARMAND. To say that I no longer think of her at all would be untrue; but Marguerite dismissed me in so sharp a manner that I found myself a pretty fool to have loved her as I did — for in truth I loved her very dearly.

PRUDENCE. Oh, I really think she loved you then, and even loves you still — that is a little. But it was time for her to leave you. Everything she had was being sold to pay her debts.

ARMAND. And now they are all paid?

PRUDENCE. Entirely.

ARMAND. And Monsieur de Varville supplied the funds?

PRUDENCE. Yes.

ARMAND. So much the better.

PRUDENCE. And so I tell her. In short, he has provided her with all her former luxuries — horses, carriage, jewels —

ARMAND. And she has returned to Paris?

PRUDENCE. Naturally; she had no wish to go back to Auteuil when you had left, so I returned to wind up her affairs there. And that reminds me, I have some things of yours at home you must collect. There was only a small card-case with your monogram that Marguerite desired to keep; but I will ask her for it, if you would like it back.

ARMAND. (*with emotion*) Let her keep it!

PRUDENCE. As for the rest, I have never seen her as she is now. She never sleeps, but chases after suppers, parties, balls, and dances the long night away. Not long ago, she was three days confined to bed, and when the doctor allowed her to get up she flung herself at once into a round of feverish excitements, risking her health and life with desperate abandon. If she continues thus, it cannot last long. Do you propose to go and see her?

ARMAND. No; the past is dead — forgotten.

PRUDENCE. Ah, I am delighted to find you take the matter so sensibly.

(*Enter Gustave.*)

ARMAND. (*seeing him*) My dear Prudence, here is a friend that I must speak with; will you have the goodness to excuse me?

PRUDENCE. By all means! (*She goes to the gaming table*) I stake ten francs!

ARMAND. So you received my letter?

GUSTAVE. I did — and here I am.

ARMAND. You wonder why I should request your presence at such a gathering?

GUSTAVE. I confess it.

ARMAND. You have not seen Marguerite of late?

GUSTAVE. No; not since I saw her in your company.

ARMAND. So you know nothing?

GUSTAVE. Nothing; instruct me.

ARMAND. And you believed that Marguerite loved me, did you not?

GUSTAVE. I believe so still.

ARMAND. (*giving him Marguerite's letter*) Read.

GUSTAVE. (*after reading it*) And Marguerite wrote this?

ARMAND. She did.

GUSTAVE. When?

ARMAND. A month since.

GUSTAVE. And what was your reply?

ARMAND. What could it be? The blow was so unexpected that I thought I should go mad. Marguerite! To deceive me! When I loved her so dearly! Oh, such women surely have no souls. Stunned by the shock, I accompanied my father as far as Tours. At first I thought to live there, but it proved impossible. I could not sleep; I stifled. I had loved Marguerite too greatly to become indifferent all at once. I had to love her or else hate her. At last, I could no longer stand the strain. I felt that I should die unless I saw her once again, heard from her own lips the words that she had written. I am here this evening because they tell me she is coming. What will occur, I know not; but I may need a friend.

GUSTAVE. My dear Armand, I am entirely at your service. But for heaven's sake reflect — your affair is with a woman. Be discreet.

ARMAND. So be it! She has a lover who will call on me for satisfaction. If I commit an indiscretion, I have blood enough to pay for it.

(*Enter Servant.*)

SERVANT. (*announcing*) Mademoiselle Marguerite Gautier! Monsieur the Baron de Varville!

ARMAND. She is here.

Enter Marguerite and De Varville.

OLYMPE. (*going to meet Marguerite*) How late you are!

VARVILLE. We have just come from the Opera.

(*Shakes hands with the gentlemen*)

PRUDENCE. (*to* Marguerite) All is well?

MARGUERITE. Very well!

PRUDENCE. (*in an undertone*) Armand is here.

MARGUERITE. (*disturbed*) Armand?

PRUDENCE. Yes.

(*At this moment, Marguerite meets the eye of Armand, who has gone to the gaming table; she smiles timidly; he bows coldly.*)

MARGUERITE. Oh, I was wrong to come to this ball tonight.

PRUDENCE. Not at all; you would have to meet some day; and it may as well be soon as late.

MARGUERITE. He has spoken to you?

PRUDENCE. Yes.

MARGUERITE. Of me?

PRUDENCE. Naturally.

MARGUERITE. What said he?

PRUDENCE. That he bore you no ill will; you were quite justified.

MARGUERITE. So much the better if he thinks so; but no — it is impossible. He bowed too coldly, and he is too pale.

VARVILLE. (*to Marguerite, aside*) Monsieur Duval is over there, Marguerite.

MARGUERITE. I know it.

VARVILLE. Will you swear to me that you were ignorant of his presence here when you arrived?

MARGUERITE. I swear it.

VARVILLE. And you will promise me not to speak to him?

MARGUERITE. I promise; but should he speak, I cannot promise that I will not reply. Prudence, stay near me.

DOCTOR. (to Marguerite) Good evening, madame.

MARGUERITE. Ah, it is you, doctor! How you scrutinise me!

DOCTOR. What better could I do when in your presence?

MARGUERITE. You find me, do you not, much changed?

DOCTOR. Take care of yourself, take care, I entreat you. I shall call on you tomorrow, to scold you at my ease.

MARGUERITE. Ah, doctor, how good and kind you are! But you are not leaving already?

DOCTOR. Presently. (He shakes her hand and retires.)

GUSTAVE. (approaching Marguerite) Good evening, Marguerite.

MARGUERITE. Ah, my dear Gustave, how glad I am to see you. And Nichette — is she here?

GUSTAVE. No.

MARGUERITE. Forgive me; she would have no desire to come. Love her well, Gustave — she must be happy, to be so truly loved.

(She wipes her eyes.)

GUSTAVE. What is the matter?

MARGUERITE. Oh, Gustave, I am so unhappy.

GUSTAVE. There, there, do not weep. Why are you here?

MARGUERITE. How else can I allay my grief?

GUSTAVE. If you will be advised by me, you will leave this ball before it is too late.

MARGUERITE. Why?

GUSTAVE. Who knows what may happen? Armand —

MARGUERITE. But surely Armand hates and despises me?

GUSTAVE. No; he loves you still. See how feverish he is — not master of himself. I know not what may yet transpire between him and Monsieur de Varville. Plead indisposition and depart.

MARGUERITE. A duel between Varville and Armand! Yes, yes, you are right, Gustave. I must leave. (She rises.)

VARVILLE. (approaching her) Where are you going?

MARGUERITE. My love, I'm suffocating and wish to withdraw.

VARVILLE. No, you are not suffocating, Marguerite. You want to withdraw because Monsieur Duval is over there and seems to pay no heed to you. But understand I have no wish to quit whatever place he honours with his presence. We are at this ball, and here will we remain.

OLYMPE. (*loudly*) What were they playing at the Opera tonight?

VARVILLE. *La Favorite.*

ARMAND. The story of a woman who deceives her lover.

PRUDENCE. Pooh! How commonplace!

ANAIS. Which means it isn't true; there's no such thing as a woman who would deceive her lover.

ARMAND. I say there is.

ANAIS. Where are they then?

ARMAND. All around you.

OLYMPE. Yes, but there are lovers and lovers.

ARMAND. As there are women and women.

GASTON. Now then! My dear Armand, you are playing like a madman.

ARMAND. To see if the proverb holds true: 'Unlucky in love, lucky at play.'

GASTON. Ah! You must be terribly unlucky in love, for you are terribly lucky at play.

ARMAND. My dear fellow, I reckon on making my fortune tonight; and when I have won it I will go and live in the country.

OLYMPE. Alone?

ARMAND. No; with someone who once accompanied me there before, and left me. Perhaps when I am rich —. (*Aside*) She will say nothing then!

GUSTAVE. (*to Armand, aside*) Be quiet, Armand, for heaven's sake! You are killing Marguerite.

ARMAND. It's a good story; I must tell it you. There is a gentleman in it who comes on at the end, a sort of *deus ex machina,* a charming type.

VARVILLE. Sir!

MARGUERITE. (*to Varville, aside*) If you challenge Monsieur Duval, you shall never see me more.

ARMAND. (*to Varville*) Are you addressing me, sir?

VARVILLE. Yes indeed, sir; you are so lucky at play that your good fortune tempts me, and I understand so well the use to which you would apply your gains that I am eager to see you win still more, and so propose a match.

ARMAND. (*looking him full in the face*) Which I accept gladly, sir.

VARVILLE. A hundred louis, sir.

ARMAND. (*astonished and contemptuous*) Agreed; a hundred louis. On which side will you —

VARVILLE. That which you do not take.

ARMAND. A hundred louis on the left.

VARVILLE. A hundred louis on the right.

GASTON. (*dealing cards*) On the right, four; on the left, nine. Armand wins.

VARVILLE. In that case, two hundred louis.

ARMAND. Agreed; two hundred louis. But take care, sir; if the proverb says 'Unlucky in love, lucky at play,' it also says 'Lucky in love, unlucky at play.'

GASTON. Six! Eight! Armand wins again.

MARGUERITE. (*to Olympe*) My God, where will this end?

OLYMPE. (*to create a diversion*) Come along, gentlemen; supper is served.

ARMAND. Shall we continue the game, sir?

VARVILLE. No — not for the present.

ARMAND. I owe you your revenge, and promise you shall have it at any game you choose.

VARVILLE. Rest easy, sir; I will take advantage of your goodwill!

OLYMPE. (*taking Armand by the arm*) You are out of luck, my dear Armand.

ARMAND. Ah, you only call me 'dear' when I've been winning.

VARVILLE. Are you coming, Marguerite?

MARGUERITE. Not yet; I would speak a word with Prudence.

VARVILLE. I warn you, Marguerite; if within ten minutes you do not rejoin us, I shall return and seek you here.

MARGUERITE. Very well, sir; go.

(*Olympe and Guests move into the saloon; Servants close folding doors behind them. Prudence is left with Marguerite.*)

Go to Armand, and in the name of all he holds most sacred implore him to come to me. I must speak with him.

PRUDENCE. Should he refuse —

MARGUERITE. He will not. He hates me too much not to seize the opportunity to tell me so. Go. (*Exit Prudence*) Let me be calm. He must continue to think of me as he does. Shall I have strength enough to keep the promise that I made his father? Oh heaven, make him despise and hate me! for only so may this duel be averted. Ah, he is here.

(*Enter Armand.*)

ARMAND. You would speak with me, madame?

MARGUERITE. Yes, Armand, I —

ARMAND. Proceed, madame; you would exonerate yourself?

MARGUERITE. No, Armand, that is not the point at issue now; do not, I
implore you, dwell upon the past.

ARMAND. You are right, madame; it covers you with too much shame.

MARGUERITE. You overwhelm me with reproaches, Armand. Hear me, I
beg you, without hatred, without anger, without contempt. Come,
Armand, give me your hand.

ARMAND. Never, madame! If this is all you have to say to me . . .

(He offers to withdraw.)

MARGUERITE. Who could believe you one day would refuse the hand I
tendered? But no matter for that now. Armand, you must leave Paris.

ARMAND. Leave Paris?

MARGUERITE. Yes — rejoin your father — and at once!

ARMAND. And why, madame?

MARGUERITE. Because Monsieur de Varville seeks to challenge you, and
I would not be the cause of such misfortune; I am alone to blame,
and I alone should suffer.

ARMAND. And so you counsel me to flee a challenge and prove myself a
coward! In truth, what other counsel could be expected from a
woman such as you?

MARGUERITE. Armand, I swear to you, I have scarce strength enough to
tell how much I have this last month suffered; my malady increases
hourly; it destroys me. In the name of our past love, Armand, in the
name of your mother and your sister, shun me, rejoin your father,
and — if you can — forget my very name.

ARMAND. I understand you, madame; you tremble for your lover and
the wealth he represents. I could bring ruin on you with a pistol-shot
or sword-thrust. That, indeed, would be a great misfortune.

MARGUERITE. You could be killed, Armand — there is the true
misfortune!

ARMAND. What matters it to you whether I live or die? Were you so
concerned about my life when you wrote to me 'Armand, forget me, I
am the mistress of another man'? This letter might have killed me,
but I live to be avenged. Ah, did you believe that I would tamely
suffer you and your accomplice there to break my heart? No,
madame, no. I am again in Paris; between Monsieur de Varville and
myself it is now a question of blood. Madame, were you also to die
for it, I swear to you that I will kill him!

MARGUERITE. Monsieur de Varville is innocent of all that has occurred.

ARMAND. You love him, madame! That is enough to make me hate
him.

MARGUERITE. You know well I do not — could not — love this man.

ARMAND. Then why did you give yourself to him?

MARGUERITE. Do not ask me, Armand! I cannot tell you. I dare not answer.

ARMAND. Then I will answer for you. You gave yourself to him because you are a woman without integrity or soul, because your love belongs to him who pays for it and you have made an auction of your heart, because when you had to make a sacrifice on my account your courage failed you and your instincts got the upper hand, because in short the man who consecrated yours his life and honour was worth less to you than the horses of your carriage and the diamonds about your neck.

MARGUERITE. Very well. Yes, all you say is true; yes, I am an infamous and wretched creature who did not love you; yes, I deceived you! But if I am so despicable, why should you remember me, why risk your life for my sake — and the lives of those who love you? Armand, on my knees I beg of you — go, leave Paris and never look behind you.

ARMAND. Then I will go — but on one condition.

MARGUERITE. Whatever it is, I agree.

ARMAND. That you go with me.

MARGUERITE. (recoiling) Never!

ARMAND. Never!

MARGUERITE. Oh heaven, give me courage!

ARMAND. (running to the door, and then returning) Listen, Marguerite. I am mad — feverish — my brain seethes, my blood is on fire — there is nothing — no infamy — of which I am not capable. A moment since, I thought that it was hatred which impelled me to you; it was love, unconquerable and infuriating love, love full of hatred, love urged on by remorse, contempt and shame — for after what has passed between us I despise myself for loving you again. No matter. Speak but one word of penitence, blame your fault on chance, on fate, on your own weakness, and it is all forgot! What is this man to me? I hate him only if you love him. Tell me only that you love me still, and I will forgive you, Marguerite; we will take flight from Paris and the past, travel to the ends of the earth if need be, until no human face remains to greet us and all the world comprises but our love.

MARGUERITE. (exhausted) I would give my life for one hour of that happiness which you propose, but such happiness is impossible.

ARMAND. Again!

MARGUERITE. An abyss divides us; we may no longer love each other. Go, forget me! — it must be so; I have sworn it.

ARMAND. To whom?

MARGUERITE. To one who had the right to ask of me this solemn oath.

ARMAND. (his anger rising) Monsieur de Varville, I presume?

MARGUERITE. Yes.

ARMAND. (*seizing Marguerite by the arm*) Monsieur de Varville, whom you love! Tell me you love him; say but that and I depart.

MARGUERITE. Very well, then. Yes, I love Monsieur de Varville.

(*Armand hurls Marguerite to the ground and offers to strike her. Then he dashes to the saloon and flings open the folding doors.*)

ARMAND. (*to Guests in the saloon*) Everybody! Come in here.

(*Enter De Varville and all the other Guests.*)

MARGUERITE. What are you doing?

ARMAND. (*to Guests*) Do you see this woman?

ALL. Marguerite Gautier?

ARMAND. Yes! Marguerite Gautier. Do you know what she has done? She sold all she possessed to live with me — so much she loved me. This was generous, was it not? But do you know what I have done? I have behaved like a scoundrel. I accepted the sacrifice without giving anything in exchange. But it is not too late; I am penitent and have come to make amends for all. You will all bear witness that now I owe this woman nothing!

(*He showers Marguerite with bank-notes. She utters a cry and falls back senseless. Varville advances on Armand, and hurls his gloves in Armand's face.*)

VARVILLE. (*with contempt*) Without equivocation, sir, you are a villain!

(*Guests rush between them.*)

ACT IV

Marguerite's sleeping chamber, meanly furnished. Window on left, with curtains half drawn; door right. Fireplace, right, with poker, tongs and fender; sofa in front of the fireplace. Table with toilette glass and tea things; chairs round. Bed at back; near it a small table with medicines, letter and night-light.

(*Marguerite discovered in bed asleep; Gaston Rieux stretched out on the sofa; no light except the night-light.*)

GASTON. (*raising his head and listening*) I must have dozed off for a moment. I hope she has not wanted anything. No; still asleep. I wonder what the time is. Seven o'clock! No daylight yet, and the fire has gone out. I must get it going again.   (*He pokes the fire.*)

MARGUERITE. (*waking up*) Nanine, give me something to drink.

GASTON. Here you are.

MARGUERITE. (*lifting her head slightly*) Who is that?

GASTON. (*preparing a cup of tea*) It's only me, Gaston.

MARGUERITE. What are you doing in my room?

GASTON. (*giving her the cup*) Drink this first, and then I will tell you. Is it sweet enough?

MARGUERITE. Yes.

GASTON. I was born to be a nurse.

MARGUERITE. But where is Nanine?

GASTON. Fast asleep. When I came at eleven last night to learn how you were, the poor girl was ready to drop with fatigue while I, as usual, was wide awake. You had already fallen asleep, so I bundled Nanine off to bed, settled myself on the sofa there near the fire, and have passed a beautiful night. You slept so quietly that it did me more good than if I had had the finest snooze in the world. And now, how are you this morning?

MARGUERITE. Very well, my good Gaston; but why should you wear yourself out like this —

GASTON. Rubbish! I spend enough nights on the town; it would do me much more good to pass some of them watching by a sick-bed! Besides, I have something to say to you.

MARGUERITE. To me?

GASTON. Yes. You are in need.

MARGUERITE. In need of what?

GASTON. Money. When I arrived here yesterday there was a bailiff in the drawing-room; I paid him off and turned him out of doors. But that's not all. You need some ready money here, and I happen to have some — not much, for I have lost a fair amount at cards and bought a pile of useless presents for New Year's Day. — May you be well and happy all the year! (*He embraces her*) — But, to be brief, look here, here are twenty-five louis anyway; I am going to put them in that table drawer over there, and when they are gone there will be more.

MARGUERITE. (*moved*) Gaston, you are very kind. And to think it should be you who takes such care of me! You, whom all suppose a scatter-brain, you who have never been more than my friend —

GASTON. Why, it is always so. Now, do you know what we are going to do?

MARGUERITE. Tell me.

GASTON. 'Twill be a splendid day! You have slept for eight good hours and must sleep a little more. From one to three the sun will be quite warm; I will come for you; wrap yourself up well; we will go for a drive in a carriage; and who will sleep well tomorrow night? Marguerite. Till then, I must go and see my mother. Heaven knows how she will receive me; it's more than a fortnight since I saw her last! I shall lunch with her and be here at one. How will that suit you?

MARGUERITE. I shall try to find the strength —

GASTON. You shall find it, never fear!

(*Enter Nanine*).

Come in, come in, Nanine. Marguerite is awake.

MARGUERITE. Were you very tired, my poor Nanine?

NANINE. A little, madame.

MARGUERITE. Open the window, I need a little air. I want to get up.

NANINE. (*opening the window and looking into the street*) Madame, the doctor is here.

MARGUERITE. He is a good man. His first visit is always here. Gaston, open the door to him as you are leaving. Nanine, help me to get up.

NANINE. But madame —

MARGUERITE. No objections now!

GASTON. Goodbye for the present!

MARGUERITE. For the present.   (*Exit Gaston.*)

(*Marguerite rises, but sinks back again exhausted. At length, supported by Nanine, she walks to the sofa; the Doctor enters in time to help her sit.*)

Good morning, doctor. How kind you are to think of me the first thing in the morning! Nanine, see if there are any letters.

(*Exit Nanine.*)

DOCTOR. Give me your hand. (*He feels her pulse*) How do you feel today?

MARGUERITE. Better and worse; better in spirit but worse in body. Last evening, I felt myself so near to death I called a priest. I was wretched, afraid of death and driven to despair. He came, talked with me for an hour, and took away with him all my remorse and terror and despair. And then I fell asleep and woke just now.

DOCTOR. All goes well, madame, and I promise you a total cure by the first days of spring.

MARGUERITE. Thank you, doctor; but I know it is your duty to speak thus. When God said it was a sin to lie, he made an exception for all doctors.

(*Re-enter Nanine.*)

(*To Nanine*) What have you there?

NANINE. Some presents for you, madame.

MARGUERITE. Ah, yes, 'tis New Year's Day. How much has happened this last year! At this hour a year ago, we were at table, singing, greeting the New Year with the self-same smile we had just given to the old. When shall we laugh again, I wonder? (*Opening the packages*) A ring, from Saint-Gaudens. Bless him! A bracelet, from the Count de Giray in London. What would he say if he could see me now? And then some bonbons. Well, the world has a better memory than I expected.

NANINE. And here is a letter, madame.

MARGUERITE. Let me see. (*Taking the letter and opening it*) 'Dear Marguerite, I have called to see you twenty times but could never be admitted. However, I must share my happiness with you. Gustave and I are to be married on the first of January in the Magdalen Chapel at St Theresa's Church. It is a New Year's present which Gustave has been keeping for me. Do, my love, try to be present: nine o'clock in the morning is the hour. Believe me, your happy and devoted friend, Nichette.' There is, then, happiness for all the world but me; yet, no, I am ungrateful! Doctor, pray close that window, I am cold, and give me pen and paper.

(*Marguerite buries her head in her hands. The Doctor places writing materials on a table near her, and retires.*)

NANINE. (*to the Doctor, in an undertone*) Well, doctor?

DOCTOR. (*shaking his head*) She is very, very ill.

MARGUERITE. (*aside*) They think I cannot hear them. (*Aloud*) Doctor, as you pass by, would you be kind enough to leave this letter at the church where Nichette is to be married, and beg them not to give it her until after the ceremony. (*She writes the letter, folds and seals it.*) There — and thank you. (*She presses his hand*) Don't forget, and come back soon if you are able!   (*Exit Doctor.*)
Now to tidy up this room a little. (*Bell rings*) Some one rings; go to the door, Nanine.   (*Exit Nanine.*)

(*Nanine re-enters.*)

NANINE. It is Madame Duvernoy, who wishes to see madame.

MARGUERITE. Show her in.   (*Exit Nanine.*)

(*Nanine re-enters with Prudence.*)

PRUDENCE. Well, my dear Marguerite, and how are you this morning?

MARGUERITE. Better, thank you, my dear Prudence.

PRUDENCE. Send Nanine away for a moment; I have something to say to you alone.

MARGUERITE. Nanine, tidy the next room, will you? I will call when I need you.   (*Exit Nanine.*)

PRUDENCE. My dear Marguerite, I have a great favour to ask you.

MARGUERITE. What is it?

PRUDENCE. Have you any money?

MARGUERITE. As you know, I have been in difficulties for some time. But, anyway, go on.

PRUDENCE. It's New Year's Day, and I have presents to give. Could you lend me two hundred francs until the end of the month?

MARGUERITE. (*casting up her eyes*) The end of the month!

PRUDENCE. If it inconveniences you —

MARGUERITE. I have but little money, of which indeed I am in urgent want.

PRUDENCE. Then we will say no more about it.

MARGUERITE. But no matter. Open that drawer.

PRUDENCE. Which one? (*She opens several*) Ah, the middle one.

MARGUERITE. How much is there?

PRUDENCE. Five hundred francs.

MARGUERITE. Well, take the two hundred that you need.

PRUDENCE. And the rest will be enough for you?

MARGUERITE. Never mind me; I have all that I shall want.

PRUDENCE. (*taking the money*) You do me a great kindness.

MARGUERITE. So much the better, dear Prudence!

PRUDENCE. Now I must go, but I shall see you again soon. You are looking much better.

MARGUERITE. Oh yes, much better.

PRUDENCE. The fine weather will come soon, and the country air will complete your recovery.

MARGUERITE. No doubt.

PRUDENCE. (*going*) Thank you again!

MARGUERITE. Send Nanine to me.

PRUDENCE. Of course.   (*Exit Prudence.*)

(*Nanine re-enters.*)

NANINE. Did she come to ask you for money again?

MARGUERITE. Yes.

NANINE. And you gave it her?

MARGUERITE. It was so small a sum, and she needed it so greatly, she said. But so do we, Nanine; there are New Year's gifts to give. So take this bracelet I was given to the jeweller's, and sell it. Come back quickly.

NANINE. But in the meantime —

MARGUERITE. I can remain alone — shall want for nothing. Besides, you will not be long, you know the way; that jeweller has bought enough from me these last three months. (*Exit Nanine; Marguerite takes a letter from her bosom and reads*) 'Madame, I have learned of the duel between Armand and Monsieur de Varville, not from my son for — you will scarcely believe it — he fled without bidding me farewell. De Varville is now out of danger, thank heaven, and I know all. You have kept your oath at hazard of your life. I have today written to Armand, explaining all. He is far distant, but will return to ask your pardon for us both; for I have been forced to do you harm, and wish to make amends. Take especial care of yourself, my child, and hope; your courage and your self-denial merit a bright future, and I promise you it shall be yours. Believe me your friend, Georges Duval. 15th November.' 'Tis six weeks since I received this letter. How many times have I re-read it, to gain a little courage! If only I could hear one word from Armand! If only I could live until the spring! (*She rises and looks in the glass*) Oh, how changed I am! And yet the doctor promised me I should recover. I will have patience. Yet, just now, with Nanine, he gave me up. I heard him; he said that I was very ill. Very ill! Yet there is hope; I have some months yet to live, and if Armand returns within that time, I shall be saved. New Year's Day! Ah, 'tis the time for hope! And I am right to do so; if I were in real danger, Gaston would not have the courage to laugh at my bedside as he did but now; the doctor would not have left me. (*At the window*) How happy the children are! Oh, how that pretty infant laughs and gambols with his toys! I should like to kiss him.

(*Nanine enters. She puts the money she has brought upon the mantelpiece, and comes to Marguerite.*)

NANINE. Madame —

MARGUERITE. What is it, Nanine?

NANINE. You feel better today, do you not?

MARGUERITE. Yes — why?

NANINE. Promise me you will be calm.

MARGUERITE. What has happened?

NANINE. I wanted to forewarn you . . . too sudden joy is difficult to bear!

MARGUERITE. Joy, you say?

NANINE. Yes, madame.

MARGUERITE. Armand! You have seen Armand? Armand is coming to see me! (*Nanine nods assent. Marguerite runs to the door.*) Armand!

(*Armand enters, looking pale. Marguerite flings her arms round his neck and holds him tight. Nanine withdraws.*)

Oh, is it really you? It is impossible that God should be so kind!

ARMAND. Yes, Marguerite, it is I — so penitent, so troubled, and so guilty that I did not dare to cross your threshold. Had I not met Nanine, I should be still weeping and praying underneath your window. Do not curse me, Marguerite! My father wrote to me, explaining everything. I was very far from you; I knew not where to go to flee my love and my remorse. I left at once, travelled like a madman, night and day, without repose or respite, without sleep, pursued by ominous foreboding, seeing from afar your house draped with mourning black. Oh, had I not found you living, I should have killed myself, knowing that I had killed you. I have not yet seen my father; Marguerite, tell me that you will forgive us both. Oh, how miraculous it is to see you once again!

MARGUERITE. Forgive you, my beloved? But I, alone, was guilty! Yet could I have acted otherwise? I sought your happiness, even at the cost of mine. But now your father will not separate us, is it not so? 'Tis not the Marguerite of former days you meet with here; but I am still young, and will grow beautiful again because I now am happy. You will forget the past. 'Tis only from today we will begin to live.

ARMAND. Oh yes, we shall no more be separated. Listen, Marguerite. We will leave this house this very minute, and never see Paris again. My father knows your true worth; he will love you as his son's good genius. My sister is married — the future is ours.

MARGUERITE. Oh, speak on, speak on! I feel my soul, my health, reviving with your words. I said this morning but a single thing could save me; I no longer hoped for it — and here you are! We have no time to lose; come, and since life is passing from me, I must arrest its passage. Oh, you do not know — Nichette and Gustave are married now, this very morning. We shall see them. It will do us good to go into a church, give thanks to God, and share in the happiness of others. What a surprise did heaven keep for me for New Year's Day! But, Armand, tell me once again you love me!

ARMAND. Yes, Marguerite, I love you; all my life is yours.

MARGUERITE. (*calling*) Nanine — my shawl; I am going out.

(*Re-enter Nanine.*)

ARMAND. Dear Nanine! You have taken such good care of her. Thank you.

MARGUERITE. Every day we talked of you, the pair of us; for no one
   else dared speak your name. It was she who consoled me, who said
   that we should meet again. And she was not mistaken.   (*She totters.*)

ARMAND. Marguerite, what is it? How pale you are!

MARGUERITE. (*with an effort*) Nothing, my beloved, nothing! When
   happiness thus floods a heart so long left desolate, it takes away the
   breath — that's all.   (*She sits down, her head falling back.*)

ARMAND. Marguerite, speak to me, I implore you — Marguerite!

MARGUERITE. (*coming to herself*) Fear nothing, my beloved. I have, you
   know, been always subject to these fainting fits; but they quickly
   pass. Look, I am smiling, I am strong! Come. 'Tis the joy of knowing
   I shall live which stifles me.

ARMAND. (*taking her hand*) You are shaking.

MARGUERITE. It is nothing! Come, Nanine, give me my shawl, my
   hat —

ARMAND. (*terrified*) My God! My God!

MARGUERITE. (*pulling off the shawl angrily, after trying to walk*) Oh, I
   cannot!   (*She falls upon the sofa.*)

ARMAND. Nanine, run and find the doctor!

MARGUERITE. Yes, yes; tell him that Armand has returned, that I want
   to live, that I must live. (*Nanine goes out*) But if your return cannot
   save me, nothing will. I have lived for love; now I am dying for it.

ARMAND. Hush now, Marguerite; you will live — you must!

MARGUERITE. Sit near me, Armand, as close as you can; and listen to
   me well. I am sorry that a moment since I was angry at death's
   approach; it is inevitable, and I welcome it, since it has awaited your
   return to strike me down. If my death had not been certain, your
   father would not have told you to return —

ARMAND. Marguerite, speak no more thus, or you will drive me mad.
   Do not tell me you are dying; tell me that you do not believe it, that
   it may not — must not — will not be.

MARGUERITE. But since God wills it, I must yield, whether I will or no.
   If my life were innocent and chaste, perhaps I would weep to leave a
   world where you remain, because the future would be full of
   promises and all my past life would give me rightful claim to them.
   When I die, all your memories of me will be pure; if I lived, there
   would always be some stain upon our love. Believe me, that which
   heaven does, is ever well done.

ARMAND. (*rising*) Ah, I am choking —

MARGUERITE. (*detaining him*) What, am I forced to give you courage?
   Come then, obey me. Open that drawer, and take the locket that you
   find there. It is my portrait, drawn at a time when I was pretty. I had
   it done for you; keep it, it will help you to remember me. But if, one

day, a beautiful young girl should fall in love with you and you should marry her — as well may be, as I sincerely hope — and she should find this portrait, tell her it is that of a friend who, if God permits her an obscure place in heaven, prays every day for her, and for thee. If she is jealous of the past, as we women often are, if she begs of you to sacrifice that portrait, then grant it her without fear, without remorse. It would be justice, and I forgive you in advance. When a woman loves, she suffers too much if she does not feel beloved. Are you listening, Armand; have you well understood me?

(*Nanine enters with Nichette, Gustave, and Gaston. Nichette enters with some fear, and becomes bolder as she sees Marguerite smile at her and Armand at her feet.*)

NICHETTE. My dear Marguerite, you wrote to me that you were dying, and I find you up and smiling.

ARMAND. (*in an undertone*) Oh, Gustave, I am utterly wretched!

MARGUERITE. I am dying, but I am happy too, and my happiness takes the sting from death. There you are now, married! You will be yet happier than before! You will think of me sometimes, will you not? Armand, give me your hand. I promise you, it is not difficult to die. And here is Gaston come to look for me. I am glad to see you once again, dear Gaston. In happiness we are ungrateful, and I had forgotten you. (*To Armand*) He has been very, very good to me. Ah, how strange! (*She rises.*)

ARMAND. What is it?

MARGUERITE. There is no more pain. Life seems to be returning to me. I feel better than ever before. Yes, yes, I shall live! Ah, how well I am! (*She sits and seems to fall asleep.*)

GASTON. She sleeps.

ARMAND. (*at first uneasily, then with terror*) Marguerite! Marguerite! Marguerite! (*A great cry. He has difficulty in withdrawing his hand from that of Marguerite*) Ah! (*He steps back, appalled*) Dead! (*Running to Gustave*) My God! My God! What will become of me?

GUSTAVE. (*to Armand*) She loved you well, poor girl!

NICHETTE. (*who has fallen on her knees*) Sleep in peace, Marguerite! Much will be forgiven you, because you greatly loved!

La Traviata

by
FRANCESCO MARIA PIAVE

ENGLISH TRANSLATION
BY WILLIAM WEAVER

Summary

by

William Weaver

ACT ONE

A gay party is in progress in the house of Violetta, a beautiful Paris courtesan. Her protector, Baron Douphol, arrives with Violetta's friend Flora and others. A few moments later, another friend, Gaston, comes in with a young man who has long wanted to meet Violetta. His name is Alfredo Germont. As all sit down to dinner, Gaston reveals that during Violetta's illness a year before, Alfredo asked every day for news of her. Violetta is amused and touched. She and Alfredo drink a toast, then, as the others go into the next room to dance, Violetta remains behind, seized with a fit of coughing. Alfredo stays with her and tells her of his concern for her health, declaring his sincere love. She dismisses the idea but invites him to return to her the next day. When she is alone, she ponders his words, then insists to herself that hers can be a life only of fleeting pleasures.

ACT TWO

Contrary to her own predictions, Violetta has been living simply and happily in the country with Alfredo. But when Alfredo discovers that, to pay for this retreat, she has sold all her belongings, he rushes to Paris to ask his father for his patrimony.

Monsieur Germont, in the meanwhile, comes to the house and persuades Violetta to give up his son, whose behavior is compromising not only the young man's own future but also the happiness of his innocent sister. Though impressed by Violetta's obvious sincerity, Germont nevertheless insists.

Violetta knows that there is only one way to make Alfredo give her up. She goes away, leaving him a letter indicating that she is going back to the baron and her former life.

Germont tries to persuade Alfredo to come home to Provence, but instead the young man pursues Violetta to Flora's house, where still another party is being given. There he insults Violetta violently and provokes a duel with the baron.

ACT THREE

Violetta is alone, ill, destitute. In the duel, the baron was wounded and Alfredo has had to go abroad. The elder Germont, however, has promised to reveal Violetta's noble sacrifice to his son, and it is this hope — and the hope of Alfredo's return — that keeps Violetta alive. Alfredo does return, but it is too late. Violetta dies in his arms.

LA TRAVIATA

Libretto by Francesco Maria Piave

First performed at the Teatro La Fenice, Venice
March 6, 1853

CHARACTERS

ALFREDO GERMONT, lover of Violetta	*Tenor*
GIORGIO GERMONT, his father	*Baritone*
GASTONE, Viscount de Letorières	*Tenor*
BARON DOUPHOL, a rival of Alfredo	*Baritone*
MARCHESE D'OBIGNY	*Bass*
DR. GRENVIL	*Bass*
GIUSEPPE, servant to Violetta	*Tenor*
VIOLETTA VALERY, a courtesan	*Soprano*
FLORA BERVOIX, her friend	*Mezzo-soprano*
ANNINA, confidante of Violetta	*Soprano*

*Friends and Guests of Violetta and Flora,
Servants, Maskers*

*The scenes are laid in Paris and environs, around 1850.
The first act takes place in August,
the second in January, the third in February.*

ACT ONE

Salon in Violetta's house. At back a door leading to another room; there are two more doors, one at either side. Left, a fireplace with a mirror over it. In the center, a richly laid table.

Violetta, sitting on a sofa, is conversing with the Doctor and some friends. Others are going to meet some guests who are just arriving, among them the Baron and Flora, on the arm of the Marquis.

CHORUS I

Dell'invito trascorsa è già l'ora . . .	The time of the invitation is already past . . .
Voi tardaste . . .	You are late . . .

CHORUS II

Giocammo da Flora,	We are gambling at Flora's,
E giocando quell'ora volâr.	And as we played, those hours flew.

VIOLETTA
(going toward them)

Flora, amici, la notte che resta	Flora, friends, you make
D'altre gioie qui fate brillar . . .	What's left of the night shine with other joys . . .
Fra le tazze più viva è la festa . . .	The party is livelier, among the cups . . .

FLORA AND MARQUIS

E goder voi potrete?	Are you able to enjoy it?

VIOLETTA

Lo voglio;	I want to;
Al piacer m'affido, ed io soglio	I entrust myself to pleasure, and with that drug
Con tal farmaco i mali sopir.	I dull my sufferings.

ALL

Sì, la vita s'addoppia al gioir.	Yes, life is doubled by enjoyment.

(Viscount Gastone de Letorières enters with Alfredo Germont. Servants are busy around the table.)

GASTONE

Io Alfredo Germont, o signora.	Here's Alfredo Germont, madame:
Ecco un altro che molto v'onora;	Another who esteems you greatly;
Pochi amici a lui simili sono.	There are few friends like him.

VIOLETTA
(gives her hand to Alfredo, who kisses it)

Mio Visconte, mercè di tal dono.	My dear Viscount, thank you for such a gift.

MARQUIS

Caro Alfredo . . .   Dear Alfredo . . .

ALFREDO

Marchese . . .   Marquis . . .

(They shake hands.)

GASTONE
(to Alfredo)

T'ho detto: As I told you:
L'amistà qui s'intreccia al diletto.   Here friendship and pleasure are joined.

(The servants in the meanwhile have set out the food.)

VIOLETTA
(to the servants)

Pronto è il tutto?   Is everything ready?

(A servant nods yes.)

Miei cari, sedete;   Dear friends, be seated;
E al convito che s'apre ogni cor.   At table all hearts are opened.

ALL

Ben diceste . . . le cure segrete   Well said . . . our friend drink
Fuga sempre l'amico licor.   Always dispels secret troubles.

*(They sit down in such a way that Violetta is between Alfredo and Gastone; opposite her,
Flora, between the Marquis and the Baron; the others sit as they please. A moment of silence,
as the plates are passed, and Violetta and Gastone talk softly between themselves, then:)*

GASTONE

Sempre Alfredo a voi pensa.   Alfredo thinks of you constantly.

VIOLETTA

Scherzate?   You're joking?

GASTONE

Egra foste, e ogni dì con affanno   When you were ill, every day he rushed
Qui volò, di voi chiese . . .   Here anxiously, and asked about you . . .

VIOLETTA

Cessate,   Stop,
Nulla son io per lui . . .   I am nothing to him . . .

GASTONE

Non v'inganno . . .   I'm not deceiving you . . .

VIOLETTA
(to Alfredo)

Vero è dunque? . . . onde è ciò? . . . Is it true then? . . . Why is this? . . .
Nol comprendo.   I don't understand.

ALFREDO
(*sighing*)

Sì, egli è ver.   Yes, it's true.

VIOLETTA
(*to Alfredo*)

Le mie grazie vi rendo.   I thank you.
                                                   (*to the Baron*)
Voi, Barone, non feste altrettanto . . .   You, Baron, didn't do as much . . .

BARON

Vi conosco da un anno soltanto.   I've known you only for a year.

VIOLETTA

Ed ei solo da qualche minuto.   And he only for a few minutes.

FLORA
(*softly to the Baron*)

Meglio fora se aveste taciuto.   You'd have done better to remain silent.

BARON
(*softly to Flora*)

M'è increscioso quel giovin . . .   That young man annoys me . . .

FLORA

Perchè?   Why?
A me invece simpatico egli è.   I find him likable, on the contrary.

GASTONE
(*to Alfredo*)

E tu dunque non apri più bocca?   Aren't you going to open your mouth any
                                                   more?

MARQUIS
(*to Violetta*)

È a madama che scuoterlo tocca.   It's up to Madame to stir him.

VIOLETTA
(*pouring wine for Alfredo*)

Sarò l'Ebe che versa . . .   I'll be Hebe and pour . . .

ALFREDO
(*chivalrous*)

E ch'io bramo   And I hope
Immortal come quella.   As immortal as she.

ALL

Beviamo, beviamo . . .   Let's drink, let's drink . . .

GASTONE

O Barone, nè un verso, nè un viva   Oh, Baron, can't you find a verse
Troverete in quest'ora giulia?   Or a toast, at this festive hour?

(The Baron shakes his head no.)

GASTONE
(to Alfredo)

Dunque a te . . . .   You then . . .

ALL

Sì, sì, un brindisi.   Yes, yes, a toast.

ALFREDO

L'estro non m'arride . . .   Inspiration isn't favoring me . . .

GASTONE

E non sei tu maestro?   But aren't you a master?

ALFREDO
(to Violetta)

Vi fia grato?   Would you like it?

VIOLETTA

Sì.   Yes.

ALFREDO
(gets up)

Sì? . . . L'ho già in cor.   Yes? . . . It's in my heart already.

MARQUIS

Dunque attenti . . .   Pay attention then . . .

ALL

Sì, attenti al cantor . . .   Yes, attention to the singer . . .

ALFREDO

Libiamo, libiamo ne' lieti calici   Let us drink, drink from the happy goblets
Che la bellezza infiora;   That beauty embellishes;
E la fuggevol ora   And let the fleeting hour
S'innebrii a voluttà.   Intoxicate itself with pleasure.
Libiam ne' dolci fremiti   Let us drink in the sweet trembling
Che suscita l'amore,   That love arouses,
                            (pointing to Violetta)
Poichè quell'occhio al core   Since that eye goes
Onnipotente va . . .   All-powerful to the heart . . .
Libiamo, amore, amor fra i calici   Let us drink, among the cups,
Più caldi baci avrà.   Love will have warmer kisses.

Ah! Libiam, amor fra' calici
Più caldi baci avrà.

    Ah! Let us drink, among the cups
    Love will have warmer kisses.

VIOLETTA
    (*rising*)

Tra voi saprò dividere
Il tempo mio giocondo;
Tutto è follia nel mondo
Ciò che non è piacer.
Godiam, fugace e rapido
È il gaudio dell'amore;
È un fior che nasce e muore,
Nè più si può goder . . .
Godiam . . . c'invita un fervido
Accento lusinghier.

    Among you I will share
    My time of joy;
    All is folly in the world
    That isn't pleasure.
    Let us enjoy ourselves, love's joy
    Is quick and fleeting;
    It's a flower that is born and dies,
    Nor can it be enjoyed again . . .
    Let us enjoy ourselves . . . feverish,
    Enchanting words invite us.

ALL

Ah! . . . godiam . . . la tazza e il cantico
Le notte abbella e il riso;
In questo paradiso
Ne scopra il nuovo dì.

    Ah! . . . Let us enjoy ourselves . . . cup and
      song
    Night embellishes, and laughter;
    In this paradise
    Let the new day find us.

VIOLETTA
    (*to Alfredo*)

La vita è nel tripudio . . .
    Life is pleasure . . .

ALFREDO
    (*to Violetta*)

Quande non s'ami ancora . . .
    When one isn't yet in love . . .

VIOLETTA
    (*to Alfredo*)

Nol dite a chi l'ignora.
    Don't speak of it to one who doesn't know
      it.

ALFREDO
    (*to Violetta*)

È il mio destin così . . .
    That is my destiny . . .

ALL

Godiamo . . . la tazza e il cantico
La notte abbella e il riso;
Godiamo . . . in questo paradiso
Ne scopra il nuovo dì.

    Let us enjoy ourselves . . . cup and song
    Night embellishes, and laughter;
    In this paradise
    Let the new day find us.

(*Music is heard from the other room.*)

ALL

Che è ciò?
    What is that?

VIOLETTA

Non gradireste ora le danze?   Wouldn't you like to dance now?

ALL

Oh, il gentil pensier! . . .   Oh, what a pleasant thought! . . .
Tutti accettiamo.   We all accept.

VIOLETTA

Usciamo dunque . . .   Let us go then . . .

(They start toward the door in the center, but Violetta suddenly turns pale.)

VIOLETTA

Ohimè! . . .   Alas! . . .

ALL

Che avete?   What is it?

VIOLETTA

Nulla, nulla.   Nothing, nothing.

ALL

Che mai v'arresta? . . .   Whatever made you stop? . . .

VIOLETTA

Usciamo . . .   Let us go . . .
(She takes a few steps, but then is again forced to stop and sit down.)

VIOLETTA

Oh Dio! . . .   Oh, God! . . .

ALL

Ancora!   Again!

ALFREDO

Voi soffrite.   You're ill.

ALL

Oh ciel! ch'è questo?   Heaven! What is this?

VIOLETTA

Un tremito che provo! . . .   I feel a trembling! . . .
Or . . . là . . . passate . . .   Now . . . go in . . . there . . .
                  (pointing to the other room)
Fra poco anch'io sarò.   I will be there too, shortly.

ALL

Come bramate.   As you wish.
(All go into the other room, except Alfredo, who remains behind.)

VIOLETTA
(stands up and goes to look at herself in the mirror)

Oh qual pallor!   Oh, what pallor!

(She turns, seeing Alfredo.)

Voi qui!   You here!

ALFREDO

Cessata è l'ansia   Is the trouble
Che vi turbò?   That upset you past?

VIOLETTA

Sto meglio.   I am better.

ALFREDO

Ah in cotal guisa   Ah, in this fashion
V'ucciderete . . . aver v'è d'uopo cura   You will kill yourself . . . You must take
Dell'esser vostro . . .   care
                              Of yourself.

VIOLETTA

E lo potrei?   How could I?

ALFREDO

Oh! se mia foste,   Oh! If you were mine,
Custode veglierei   Like a guardian, I'd watch over
Pe' vostri soavi dì.   Your peaceful days.

VIOLETTA

Che dite? . . . ha forse alcuno   What are you saying? . . . Does anyone
Cura di me?   Really care for me?

ALFREDO
(with fire)

Perchè nessuno al mondo v'ama . . .   Because no one in the world loves you . . .

VIOLETTA

Nessun? . . .   No one? . . .

ALFREDO

Tranne sol io.   Only I, I alone.

VIOLETTA
(laughing)

Gli è vero! . . .   That's true! . . .
Si grande amor dimenticato avea.   I had forgotten such a great love.

ALFREDO

Ridete! . . . e in voi v'ha un core?   You laugh! . . . Have you a heart?

VIOLETTA

Un cor? . . . sì . . . forse . . .	A heart? . . . Yes . . . perhaps . . .
E a che lo richiedete?	Why do you ask?

ALFREDO

Ah se ciò fosse . . .	Ah, if that were so . . .
Non potreste allora celiar . . .	Then you wouldn't be able to mock . . .

VIOLETTA

Dite davvero?	Are you speaking the truth?

ALFREDO

Io non v'inganno.	I'm not deceiving you.

VIOLETTA

Da molto è che mi amate?	Have you loved me for a long time?

ALFREDO

Ah sì, da un anno.	Ah yes, for a year.
Un dì felice, eterea	One day, happy and ethereal,
Mi balenaste innante,	You appeared before me,
E da quel dì tremante	And since that day I've lived,
Vissi d'ignoto amor.	Trembling, in an unknown love.
Di quell'amor, quell'amor ch'è palpito	In that love which is the pulse
Dell'universo, dell'universo intero,	Of the universe, the whole universe,
Misterioso, altero,	Mysterious, aloof,
Croce e delizia al cor.	The heart's cross and delight.

VIOLETTA

Ah se ciò è ver, fuggitemi . . .	Ah, if that is true, flee from me . . .
Solo amistade io v'offro;	I offer you only friendship;
Amar non so, nè soffro	I cannot love, nor can I bear
Un così eroico amore.	Such a heroic love.
Io sono franca, ingenua;	I am frank, simple;
Altra cercar dovete;	You must look for another woman;
Non arduo troverete	You won't find it difficult
Dimenticarmi allor.	To forget me then.

ALFREDO

Oh amore misterioso,	Oh, mysterious love,
Misterioso, altero,	Mysterious, aloof,
Croce e delizia al cor.	The heart's cross and delight.

VIOLETTA

Non arduo troverete	You won't find it difficult
Dimenticarmi allor.	To forget me then.

(Gastone appears at the door in the center.)

GASTONE

Ebben? che diavol fate?	Well? What the devil are you doing?

VIOLETTA

Si folleggiava . . .   We were talking nonsense . . .

GASTONE

Ah! ah! . . . sta ben . . . restate . . .   Ha! Ha! . . . very well . . . stay . . .
(He goes back in.)

VIOLETTA

Amor dunque non più . . .   No more love then . . .
Vi garba il patto?   Does this agreement suit you?

ALFREDO

Io v'obbedisco . . . Parto . . .   I obey you . . . I'm leaving . . .

VIOLETTA
(takes a flower from her bosom)
A tal giungeste?   You go that far?
Prendete questo fiore.   Take this flower.

ALFREDO

Perchè?   Why?

VIOLETTA

Per riportarlo.   To bring it back.

ALFREDO
(coming back)
Quando?   When?

VIOLETTA

Quando sarà appassito.   When it has withered.

ALFREDO

Oh ciel! . . . Domani . . .   Heaven! . . . Tomorrow . . .

VIOLETTA

Ebben . . . domani.   Very well . . . tomorrow.

ALFREDO
(ecstatically taking the flower)
Io son, io son felice!   I . . . I am happy!

VIOLETTA

D'amarmi dite ancora?   You still say you love me?

ALFREDO
(about to leave)
Oh, quanto, quanto v'amo!   Ah, how much, how much, I love you!

VIOLETTA

Partite?   Are you going?

ALFREDO
(comes back to her and kisses her hand)
Parto.   I go.

VIOLETTA

Addio.   Good-bye.

ALFREDO

Di più non bramo.   I long for nothing more.

VIOLETTA AND ALFREDO

Addio. Addio.   Good-bye, good-bye.

(Alfredo goes out. The others, flushed from their dancing, come back from the other room.)

ALL

Si ridesta in ciel l'aurora,	Dawn is reawakening in the sky,
E n'è forza di partire;	And we must leave;
Mercè a voi, gentil signora,	Our thanks to you, kind lady,
Di sì splendido gioir.	For such splendid entertainment.
La città di feste è piena,	The city is filled with parties,
Volge il tempo dei piacer;	The season of pleasures is coming;
Nel riposo ancor la lena	We must restore our vigor by resting
Si ritempri per goder.	So that we can enjoy ourselves more.

(They go out at right. Violetta is alone.)

VIOLETTA

E strano! . . . è strano! . . . in core	It's strange! . . . strange! . . . those words
Scolpiti ho quegli accenti!	Are carved in my heart!
Saria per me sventura un serio amore?	Would a serious love be a misfortune for me?
Che risolvi, o turbata anima mia?	What are you resolving, O my anguished spirit?
Null'uomo ancor t'accendeva . . .	No man ever aroused you before . . .
Oh gioia ch'io non conobbi,	Oh joy I did not know,
Esser amata amando! . . .	To be loved and to love! . . .
E sdegnarla poss'io	And can I spurn it
Per l'aride follie del viver mio? . . .	For the barren follies of my life? . . .
Ah fors'è lui che l'anima	Ah, perhaps he is the one whom my spirit,
Solinga ne' tumulti	Alone amid tumults,
Godea sovente pingere	Often enjoyed painting
De' suoi colori occulti . . .	With its mysterious colors . . .
Lui, che modesto e vigile	He who, modest and constant,
All'egre soglie ascese,	Came to my sickroom door,
E nuova febbre accese	And kindled a new fever
Destandomi all'amor.	Waking me to love.
A quell'amor, quell'amor ch'è palpito	To that love which is the pulse
Dell'universo, dell'universo intero,	Of the universe, the whole universe,
Misterioso, altero,	Mysterious, aloof,
Croce e delizia al cor.	

*[A me, fanciulla, un candido
E trepido desire
Quest'effigiò dolcissimo
Signor dell'avvenire,
Quando ne' cicli il raggio
Di sua beltà vedea,
E tutta me pascea
Di quel divino error.
Sentia che amore è palpito
Dell'universo intero,
Misterioso, altero,
Croce e delizia al cor.]

The heart's cross and delight.
[When I was a girl, an innocent
And timid desire
Depicted him, the tender
Lord of my future,
When I saw in the skies
The glow of his beauty,
And I fed myself wholly
On that divine fancy.
I felt that love is the pulse
Of the whole universe,
Mysterious, aloof,
The heart's cross and delight.]

(She is lost in thought for a moment, then she recovers herself.)

Follie! . . . follie! . . .
Delirio vano è questo! . . .
Povera donna, sola,
Abbandonata in questo
Popoloso deserto
Che appellano Parigi,
Che spero or più? . . .
Che far degg'io? . . . Gioire!
Di voluttà ne' vortici perir!
Gioir! . . . gioir! . . .
Sempre libera degg'io
Folleggiare di gioia in gioia,
Vo' che scorra il viver mio
Pe' sentieri del piacer.
Nasca il giorno, o il giorno muoia,
Sempre lieta ne' ritrovi,
A diletti sempre nuovi
Dee volar il mio pensier.

Folly! . . . folly! . . .
This is vain raving! . . .
A poor woman, alone,
Abandoned in this
Crowded desert
That they call Paris,
What more can I hope for now? . . .
What must I do? . . . Enjoy myself!
Perish in the giddy whirl of pleasure!
Enjoy myself! . . . Enjoy! . . .
Always free I must
Dart lightheadedly from joy to joy,
I want my life to glide
Along the paths of pleasure.
Whether the day is born or dying,
Always gay at parties,
My thought must fly
Always to new delights.

ALFREDO
(below the balcony)

Amor è palpito dell'universo, ecc.   Love is the pulse of the universe, etc.

VIOLETTA

Dee volar, ah! il mio pensier!   Ah! My thought must fly!
(She leaves through the door, left.)

---

* Brackets denote passages often omitted in performance.

ACT TWO

Scene One

A country house near Paris. Drawing room on the ground floor. In the back, facing the audience, there is a fireplace, with a clock and a mirror over it, between two French windows that give onto a garden. Downstage, two other doors, facing each other. Chairs, tables, some books, and writing materials.
Alfredo comes in, wearing hunting clothes. He puts down his gun.

ALFREDO

Lunge da lei per me non v'ha diletto! . . .	Away from her, there's no joy for me! . . .
Volaron già tre lune	Three months have flown past already
Dacchè la mia Violetta	Since for me my Violetta
Agi per me lasciò, dovizie, amori	Abandoned comforts, riches, loves
E le pompose feste,	And the elaborate parties,
Ov'agli omaggi avvezza,	Where, accustomed to admiration,
Vedea schiavo ciascun di sua bellezza . . .	She saw every man enslaved by her beauty . . .
Ed or contenta in questi ameni luoghi	And now, content in these pleasant surroundings,
Tutto scorda per me. Qui presso a lei	
Io rinascer mi sento,	She forgets it all for me. Here with her
E dal soffio d'amor rigenerato	I feel myself reborn,
Scordo ne' gaudi suoi tutto il passato.	And regenerated by the breath of love,
De' miei bollenti spiriti	In its ecstasies, I forget all the past.
Il giovanile ardore	The youthful ardor
Ella temprò col placido	Of my ebullient spirits
Sorriso dell'amor! . . .	She tempered with the calm
Dal dì che disse: "Vivere	Smile of love! . . .
Io voglio a te fedel,"	Since the day she said:
Dell'universo immemore	"I want to live, faithful to you,"
Io vivo quasi in ciel.	Not heeding the universe,
	I live as if in heaven.

(Annina comes in hastily, in traveling attire.)

ALFREDO

Annina, donde vieni?	Annina, where are you coming from?

ANNINA

Da Parigi.	From Paris.

ALFREDO

Chi tel commise?	Who sent you there?

ANNINA

Fu la mia signora.	It was my mistress.

ALFREDO

Perchè?	Why?

ANNINA

Per alienar cavalli, cocchi	To sell off her horses, carriages
E quanto ancor possiede.	And everything she still owns.

ALFREDO

Che mai sento!	What's this I hear!

ANNINA

Lo spendio è grande a viver qui so- linghi . . .	The expense is great, living here alone . . .

ALFREDO

E tacevi?	And you were silent?

ANNINA

Mi fu il silenzio imposto.	I was ordered to be silent.

ALFREDO

Imposto?! . . . or v'abbisogna? . . .	Ordered?! . . . Now how much is needed? . . .

ANNINA

Mille luigi.	A thousand louis.

ALFREDO

Or vanne . . . Andrò a Parigi . . .	Go now . . . I'll go to Paris . . .
Questo colloquio non sappia la signora;	Madame must not know of this talk;
Il tutto valgo a riparar ancora.	I can still set everything right.
Va! va!	Go! Go!

(*Annina goes out.*)

ALFREDO

*[Oh mio rimorso! oh infamia!	[Oh, my remorse! Oh, disgrace!
Io vissi in tale errore! . . .	I lived in such ignorance! . . .
Ma il turpe sonno a frangere	But the truth appeared to me
Il ver mi balenò! . . .	To break off my shameful slumber! . . .
Per poco in seno acquetati,	Be silent in my breast a little while,
O grido dell'onore;	O cry of honor;
M'avrai securo vindice;	I'll be your certain avenger;
Quest'onta laverò.	I'll wash away this shame.
Oh mio rossor! oh infamia!	Oh, my blushes! Oh, shame!
Ah sì, quest'onta laverò!]	Ah yes, I'll wash away this shame!]

(*He goes out. Violetta comes in with some papers, talking with Annina.*)

VIOLETTA

Alfredo?	Alfredo?

---

* Brackets denote passages often omitted in performance.

ANNINA

Per Parigi or or partiva.   He just left for Paris.

VIOLETTA

E tornerà?   When will he come back?

ANNINA

Pria che tramonti il giorno . . .   Before sunset . . .
Dirvel m'impose . . .   He told me to tell you . . .

VIOLETTA

È strano!   That's strange!

(Giuseppe comes in and hands her a letter.)

GIUSEPPE

Per voi.   For you.

VIOLETTA
(sits down, taking it)

Sta ben . . . In breve   Very well . . . Shortly
Giungerà un uom d'affari . . .   A man will come on business . . .
Entri all'istante.   Show him in at once.

(Annina and Giuseppe go out. Violetta opens the letter.)

VIOLETTA

Ah, ah! scopriva Flora il mio ritiro,   Ha, ha! Flora has discovered my retreat,
E m'invita a danzar per questa sera! . . . And she invites me to a dance this eve-
Invan m'aspetterà . . .   ning! . . .
                                         She'll wait for me in vain . . .
(She throws the letter on the table and sits down. Giuseppe comes back in.)

GIUSEPPE

È qui un signore.   A gentleman is here.

VIOLETTA

Sarà lui che attendo.   It will be the one I'm expecting.
*(She nods to Giuseppe to show him in. Monsieur Germont enters, preceded by Giuseppe,
who draws up two chairs and leaves.)*

GERMONT

Madamigella Valery? . . .   Mademoiselle Valery? . . .

VIOLETTA

Son io.   I am she.

GERMONT

D'Alfredo il padre in me vedete!   In me you see Alfredo's father!

VIOLETTA

(*surprised, motions him to be seated*)

Voi!   You!

GERMONT

(*sitting down*)

Sì, dell'incauto, che a ruina corre,   Yes, father of the heedless boy, who rushes
Ammaliato da voi.   To his ruin, bewitched by you.

VIOLETTA

(*rising, offended*)

Donna son io, signore, ed in mia casa;   I am a woman, sir, and in my own house;
Ch'io vi lasci assentite,   Allow me to leave you,
Più per voi, che per me.   More for your sake, than for mine.

(*She starts to go.*)

GERMONT

(Quai modi!) Pure . . .   (What manners!) And yet . . .

VIOLETTA

Tratto in error voi foste . . .   You were mistaken . . .

(*She sits down again.*)

GERMONT

De' suoi beni   He wants to make you a gift
Dono vuol farvi . . .   Of his possessions . . .

VIOLETTA

Non l'osò finora . . .   He never dared before . . .
Rifiuterei.   I would refuse.

GERMONT

(*looking around*)

Pur tanto lusso . . .   Still, all this luxury . . .

VIOLETTA

(*gives him a paper*)

A tutti è mistero quest'atto . . .   This deed is a secret from everyone . . .
A voi nol sia . . .   But not from you . . .

GERMONT

(*glancing over the papers*)

Ciel! che discopro!   Heavens! What's this I discover!
D'ogni vostro avere   You mean to deprive yourself
Or volete spogliarvi?   Of everything you own?
Ah il passato perchè, perchè v'accusa? . . .   Ah, why, why does the past accuse you? . . .

VIOLETTA
(with enthusiasm)

Più non esiste . . .	It exists no more . . .
Or amo Alfredo, e Dio	Now I love Alfredo, and God
Lo cancellò col pentimento mio!	Erased it, with my repentance!

GERMONT

Nobili sensi invero!	Noble feelings, indeed!

VIOLETTA

Oh come dolce	Ah, how sweet your words
Mi suona il vostro accento!	Sound to me!

GERMONT
(rising)

Ed a tai sensi	And I ask a sacrifice
Un sacrifizio chieggo.	Of those feelings.

VIOLETTA
(rising)

Ah no . . . tacete . . .	Ah no . . . don't speak . . .
Terribil cosa chiedereste certo . . .	You'd surely ask something terrible . . .
Il previdi . . . v'attesi . . .	I foresaw it . . . I was expecting you . . .
Era felice troppo . . .	I was too happy . . .

GERMONT

D'Alfredo il padre	Alfredo's father here
La sorte, l'avvenir domanda or qui	Asks of you the destiny, the future
De' suoi due figli! . . .	Of his two children! . . .

VIOLETTA

Di due figli!	Two children!

GERMONT

Sì.	Yes.
Pura siccome un angelo	Pure as an angel
Iddio mi diè una figlia;	God gave me a daughter;
Se Alfredo nega riedere	If Alfredo refuses to return
In seno alla famiglia,	To his family's bosom,
L'amato e amante giovine,	The beloved and loving youth
Cui sposa andar dovea,	Whose bride she was to be,
Or si ricusa al vincolo	Will now reject the tie
Che lieti ne rendeva.	That made them so happy.
Deh non mutate in triboli	Ah, don't change into trials
Le rose dell'amor . . .	The roses of love . . .
A' prieghi miei resistere	Your heart must not resist
Non voglia il vostro cor, no, no.	My entreaties, no, no.

VIOLETTA

Ah! comprendo . . .
Dovrò per alcun tempo
Da Alfredo allontanarmi . . . doloroso
Fora per me . . . pur . . .

Ah! I understand . . .
I'll have to go away
From Alfredo for a while . . .
It will be painful for me . . . still . . .

GERMONT

Non è ciò che chiedo . . .

That isn't what I'm asking . . .

VIOLETTA

Cielo! che più cercate? . . .
Offersi assai! . . .

Heaven! What more do you want? . . .
I've offered so much! . . .

GERMONT

Pur non basta.

And yet it's not enough.

VIOLETTA

Volete che per sempre
A lui rinunzi?

You want me to give him up
Forever?

GERMONT

È d'uopo.

It's necessary.

VIOLETTA

Ah no! giammai! . . . no, mai!
Non sapete quale affetto
Vivo, immenso m'arda in petto?
Che nè amici, nè parenti
Io non conto tra' viventi?
E che Alfredo m'ha giurato
Che in lui tutto troverò?
Non sapete che colpita
D'atro morbo è la mia vita?
Che già presso il fin ne vedo? . . .
Ch'io mi separi da Alfredo! . . .
Ah il suppizio è sì spietato,
Che a morir preferiro.

Ah no! Never! . . . no, never!
Don't you know the love,
Vital, immense, that burns in my heart?
That I have no friends,
No relatives among the living?
And that Alfredo has sworn to me
That in him I'll find everything?
Don't you know that my life
Is stricken by a dire disease?
That I can already see its end near? . . .
For me to leave Alfredo! . . .
Ah, the torment is so merciless,
That I'd prefer to die.

GERMONT

È grave il sagrifizio;
Ma pur tranquilla uditemi.
Bella voi siete e giovine . . .
Col tempo . . .

The sacrifice is hard;
Yet listen to me calmly.
You are beautiful and young . . .
In time . . .

VIOLETTA

Ah più non dite . . .
V'intendo . . . m'è impossibile . . .
Lui solo amar vogl'io . . .

Ah, say no more . . .
I understand you . . . it's impossible for
me . . .
I want to love only him . . .

GERMONT

Sia pure . . . ma volubile   That may be . . . But men
Sovente è l'uom . . .   Are often fickle . . .

VIOLETTA
(stricken)

Gran Dio!   Good God!

GERMONT

Un dì, quando le veneri   One day, when time has put
Il tempo avrà fugale,   Carnal desire to flight,
Fia presto il tedio a sorgere . . .   Boredom will follow quickly . . .
Che sarà allor? . . . Pensate . . .   Then what will happen? . . . Think . . .
Per voi non avran balsamo   You won't have the solace
I più soavi affetti!   Of tenderer affections!
Poichè dal ciel non furono . . .   Since these bonds were not . . .
Tai nodi benedetti . . .   Blessed by heaven . . .

VIOLETTA

È vero! è vero!   It's true! It's true!

GERMONT

Ah dunque sperdasi   Ah, then let this seductive dream
Tal sogno seduttore . . .   Be dispelled . . .
Siate di mia famiglia   Be the consoling angel
L'angel consolatore . . .   Of my family . . .
Violetta, deh pensateci,   Violetta, ah, think it over,
Ne siete in tempo ancor . . .   You are still in time . . .
È Dio che ispira, o giovine,   Ah, young lady, it is God
Tai detti a un genitor.   Who inspires a father's words.

VIOLETTA
(to herself, with great grief)

(Così alla misera, ch'è un di caduta,   (So, for the wretched girl, who one day fell,
Di più risorgere speranza è muta!   Any hope of rising again is silent!
Se pur benefico le indulga Iddio,   Even if God is kind and indulgent to her,
L'uomo implacabile per lei sarà.)   Mankind will always be implacable.)

GERMONT

Siate di mia famiglia   Be the consoling angel
L'angiol consolator.   Of my family.

VIOLETTA
(weeping)

Dite alla giovine sì bella e pura,   Tell the young girl, so beautiful and pure,
Ch'avvi una vittima della sventura,   That there is a victim of misfortune
Cui resta un unico raggio di bene . . .   Who has a single ray of happiness . . .
Che a lei il sacrifica a che morrà.   Which she sacrifices to her, and who will die.

GERMONT

Piangi, piangi, o misera.	Weep, weep, O unhappy girl.
Supremo, il veggo, è il sagrifizio	I am asking, I see,
Ch'ora ti chieggo . . .	The supreme sacrifice of you now . . .
Sento nell'anima già le tue pene . . .	Already in my spirit I feel your sufferings . . .
Coraggio, e il nobil tuo cor	Courage, your noble heart
Vincerà!	Will win out!

VIOLETTA

Dite alla giovine, ecc.	Tell the young girl, etc.
	(Silence.)
Imponete.	Command me.

GERMONT

Non amarlo ditegli.	Say you don't love him.

VIOLETTA

Nol crederà.	He won't believe it.

GERMONT

Partite . . .	Leave . . .

VIOLETTA

Seguirammi.	He will follow me.

GERMONT

Allor . . .	Then . . .

VIOLETTA

Qual figlia m'abbraciate . . .	Embrace me as a daughter . . .
Forte così sarò.	Then I will be strong.
	(They embrace.)
Tra breve ei vi fia reso,	He will be given back to you soon,
Ma afflitto oltre ogni dire . . .	But unspeakably grieved . . .
A suo conforto di colà volerete.	From there you will hasten to console him.

(Violetta points to the garden, then goes to write.)

GERMONT

Che pensate?	What are you thinking of?

VIOLETTA

Sapendol, v'opporreste	If you knew, you would oppose
Al pensier mio . . .	My idea . . .

GERMONT

Generosa! . . . e per voi che far poss'io?	Generous girl! . . . What can I do for you?

VIOLETTA
(coming back to him)

Morrò! . . . morro! . . . la mia memoria	I'll die . . . I'll die . . . Don't allow him
Non fia ch'ei malediea,	To curse my memory,
Se le mie pene orribili	Let someone at least tell him
Vi sia chi almen gli dica.	Of my horrible sufferings.

GERMONT

No, generosa vivere	No, you must live,
E lieta voi dovrete . . .	Generous and happy . . .
Mercè di queste lagrime	One day you'll receive from heaven
Dal cielo un giorno avrete.	A reward for these tears.

VIOLETTA

Conosca il sagrifizio	Let him know the sacrifice
Ch'io consumai d'amore . . .	That I made for love . . .
Che sarà suo fin l'ultimo	And that even the last sigh
Sospiro del mio cor.	Of my heart will be his.

GERMONT

Premiato il sagrifizio	The sacrifice of your love
Sarà del vostro amore,	Will be rewarded,
D'un'opra così nobile	You'll be proud then
Sarete fiera allor, sì, sì.	Of such a noble deed, yes, yes.

VIOLETTA

Qui giunge alcun: partite.	Someone is coming; leave.

GERMONT

Oh grato v'è il cor mio!	Oh, my heart is grateful to you!

VIOLETTA

Partite.	Leave.
Non ci vedrem più forse . . .	Perhaps we won't see each other again . . .

VIOLETTA AND GERMONT
(embracing)

Siate felice . . . Addio!	Be happy . . . farewell!

(Germont is at the door.)

VIOLETTA
(weeping)

Conosca il sagrifizio	Let him know the sacrifice
Che consumai d'amore . . .	That I made for love . . .
Che sarà suo fin l'ultimo . . .	And that even the last sigh . . .

(Her tears choke her words.)

Addio!	Farewell!

VIOLETTA AND GERMONT

Felice siate . . . Addio!	Be happy . . . farewell!

(Germont goes out of the door into the garden. Violetta sits down and writes.)

VIOLETTA

Dammi tu forza, o cielo!   Give me the strength, O heaven!
(She rings the bell. Annina comes in.)

ANNINA

Mi richiedeste? . . .   You sent for me? . . .

VIOLETTA

Sì, reca tu stessa   Yes,
Questo foglio.   Take this letter yourself.

ANNINA
(looks at the address and shows her surprise)
Oh!   Oh!

VIOLETTA

Silenzio . . . va all'istante.   Silence . . . go at once.
(Annina goes.)
Ed or si scriva a lui . . .   And now I must write to him . . .
Che gli dirò? . . .   What will I tell him? . . .
Chi men darà il coraggio?   Who will give me the courage?
(She writes, then seals the letter. Alfredo enters.)

ALFREDO

Che fai?   What are you doing?

VIOLETTA
(hiding the letter)
Nulla.   Nothing.

ALFREDO

Scrivevi?   Were you writing?

VIOLETTA
(confused)
Sì . . . no . . .   Yes . . . no.

ALFREDO

Qual turbamento! . . .   What agitation! . . .
A chi scrivevi? . . .   To whom were you writing? . . .

VIOLETTA

A te . . .   To you . . . .

ALFREDO

Dammi quel foglio.   Give me that paper.

VIOLETTA

No, per ora.   No, not now.

ALFREDO

Mi perdona . . . son io preoccupato.   Forgive me . . . I'm worried.

VIOLETTA
(*rising*)

Che fu?   What is it?

ALFREDO

Giunse mio padre . . .   My father came . . .

VIOLETTA

Lo vedesti?   Did you see him?

ALFREDO

Ah no; severo scritto mi lasciava!   Ah, no; he left me a stern note!
Però l'attendo . . .   However, I expect him . . .
T'amerà in vederti . . .   When he sees you, he'll love you . . .

VIOLETTA
(*agitated*)

Ch'ei qui non mi sorprenda . . .   He mustn't surprise me here . . .
Lascia che m'allontani . . .   Let me go away . . .
Tu lo calma . . . Ai suoi piedi   You calm him . . . I'll throw myself
Mi getterò . . .   At his feet . . .
(*controlling her tears with effort*)
Divisi ei più . . . non ne vorrà . . . He won't want us . . . separated any
Sarem felici . . . sarem felici . . .   more . . .
Perchè tu m'ami, Alfredo,   We will be happy . . . we will be happy . . .
Tu m'ami, non è vero? Tu m'ami?   Because you love me, Alfredo,
Alfredo, non è vero?   You love me, don't you? You love me?
                                        Alfredo, don't you?

ALFREDO

Oh quanto! Perchè piangi?   Oh, so much! Why are you crying?

VIOLETTA

Di lagrime avea d'uopo . . .   I needed tears . . .
Or son tranquilla . . . lo vedi? . . . Now I'm calm . . . you see? . . .
(*forcing herself*)
Or son tranquilla . . . ti sorrido . . . Now I'm calm . . . I'm smiling at you . . .
Sarò là, tra quei fior,   I'll be there, among those flowers,
Presso a te sempre, sempre . . .   Near you always, always . . .
Amami, Alfredo, amami quant'io t'amo . . . Love me, Alfredo, love me as I love you . . .
Addio! . . .   Farewell! . . .
(*She runs into the garden.*)

ALFREDO

Ah, vive sol quel core	Ah, that heart lives only
All'amor mio!	For love of me!

(He sits down, picks up a book at random, reads a bit, then stands up,
looks at the time on the clock over the fireplace.)

È tardi . . . ed oggi forse	It's late . . . and perhaps my father
Più non verrà mio padre.	Will not come today.

(Giuseppe hurries in.)

GIUSEPPE

La signora è partita . . .	Madame has gone . . .
L'attendeva un calesse,	A coach was waiting for her,
E sulla via già corre di Parigi . . .	And it is already hurrying toward Paris . . .
Annina pure prima di lei spariva . . .	Annina also disappeared, before her . . .

ALFREDO

Il so . . . ti calma.	I know . . . calm yourself.

GIUSEPPE

(Che vuol dir ciò?)	(What can this mean?)

(He goes out.)

ALFREDO

Va forse d'ogni avere	Perhaps she is going
Ad affrettar la perdita . . .	To hasten the loss of all her posses-
Ma Annina lo impedirà.	sions . . .
	But Annina will prevent that.

(His father is seen crossing the garden in the distance.)

Qualcuno è nel giardino . . .	Someone is in the garden . . .
Chi è là? . . .	Who is there? . . .

(He starts to go out, but a messenger appears in the doorway.)

MESSENGER

Il signor Germont?	Monsieur Germont?

ALFREDO

Son io.	I am he.

MESSENGER

Una dama da un cocchio,	A lady in a carriage,
Per voi, di qua non lunge,	Not far from here,
Mi diede questo scritto . . .	Gave me this letter for you . . .

(He gives a letter to Alfredo, accepts a tip, and leaves.)

ALFREDO

Di Violetta! . . . Perchè son io com-	From Violetta! . . . Why am I upset! . . .
mosso! . . .	Perhaps she's inviting me to join her . . .

A raggiungerla forse ella m'invita . . .   I'm trembling . . . O heaven! . . . Cour-
Io tremo! . . . Oh ciel! . . . Coraggio! . . .   age! . . .
                    (*He opens and reads the letter.*)
"Alfredo, al giungervi di questo foglio . . ."   "Alfredo, when you receive this letter . . ."
                    (*He shouts, thunderstruck.*)
Ah!   Ah!
          (*Turning, he finds himself facing his father, into whose arms he falls, crying:*)
Padre mio!   Father!

GERMONT

Mio figlio! Oh quanto soffri! . . .   My son! Oh how you are suffering! . . .
Oh tergi il pianto,   Oh, dry your tears,
Ritorna di tuo padre orgoglio e vanto.   Come back, your father's pride and boast.

(*Alfredo, in despair, sits at the table, his face in his hands.*)

GERMONT

Di Provenza il mar, il suol   Who erased the sea, the land
Chi dal cor ti cancellò?   Of Provence from your heart?
Al natio fulgente sol   What fate stole you
Qual destino ti furò?   From your splendid native sun?
Oh rammenta pur nel duol   Ah, recall even in your grief
Ch'ivi gioia a te brillò,   That joy glowed for you there,
E che pace colà sol   And that only there
Su te splendere ancor può . . .   Can peace still shine on you . . .
Dio mi guidò . . . Dio mi guidò!   God led me . . . God led me!
Ah il tuo vecchio genitor   Ah, you don't know how much
Tu non sai quanto soffrì!   Your old father suffered!
Te lontano, di squallor   With you far away, his roof
Il suo tetto si coprì . . .   Was covered with shame . . .
Ma se alfin ti trovo ancor,   But if I've found you at last,
Se in me speme non fallì,   If my hope didn't fail,
Se la voce dell'onor   If the voice of honor
In te appien non ammutì   Isn't completely dumb in you
Dio m'esaudì . . . Dio m'esaudì.   God answered my prayer . . . God an-
                                        swered my prayer.
                    (*shaking Alfredo*)
Ne rispondi d'un padre all'affetto?   Don't you respond to your father's love?

ALFREDO

Mille serpi divoranmi il petto . . .   A thousand serpents are devouring my
                                        breast . . .
                    (*rejecting his father*)
Mi lasciate . . .   Leave me . . .

GERMONT

Lasciarti!   Leave you!

ALFREDO
                    (*resolved*)
(Oh vendetta!)   (Oh, vengeance!)

GERMONT

Non più indugi, partiamo . . .   No more delay, we are leaving . . .
T'affretta . . .   Hurry . . .

ALFREDO

(Ah fu Douphol!)   (Ah, it was Douphol!)

GERMONT

M'ascolti tu?   Are you listening to me?

ALFREDO

No!   No!

GERMONT

Dunque invano trovato t'avrò?   Then have I found you in vain?
*[No, non udrai rimproveri;   [No, you will hear no reproaches;
Copriam d'oblio il passato;   Let us cover the past with oblivion;
L'amor che m'ha guidato   The love that has guided me
Sa tutto perdonar.   Can pardon everything.
Vieni, i tuoi cari in giubilo   Come, you will see with me
Con me rivedi ancora;   Your loved ones rejoice again;
A chi penò finora   Don't deny such joy
Tal gioia non negar.   To those who have suffered till now.
Un padre ed una suora   Hasten to console
T'affretta a consolar.]   A father and a sister.]

ALFREDO
            (recovering himself, glances at the table and sees Flora's letter)
Ah! . . . ell'è alla festa! volisi   Ah! . . . She is at the ball! Let me fly
L'offesa a vendicar.   To avenge the offense.
                    (He rushes out, followed by his father.)

GERMONT

Che dici? ah ferma!   What are you saying? Ah, stop!

ACT TWO

Scene Two

A salon in Flora's town house, richly decorated and lighted. A door in the back, and one
at either side. Downstage, right, a table equipped for gambling; at left, a table richly laden
with flowers and refreshments; various chairs and a sofa.
    Flora, the Marquis, the Doctor, and other guests come in from the left, conversing.

FLORA

Avrem lieta di maschere la notte;   We'll have a gay night, with masquers;
N'è duce il Viscontino . . .   The Viscount is the leader . . .
Violetta ed Alfredo anco invitai . . .   I invited Violetta and Alfredo, too . . .

---

*Brackets denote passages often omitted in performance.

MARQUIS

La novità ignorate?	Don't you know the news?
Violetta e Germont sono disgiunti.	Violetta and Germont have separated.

FLORA AND DOCTOR

Fia vero?	Can it be true?

MARQUIS

Ella verrà qui col Barone.	She'll come here with the Baron.

DOCTOR

Li vidi ieri ancor . . . parean felici.	I saw them just yesterday . . . they seemed happy.

(*A noise is heard at right.*)

FLORA

Silenzio . . . Udite? . . .	Silence . . . You hear? . . .

(*They go toward the right.*)

FLORA, DOCTOR, AND MARQUIS

Giungono gli amici.	Our friends are coming.

(*Many ladies disguised as gypsies come in at right.*)

GYPSIES

Noi siamo zingarelle	We are gypsy girls
Venute da lontano;	Who've come from afar;
D'ognuno sulla mano	In everyone's hand
Leggiamo l'avvenir.	We read the future.
Se consultiam le stelle	If we consult the stars
Null'avvi a noi d'oscuro,	Nothing is dark to us,
E i casi del futuro	And future events
Possiamo altrui predir.	We can predict for others.
Vediamo!	Let's see!

(*A first part of the chorus looks at Flora's hand.*)

GYPSIES I

Voi, signora . . .	You, madame . . .
Rivali alquanti avete . . .	Have many rivals . . .

GYPSIES II

(*looking at the Marquis's hand*)

Marchese, voi non siete	Marquis, you are not
Model di fedeltà.	A model for faithfulness.

FLORA

(*to the Marquis*)

Fate il galante ancora?	Are you still playing the swain?
Ben, vo' me la paghiate.	Well, you'll pay me for it.

MARQUIS
(*to Flora*)

Che diamin vi pensate? . . .	Whatever are you thinking? . . .
L'accusa e falsità.	The charge is a falsehood.

FLORA

La volpe lascia il pelo,	A fox will leave his skin,
Non abbandona il vizio . . .	But not his wickedness . . .
Marchese mio, giudizio,	My dear Marquis, be careful,
O vi farò pentir . . .	Or I'll make you regret it . . .

ALL

Su via, si stenda un velo	Come, let's draw a curtain
Sui fatti del passato;	Over the deeds of the past;
Già quel ch'è stato è stato,	What has been has been,
Badate (badiamo) all'avvenir.	Look (let us look) only to the future.

(*Flora and the Marquis shake hands. Gastone and others, disguised as Spanish matadors and picadors, come running in from the right.*)

GASTONE AND MATADORS

Di Madride noi siam mattadori,	We are matadors from Madrid,
Siamo i prodi del circo dei tori,	We're the heroes of the bull ring,
Testè giunti a godere del chiasso	Just arrived to enjoy the fuss
Che a Parigi si fa pel Bue grasso;	They're making in Paris for Mardi Gras;
E una storia, se udire vorrete,	And if you care to hear a story,
Quali amanti noi siamo saprete.	You'll learn what lovers we are.

THE OTHERS

Sì, sì bravi; narrate, narrate,	Yes, yes, good for you; tell us, tell,
Con piacere l'udremo.	We'll hear it with pleasure.

GASTONE AND MATADORS

Ascoltate.	Listen.
È Piquillo un bel gagliardo	Piquillo's a bold and handsome
Biscaglino mattador;	Matador from Biscay;
Forte il braccio, fiero il guardo,	Strong of arm, fierce of eye,
Delle giostre egli è signor.	He's the lord of the arena.
D'andalusa giovinetta	He fell madly in love
Follemente innamorò;	With an Andalusian maiden;
Ma la bella ritrosetta	But the pretty, coy girl
Così al giovine parlò:	Spoke to the young man thus:
"Cinque tori in un sol giorno	"I want to see you bring down
Vo'vederti ad atterrar;	Five bulls in a single day;
E, se vinci, al tuo ritorno	If you win, at your return
Mano e cor ti vo' donar."	I'll give you my hand and heart."
"Sì," gli disse, e il mattadore	"Yes," he said, and the matador
Alle giostre mosse il piè;	Went off to the arena;
Cinque tori, vincitore,	And, a winner, five bulls then
Sull'arena egli stendè.	He laid out on the sand.

THE OTHERS

Bravo, bravo il mattadore,	Good for him, the matador,
Ben gagliardo si mostrò,	He showed how bold he was,
Se alla giovane l'amore	If that was how he proved
In tal guisa egli provòl	His love to the young girl!

GASTONE AND MATADORS

Poi, tra plausi, ritornato	Then, amid applause, he went
Alla bella del suo cor,	Back to his heart's beauty,
Colse il premio desiato	He took the prize he wanted
Tra le braccia dell'amor.	In the arms of love.

THE OTHERS

Con tai prove i mattadori	With such exploits matadors
San le belle conquistar.	Know how to win the fair.

GASTONE AND MATADORS

Ma qui son più miti i cori;	But here the hearts are milder;
A noi basta folleggiar.	We have only to amuse.

ALL

Sì, allegri, or pria tentiamo	Yes, be merry . . . first let's test
Della sorte il vario umor;	Luck's fickle mood;
La palestra dischiudiamo	Let's open the arena
Agli audaci giuocator.	To the bold gamblers.

(The men take off their masks; some walk up and down and others prepare to gamble. Alfredo enters.)

ALL

Alfredo! . . . Voi! . . .	Alfredo! . . . You! . . .

ALFREDO

Sì, amiei . . .	Yes, friends.

FLORA

Violetta?	Violetta?

ALFREDO

Sì, amici . . .	Yes, friends.

FLORA

Violetta?	Violetta?

ALFREDO

Non ne so.	I know nothing about her.

ALL

Ben disinvolto! . . . bravo! . . .	Such nonchalance! . . . Bravo! . . .
Or via, giuocar si può	Come, now we can gamble.

(Gastone starts to cut the cards, Alfredo and others place bets. Violetta comes in, on the Baron's arm. Flora goes toward them.)

FLORA

Qui desiata giungi . . .   We hoped you would come . . .

VIOLETTA

Cessi al cortese invito.   I accepted the kind invitation.

FLORA

Grata vi son, Barone,   I'm grateful to you, Baron,
D'averlo pur gradito.   Also for having accepted it.

BARON
(softly to Violetta)

Germont è qui! . . . il vedete?   Germont is here! . . . Do you see him?

VIOLETTA

(Cielo! gli è vero!)   (Heaven! It's true!)
           (softly to the Baron)
Il vedo.   I see him.

BARON

Da voi non un sol detto   Don't you say a single word
Si volga a questo Alfredo . . .   To this Alfredo . . .
Non un detto!   Not a word!

VIOLETTA

(Ah perchè venni, incauta!   (Ah, reckless me, why did I come!
Pietà, gran Dio, pietà di me!)   Have mercy on me, God!)

(Flora has Violetta sit down near her on the sofa. The Doctor comes over to them; the Marquis stays to one side with the Baron; Gastone cuts the cards, Alfredo and the others bet, other guests stroll about.)

FLORA
(to Violetta)

Meco t'assidi; narrami: Sit with me; tell me:
Quai novità vegg'io? . . .   What do I see that's new? . . .

(Flora and Violetta talk together.)

ALFREDO

Un quattro!   A four!

GASTONE

Ancora hai vinto!   You've won again!

ALFREDO

Sfortuna nell'amore   Misfortune in love
Fortuna reca al giuoco . . .   Brings luck in gambling . . .
     (He bets and wins.)

ALL

È sempre vincitore! . . .   He's still the winner! . . .

ALFREDO

Oh vincerò stasera; c l'oro guadagnato   Oh, I'll win this evening; and then I'll go
Poscia a goder tra' campi tornerò beato.   Back to the country to enjoy the gold I've
                                             won.

FLORA

Solo?   Alone?

ALFREDO

No . . . no . . .   No . . . no . . .
Con tale che vi fu meco ancora,   With her who was with me before,
Poi mi sfuggia . . .   Then ran away from me . . .

VIOLETTA

(Mio Dio! . . .)   (My God! . . .)

GASTONE
(*to Alfredo, pointing at Violetta*)
(Pietà di lei!)   (Have pity on her!)

BARON
(*to Alfredo, with ill-concealed wrath*)
Signor!   Sir!

VIOLETTA
(*softly to the Baron*)
(Frenatevi, o vi lascio.)   (Control yourself, or I'll leave you.)

ALFREDO
(*nonchalant*)
Barone, m'appellaste?   Did you call me, Baron?

BARON

Siete in sì gran fortuna,   You're so lucky,
Che al giuoco mi tentaste . . .   That you've tempted me to gamble . . .

ALFREDO
(*ironic*)
Sì? . . . La disfida accetto.   Yes? . . . I accept the challenge.

VIOLETTA

(Che fia? . . . morir mi sento! . . .   (What is this? . . . I feel as I were
Pietà, gran Dio, pietà di me!)   dying! . . .
                                             Have mercy on me, God!)

BARON
(*betting*)

Cento luigi a destra.

A hundred louis on the right.

ALFREDO
(*betting*)

Ed alla manca cento . . .

And a hundred on the left . . .

GASTONE
(*cutting*)

Un asso . . . un fante . . .

An ace . . . a knave . . .

(*to Alfredo*)

Hai vinto!

You've won!

BARON

Il doppio? . . .

Double? . . .

ALFREDO

Il doppio sia.

Double it is.

GASTONE
(*cutting*)

Un quattro . . . un sette . . .

A four . . . a seven . . .

ALL

Ancora! . . .

Again! . . .

ALFREDO

Pur la vittoria è mia!

The victory is still mine!

ALL

Bravo davver! . . . la sorte è tutta per Alfredo! . . .

Good for him! . . . Luck is all with Alfredo! . . .

FLORA

Del villeggiar la spesa
Farà il baron, già il vedo.

The Baron will pay his holiday's expenses,
I see that already.

ALFREDO
(*to the Baron*)

Seguite pur!

Continue!

(*A servant comes in.*)

SERVANT

La cena è pronta.

Supper is ready.

FLORA

Andiamo.

Let's go.

ALL

Andiamo.   Let's go.

VIOLETTA

(Che fia? . . . morir mi sento!   (What is this? I feel as if I were dying!
Pietà, gran Dio, pictà di me!)   Have mercy on me, God!)

(All go out, only Alfredo and the Baron remain behind.)

ALFREDO

Se continuar v'aggrada . . .   If you care to go on . . .

BARON

Per ora nol possiamo: We can't for the moment:
Più tardi la rivineita.   I'll have my return chance later.

ALFREDO

Al giuoco che vorrete.   At any game you wish.

BARON

Seguiam gli amici . . . poscia . . . Let us follow our friends . . . then . . .

ALFREDO

Sarò qual bramerete.   I will be yours to command.
Andiam.   Let us go.

BARON

Andiam.   Let us go.

(They go off. The stage is deserted for a moment. Then Violetta comes back, distressed.)

VIOLETTA

Invitato a qui seguirmi,   Will he come after me here,
Verrà desso? . . . vorrà udirmi?   As I've asked him? . . . Will he listen to me?
Ei verrà . . . chè l'odio atroce   He'll come . . . for his terrible hatred
Puote in lui più di mia voce . . .   Has more power over him than my voice.

(Alfredo enters.)

ALFREDO

Mi chiamaste? . . . che bramate? . . . You called me? . . . What do you want?

VIOLETTA

Questi luoghi abbandonate;   Leave this place;
Un periglio vi sovrasta . . .   Danger threatens you . . .

ALFREDO

Ah comprendo! . . . Basta, basta . . . Ah, I understand! . . . Enough, enough . . .
E sì vile mi credete?   You think I'm so cowardly?

VIOLETTA

Ah no, no, mai . . .   Ah, no, no, never . . .

ALFREDO

Ma che temete?   But what do you fear?

VIOLETTA

Tremo sempre del Barone . . .   I'm always afraid the Baron . . .

ALFREDO

È fra noi mortal quistione . . .   It's a life-and-death matter between us . . .
S'ei cadrà per mano mia,   If he falls by my hand,
Un sol colpo vi torria   A single blow would deprive you
Coll'amante il protettore . . .   Of lover and keeper . . .
V'atterrisce tal seiagura?   Does such a disaster terrify you?

VIOLETTA

Ma s'ei fosse l'uccisore! . . .   But if he were the killer! . . .
Ecco l'unica sventura   That is the only misfortune
Ch'io pavento a me fatale.   I fear, a fatal one for me.

ALFREDO

La mia morte! . . . che ven cale? . . .   My death! What does it matter to you? . . .

VIOLETTA

Deh, partite . . . e sull'istante.   Please, leave . . . and at once.

ALFREDO

Partirò, ma giura innante   I'll leave, but swear first
Che dovunque seguirai   That you'll follow my steps
I passi miei . . .   Anywhere . . .

VIOLETTA

Ah no, giammai.   Ah no, never.

ALFREDO

No! . . . giammai! . . .   No! . . . never! . . .

VIOLETTA

Va, sciagurato!   Go, unhappy man!
Scorda un nome ch'è infamato . . .   Forget a name that is dishonored . . .
Va, mi lascia sul momento . . .   Go, leave me at once.
Di fuggirti un giuramento   I took a sacred oath
Sacro io feci . . .   To flee from you . . .

ALFREDO

A chi? . . . Dillo . . . Chi potea? . . .   To whom? . . . Tell me . . . Who could
                                                   make you? . . .

VIOLETTA

A chi dritto pien n'avea.   One who had every right.

ALFREDO

Fu Douphol? . . .   Was it Douphol? . . .

VIOLETTA
(*making a supreme effort*)

Sì.   Yes.

ALFREDO

Dunque l'ami?   Then you love him?

VIOLETTA

Ebben . . . l'amo . . .   Very well . . . I love him . . .

(*Furious, Alfredo runs and flings open the door.*)

ALFREDO

Or tutti a me.   Everyone come here to me.

(*All come in, confused.*)

ALL

Ne appellaste? . . . che volete?   You called us? . . . What do you want?

(*Alfredo points to Violetta, who leans against the table, crushed.*)

ALFREDO

Questa donna conoscete?   You know this woman?

ALL

Chi? Violetta?   Who? Violetta?

ALFREDO

Che facesse non sapete?   You don't know what she did?

VIOLETTA

(Ah! taci.)   (Ah! Be silent!)

ALL

No.   No.

ALFREDO

Ogni suo aver tal femmina   This woman squandered
Per amor mio sperdea . . .   All she owned for love of me . . .
Io cieco, vile, misero,   Blind, cowardly, wretched,
Tutto accettar potea.   I could accept it all.
Ma è tempo ancora! . . . tergermi   But I'm still in time! . . . I want
Da tanta macchia bramo . . .   To cleanse myself of such a stain . . .
Qui testimon vi chiamo,   I call you here as witnesses,

Or testimon vi chiamo	Now I call you as witnesses
Che qui pagata io l'ho.	That here I have repaid her.

(With furious contempt he throws a purse at the feet of Violetta, who faints in Flora's arms. At the last words Monsieur Germont comes in.)

ALL

Oh, infamia orribile	Oh, you've committed
Tu commettesti!	A horrible infamy!
Un cor sensible	In this way, you've killed
Così uccidesti! . . .	A sensitive heart! . . .
Di donne ignobile	Ignoble insulter
Insultatore,	Of women,
Di qua allontanati,	Go away from here,
Ne desti orror!	You fill us with horror!
Va! Va! Ne desti orror!	Go! Go! You fill us with horror!

GERMONT
(with dignity and fire)

Di sprezzo degno sè stesso rende	A man who, even in anger, offends a woman
Chi pur nell'ira la donna offende.	Renders himself deserving of contempt.
Dov'è mio figlio? . . . più non lo vedo;	Where is my son? . . . I see him no more;
In te, in te più Alfredo trovar non so.	I cannot discover Alfredo in you.

ALFREDO

(Ah sì! che feci! . . . ne sento orrore!	(Ah yes! What have I done? . . . I feel horror at it!
Gelosa smania, deluso amore	Jealous raving, disappointed love
Mi strazian l'alma . . . più non ragiono . . .	Tear my soul . . . I can reason no more . . .
Da lei perdono più non avrò.	I'll never receive her pardon now.
Volea fuggirla . . . non ho potuto . . .	I wanted to flee her, but I wasn't able to . . .
Dall'ira spinto son qui venuto!	Driven by anger, I came here!
Or che lo sdegno ho disfogato,	Now that I've unburdened my scorn,
Me sciagurato! rimorso n'ho!)	Wretched, I feel remorse for it!)

GERMONT

(Io sol fra tanti so qual virtude	(Only I, among them all, know what virtue
Di quella misera il sen racchiude . . .	Is contained in the heart of that poor girl . . .
Io so che l'ama, che gli è fedele;	I know she loves him, that she is faithful to him;
Eppur crudele tacer dovrò!)	And yet I must be cruelly silent!)

BARON
(softly to Alfredo)

A questa donna l'atroce insulto	The terrible insult to this woman
Qui tutti offese, ma non inulto	Offended all here, but such an outrage
Fia tanto oltraggio . . . provar vi voglio	Must not go unpunished . . . I want to prove
Che il vostro orgoglio fiaccar saprò.	That I can humble your pride.

FLORA, GASTONE, DOCTOR, MARQUIS AND CHORUS
(to Violetta)

Oh quanto peni! ma pur fa cor . . .   Ah, how you suffer! But still, take heart . . .
Qui soffre ognuno del tuo dolor;   Here everyone suffers at your grief;
Fra cari amici qui sei soltanto,   Here you are among dear friends only;
Rasciuga il pianto che t'inondò.   Dry the tears that bathed you.

VIOLETTA
(coming around)

Alfredo, Alfredo, di questo core   Alfredo, Alfredo, you can't understand
Non puoi comprendere tutto l'amore . . .   All the love in this heart . . .
Tu non conosci che finò a prezzo   You don't know that I have subjected it
Del tuo disprezzo provato io l'ho.   Even to the price of your contempt.
Ma verrà tempo, in che il saprai . . .   But the time will come, when you will
Come t'amassi confesserai . . .   know . . .
Dio dai rimorsi ti salvi allor . . .   You will admit how much I loved you . . .
Ah! io spenta ancora t'amerò.   May God save you from remorse then . . .
                                            Ah! Even when I'm dead, I'll love you still.

ALFREDO

(Ohimè! che feci! ne sento orror! ecc.)   (Alas, what have I done? I feel horror at it!
                                              etc.)

BARON

Provar vi voglio, ecc.   I want to prove, etc.

ALL

Quanto peni! fa cor! ecc.   How you suffer! Take heart! etc.
    (Germont takes his son away with him. The Baron follows. Violetta is led into another
room by the Doctor and Flora; the others disperse.)

ACT THREE

*Violetta's bedroom. In the back there is a bed with curtains half-drawn; a window with
shut blinds on the inside; near the bed a stool with a carafe of water on it, a crystal cup, and
various medicines. Halfway downstage there is a dressing table near a sofa; farther away
another piece of furniture with a night light burning on it; various chairs and other pieces.
The door is at left; opposite, a fireplace with a fire burning.*
    Violetta is sleeping in the bed. Annina, sitting near the fire, is also asleep.

VIOLETTA
(waking)

Annina?   Annina?

ANNINA
(waking, confused)

Comandate?   Yes, Madame?

VIOLETTA

Dormivi? poveretta!   Were you asleep? Poor thing!

ANNINA

Sì, perdonate.   Yes, forgive me.

VIOLETTA

Dammi d'acqua un sorso.   Give me a sip of water.

(Annina obeys.)

VIOLETTA

Osserva . . . È pieno il giorno?   Look . . . Is it broad daylight?

ANNINA

Son sett'ore.   It's seven o'clock.

VIOLETTA

Dà accesso a un po' di luce.   Let a little light in.

(Annina opens the shutters and looks into the street.)

ANNINA

Il signor di Grenvil . . .   Monsieur de Grenvil . . .

VIOLETTA

Oh il vero amico!   Oh, a true friend!

Alzar mi vo' . . . M'aita.   I want to get up . . . Help me.

(She starts to rise, but falls back, then, with Annina supporting her, she goes slowly to the sofa. The Doctor enters in time to help settle her on it. Annina adds some cushions.)

VIOLETTA

Quanta bontà! . . . Pensaste a me per tempo!   How kind! . . . You thought of me early!

DOCTOR

(touching her wrist)

Sì . . . Come vi sentite?   Yes . . . How do you feel?

VIOLETTA

Soffre il mio corpo, ma tranquilla ho l'alma.   My body suffers, but my spirit is serene.

Mi confortò iersera un pio ministro . . .   A priest comforted me yesterday eve-

Ah! religione è sollievo ai sofferenti.   ning . . .

                     Ah! Religion is a relief to those who suffer.

DOCTOR

E questa notte?   And last night?

VIOLETTA

Ebbi tranquillo il sonno.   My sleep was peaceful.

DOCTOR

Coraggio adunque . . .	Courage then . . .
La convalescenza non è lontana . . .	Your convalescence isn't far off . . .

VIOLETTA

Oh, la bugia pietosa	Ah, doctors are allowed
Ai medici è concessa!	Merciful lies!

DOCTOR
(*shaking her hand*)

Addio . . . a più tardi!	Good-bye . . . until later.

VIOLETTA

Non mi scordate.	Don't forget me.

(*The Doctor leaves. Annina accompanies him to the door, saying softly and hastily:*)

ANNINA

Come va, signore?	How is she, sir?

DOCTOR

La tisi non le accorda che poche ore.	Her consumption grants her only a few hours more.

(*He goes out.*)

ANNINA

Or fate cor . . .	Now take heart . . .

VIOLETTA

Giorno di festa è questo?	Is this a holiday?

ANNINA

Tutta Parigi impazza . . . è carnevale.	All Paris is going mad . . . it's carnival.

VIOLETTA

Ah nel comun tripudio, sallo Iddio	Ah, God knows, in the general festivity,
Quanti infelici soffrn!	How many unfortunates are suffering!

(*pointing*)

Quale somma v'ha in quelio stipo?	How much is there in that cupboard?

ANNINA
(*opens and counts*)

Venti luigi.	Twenty louis.

VIOLETTA

Dieci ne reca a' poveri tu stessa.	Take ten to the poor yourself.

ANNINA

Poco rimanvi allora . . .	Little is left then . . .

VIOLETTA

Oh mi saran bastanti! . . .	Oh, it will be enough for me! . . .
Cerca poscia mie lettere.	Then see if I have any letters.

ANNINA

Ma voi?	But what about you?

VIOLETTA

Null' occorrà . . .	I won't need anything . . .
Sollecita, se puoi.	Hurry, if you can.

(*Annina leaves. Violetta takes a letter from her bosom and reads.*)

VIOLETTA

"Teneste la promessa . . . La disfida	"You kept the promise . . . The duel
Ebbe luogo! Il Barone fu ferito,	Took place! The Baron was wounded,
Però migliora . . . Alfredo	But is improving . . . Alfredo
È in stranio suolo. Il vostro sagrifizio	Is in a foreign land. I myself
Io stesso gli ho svelato.	Revealed your sacrifice to him.
Egli a voi tornerà pel suo perdono;	He will come back to you for your forgive-
Io pur verrò . . . Curatevi . . . mertate	ness;
Un avvenir migliore.	I too will come . . . Take care of your-
Giorgio Germont."	self . . .
È tardi!	You deserve a better future.
	Giorgio Germont."
	It's late!

(*She rises.*)

Attendo, attendo, nè a me giungon mai! . . .	I wait and wait, but they never come to me! . . .

(*She looks at herself in the mirror.*)

Oh come son mutata! . . .	Oh, how I've changed! . . .
Ma il Dottore a sperar pure m'esorta! . . .	Still the Doctor urges me to hope! . . .
Ah con tal morbo ogni speranza è morta!	Ah, with this disease, all hope is dead!
Addio, del passato bei sogni ridenti,	Farewell, lovely, happy dreams of the past,
Le rose del volto già sono pallenti;	The roses in my face are fading already;
L'amore d'Alfredo perfino mi manca,	And I am without Alfredo's love also,
Conforto, sostegno dell'anima stanca . . .	The comfort and support of my weary soul . . .
Ah! della traviata sorridi al desio,	Ah! Smile at the wish of the lost one,
A lei, deh perdona, tu accoglila, o Dio!	Forgive her, and receive her, O God!
Ah! tutto . . . or tutto finì.	Ah! All . . . now all is finished.
* [Le gioie, i dolori tra poco avran fine;	[The joys, the griefs will soon have an end;
La tomba ai mortali di tutto è confine!	The tomb is the end of everything for mor-
Non lagrima o fiore avrà la mia fossa!	tals!
Non croce col nome che copra quest'ossa!	No tear or flower will my grave have!
Ah! della traviata sorridi al desio,	Nor a cross with a name to cover these bones!
A lei, deh perdona, tu accoglila, o Dio!	Ah! Smile at the wish of the lost one,
Ah! tutto . . . or tutto finì.]	Forgive her, and receive her, O God!
	Ah! All . . . now all is finished.]

(*She sits down.*)

---

* Brackets denote passages often omitted in performance.

Chorus of Masquers
(outside)

Largo al quadrupede sir della festa,
Di fiori e pampini cinta la testa . . .
Largo al più docile d'ogni cornuto,
Di corni e pifferi abbia il saluto.
Parigini, date passo
Al trionfo del Bue grasso.

Make way for the quadruped lord of the
   feast,
His head garlanded with flowers and vine
   leaves . . .
Make way for the mildest of all horned
   beasts,
Let him be greeted by horns and fifes.
Parisians, step aside
For the triumph of the fat Ox.

L'Asia, nè l'Africa vide il più bello,
Vanto ed orgoglio d'ogni macello . . .
Allegre maschere, pazzi garzoni,
Tutti plauditelo con canti e suoni.
Parigini, date passo
Al trionfo del Bue grasso.
Largo al quadrupede, ecc.

Not Asia nor Africa ever saw a handsomer,
Pride and joy of every butcher shop . . .
Merry masquers, mad apprentices,
All applaud him with songs and music.
Parisians, step aside
For the triumph of the fat Ox.
Make way for the quadruped, etc.

(Annina comes back, hurrying.)

Annina
(hesitating)

Signora . . .

Madame · . . .

Violetta

Che t'accadde?

What's happened to you?

Annina

Quest'oggi, è vero? . . . vi sentite meglio?

You do feel better today, don't you?

Violetta

Sì, perchè?

Yes, why?

Annina

D'esser calma promettete? . . .

You promise to be calm? . . .

Violetta

Sì, che vuoi dirmi?

Yes, what do you want to tell me?

Annina

Prevenir vi volli . . .
Una gioia improvvisa . . .

I wanted to prepare you . . .
A sudden joy . . .

Violetta

Una gioia! . . . dicesti?

A joy! . . . you said?

Annina

Sì, o signora . . .

Yes, madame . . .

(Annina nods and goes to open the door.)

VIOLETTA

Alfredo! . . . Ah tu il vedesti!	Alfredo! . . . Ah, you saw him!
Ei vien! . . . t'affretta . . .	He's coming! . . . Hurry . . .
Alfredo?	Alfredo?

(*Alfredo appears, pale with emotion; they throw themselves into each other's arms, exclaiming:*)

VIOLETTA

Amato Alfredo, oh gioia! Beloved Alfredo, oh joy!

ALFREDO

Oh mia Violetta, oh gioia!	Oh, my Violetta, oh, joy!
Colpevol sono . . . so tutto, o cara . . .	I'm to blame . . . I know all, my dear . . .

VIOLETTA

Io so che alfine reso mi sei! I know that at last you've been restored to me!

ALFREDO

Da questo palpito	See how I love you
S'io t'ami impara,	From my heart's beating,
Senza te esistere	I could exist no longer
Più non potrei.	Without you.

VIOLETTA

Ah s'anco in vita	Ah, if you've found me
M'hai ritrovata,	Still alive,
Credi che uccidere	You must believe
Non può il dolor.	That grief cannot kill.

ALFREDO

Scorda l'affanno, donna adorata,	Forget your grief, adored woman,
A me perdona e al genitor.	Forgive me and my father.

VIOLETTA

Ch'io ti perdoni? le rea son io:	I, forgive you? I'm the guilty one:
Ma solo amor tal me rendè.	But it was love alone that made me so.

ALFREDO AND VIOLETTA

Null'uomo o demon, angiol mio,	No man or demon, my angel,
Mai più dividermi potrà da te.	Will ever again separate me from you.

ALFREDO

Parigi, o cara, noi lasceremo,	We will leave Paris, O beloved,
La vita uniti trascorreremo . . .	We'll spend our life together . . .
De' corsi affanni compenso avrai,	You'll be rewarded for your past sufferings,
La tua salute rifiorirà . . .	Your health will bloom again . . .
Sospiro e luce tu mi sarai,	You'll be my light, my breath,
Tutto il futuro ne arriderà.	All the future will smile on us.

VIOLETTA (AND ALFREDO)

Parigi, o caro, noi lasceremo, ecc.   We will leave Paris, O beloved, etc.
La mia salute rifiorirà, ecc.   My health will bloom again, etc.

VIOLETTA

Ah non più . . . a un tempio . . .   Ah, no more . . . to a church . . .
Alfredo, andiamo,   Alfredo, let us go,
Del tuo ritorno grazie rendiamo.   Let us give thanks for your return.
                                              (She falters.)

ALFREDO

Tu impallidisci! . . .   You're pale! . . .

VIOLETTA

È nulla, sai?   It's nothing, you know.
Gioia improvvisa non entra mai,   Sudden joy never enters
Senza turbarlo, in mesto core.   A sad heart, without upsetting it.
   (Violetta, exhausted, sinks into a chair. Frightened, Alfredo holds her up.)

ALFREDO

Gran Dio! . . . Violetta!   Oh God! . . . Violetta!

VIOLETTA

È il mio malore! . . . fu debolezza . . .   It's my illness! . . . weakness . . .
Ora son forte . . . vedi? sorrido . . .   Now I'm strong . . . you see? I'm smil-
                                                  ing . . .
                            (Making an effort.)

ALFREDO
                            (desolate)
(Ahi cruda sorte!)   (Alas, cruel fate!)

VIOLETTA

Fu nulla! . . . Annina, dammi a vestire.   It was nothing! . . . Annina, give me my
                                                  clothes.

ALFREDO

Adesso? . . . attendi . . .   Now? . . . Wait . . .

VIOLETTA
                            (standing up)
No! . . . voglio uscire.   No! . . . I want to go out.
   (Annina brings her a dress, which she starts to put on, but her weakness prevents her, she
throws it away crossly and sinks back in the chair.)

VIOLETTA

Gran Dio! . . . non posso!   Good God! . . . I can't!

ALFREDO

(Cielo! che vedo!)   (Heaven! What do I see?!)
                                            (to Annina)
Va pel Dottore . . .   Go for the Doctor . . .

VIOLETTA
(to Annina)
Ah! digli . . . digli che Alfredo   Ah! Tell him . . . tell him that Alfredo
È ritornato . . . all'amor mio . . .   Has come back . . . to my love . . .
Digli che vivere . . . ancor vogl'io . . . Tell him . . . I want to live again . . .
(Annina leaves.)

VIOLETTA
(to Alfredo)
Ma se tornando non m'hai salvato,   But if, by coming back, you haven't saved
A niuno in terra salvarmi è dato.   me,
                                            Then no one on earth has the power to save
                                            me.
(impetuously rising)
Ah! gran Dio! . . . morir sì giovine,   Ah! Great God! . . . to die so young,
Io che penato ho tanto!   I who have suffered so much!
Morir sì presso a tergere   To die so close to drying
Il mio sì lungo pianto!   My many, many tears!
Ah! dunque fu delirio   Ah! So my credulous hope
La credula speranza! . . .   Was delirium! . . .
Invano di costanza   I've armed my heart
Armato avrò il mio cor! . . .   With constancy, in vain! . . .

ALFREDO
Oh mio sospiro e palpito,   Oh, my breath and pulse,
Diletto del cor mio!   Delight of my heart!
Le mie colle tue lagrime   I must mingle
Confondere degg'io! . . .   My tears with yours! . . .
Ma più che mai, deh! credilo   But more than ever, believe me,
M'è d'uopo di costanza . . .   I need your constancy . . .
Ah tutto alla speranza   Ah, don't close your heart
Non chiudere il tuo cor!   To hope entirely!

VIOLETTA
Oh Alfredo, il crudo termine . . .   Oh, Alfredo, the cruel end . . .

ALFREDO
Ah! Violetta mia, deh! calmati.   Ah! My Violetta, please be calm!

VIOLETTA
. . . serbato al nostro amor!   . . . destined for our love!

ALFREDO
M'uccide il tuo dolor.   Your grief destroys me.
(Violetta sinks back on the sofa. Monsieur Germont enters, followed by the Doctor, with Annina.)

GERMONT

Ah Violetta! . . .   Ah, Violetta! . . .

VIOLETTA

Voi, signor!   You, monsieur!

ALFREDO

Mio padre!   Father!

VIOLETTA

Non mi scordaste?   You haven't forgotten me?

GERMONT

La promessa adempio . . .   I'm keeping my promise . . .
A stringervi qual figlia al seno,   To clasp you to my bosom as a daughter,
O generosa!   O generous girl!

VIOLETTA

Ahimè! tardi giungeste!   Alas. You've come late!
                                                      (embracing him)
Pure, grata ven sono . . .   Still I'm grateful to you . . .
Grenvil, vedete? fra le braccia   Grenvil, you see? I die in the arms
Io spiro di quanti cari ho al mondo . . .   Of those dearest to me in the world . . .

GERMONT

Che mai dite!   What are you saying?!
                                                      (observing Violetta)
(Oh cielo! . . . è ver!)   (Oh heaven! . . . It's true!)

ALFREDO

La vedi, padre mio?   You see her, Father?

GERMONT

Di più non lacerarmi,   Don't distress me further,
Troppo rimorso l'alma mi divora . . .   Too much remorse is consuming my
Quasi fulmin m'atterra ogni suo detto . . .   soul . . .
Ah mal cauto vegliardo!   Her every word strikes me like a thunder-
Il mal ch'io feci ora sol vedo!   bolt . . .
                                                      Ah, ill-advised old man!
                                                      Only now do I see the harm I did!

(*Violetta meanwhile has painfully opened a drawer in the dressing table, and taking out a miniature, she says:*)

VIOLETTA

Più a me t'appressa . . .   Come closer to me . . .
Ascolta, amate Alfredo,   Listen, beloved Alfredo.
Prendi: quest'è l'immagine   Take this: this is the picture
De' miei passati giorni,   Of my former days,

A rammentar ti torni
Colei che sì t'amò.

Let it remind you again
Of her who loved you so.

ALFREDO

No, non morrai, non dirmelo . . .
Dèi viver, amor mio . . .
A strazio sì terribil
Qui non mi trasse Iddio.

No, you won't die, don't say it to me . . .
You must live, my love . . .
God didn't bring me here
For such terrible torment.

GERMONT

Cara, sublime vittima
D'un disperato amore,
Perdonami io strazio
Recato al tuo bel cor.

Beloved, sublime victim
Of a desperate love,
Forgive me for the torture
I caused your noble heart.

VIOLETTA

Se una pudica vergine,
Degli anni suoi sul fiore,
A te donasse il core . . .
Sposa ti sia . . . lo vo' . . .
Le porgi quest'effigie;
Dille che dono ell'è
Di chi nel ciel fra gli angeli
Prega per lei, per te.

If an innocent maiden,
In the flower of her years,
Should give her heart to you . . .
Let her be your bride . . . I wish it . . .
Give her this portrait;
Tell her it is the gift
Of one who, among the angels in heaven,
Is praying for her, for you.

ALFREDO

Si presto, ah no, dividerti
Morte non può da me.
Ah vivi, o solo un feretro
M'accoglierà con te.

Ah no, death cannot separate
You from me so quickly.
Ah, live . . . or a single coffin
Will receive me, with you.

GERMONT, DOCTOR, AND ANNINA

Finchè avrà il ciglio lagrime
Io piangerò per te.
Vola a' beati spiriti,
Iddio ti chiama a sè.

As long as my eyes have tears
I will weep for you.
Fly to the blessed spirits;
God is calling you to Him.

VIOLETTA
(rising again, animated)

È strano!

It's strange!

ALL

Che!

What!

VIOLETTA

Cessarono gli spasimi del dolore . . .
In me . . . rinasce . . . m'agita
Insolito vigor! . . .

The seizures of pain have stopped . . .
An unfamiliar strength
Is born in me . . . stirs me! . . .

Ah! . . . ma io . . . ah! ma io ritorno a viver!   Ah! . . . Why, I . . . I am returning to life!
Oh gioia!   Oh joy!

(She falls back on the sofa.)

ALL

O cielo! . . . muor!   Oh, heaven! . . . She's dying!

ALFREDO

Violetta?   Violetta?

ANNINA AND GERMONT

Oh Dio, soccorrasi . . .   Oh, God, help her . . .

The Doctor touches her wrist.

DOCTOR

È spenta!   She's dead!

ANNINA

Oh rio dolor!   Oh, cruel grief!

ALFREDO AND GERMONT

Oh mio dolor!   Oh, my grief!

NOTES

La Traviata

AT THE METROPOLITAN OPERA

[EDITOR'S NOTE: The first performance of *La Traviata* was in Venice, at the Teatro La Fenice, on March 6, 1853. The first performance at the Metropolitan Opera was on November 5, 1883. The role of Violetta was sung by Marcella Sembrich, the role of Alfredo by Victor Capoul, and the role of Germont by Giuseppe Del Puente. The conductor was Augusto Vianesi. The production was designed by James Fox and members of the artistic staff at the Metropolitan. In 1921 Joseph Urban designed a new production for the Met debut of Amelita Galli-Curci. Jonel Jorgulesco designed a new production in 1935, which, except for a new Act II, painted by Joseph Novak in 1946, remained in use until 1957. In 1957 Oliver Smith designed new sets, with costumes by Rolf Gérard, for a production staged by Tyrone Guthrie. Cecil Beaton designed a new *La Traviata* in 1966 for a production staged by Alfred Lunt. The most recent production was designed by Tanya Moiseiwitch and staged by Colin Graham, with lighting by Gil Wechsler. The premiere of this production was on March 17, 1981. Through the season of 1981–1982, *La Traviata* has amassed a total of 482 performances at the Met in 76 seasons. Thirteen performances are scheduled for the 1983–1984 season, the season which marks the hundredth year since *La Traviata* was first seen at the Met.]

NOVEMBER 5, 1883

VIOLETTA	*Marcella Sembich*
ALFREDO	*Victor Capoul*
GIORGIO GERMONT	*Giuseppe Del Puente*
FLORA BERVOIX	*Emily Lablache*
GASTONE	*Vincenzo Fornaris*
BARON DOUPHOL	*Achile Augier*
MARQUIS D'OBIGNY	*Baldassare Corsini*
DOCTOR GRENVIL	*Ludovico Contini*
ANNINA	*Imogene Forti*
GIUSEPPE	*Signor Barberis*

CONDUCTOR   *Augusto Vianesi*

DECEMBER 22, 1894

VIOLETTA	*Lillian Nordica*
ALFREDO	*Giuseppe Russitano*
GIORGIO GERMONT	*Italo Campanini*

FLORA BERVOIX	*Marie Van Cauteren*
GASTONE	*Roberto Vanni*
BARON DOUPHOL	*Lodovico Viviani*
DOCTOR GRENVIL	*Antonio de Vaschetti*
ANNINA	*Mathilde Bauermeister*

CONDUCTOR   *Emilio Bevignani*

DECEMBER 21, 1896

VIOLETTA	*Nellie Melba*
ALFREDO	*Giuseppe Cremonini*
GIORGIO GERMONT	*Mario Ancona*
FLORA BERVOIX	*Marie Van Cauteren*
GASTONE	*Roberto Vanni*
BARON DOUPHOL	*Jacques Bars*
MARQUIS D'OBIGNY	*Igenio Corsi*
DOCTOR GRENVIL	*Antonio de Vaschetti*
ANNINA	*Mathilde Bauermeister*

CONDUCTOR   *Emilio Bevignani*

DECEMBER 5, 1898

VIOLETTA	*Marcella Sembrich*
ALFREDO	*Thomas Salignac*
GIORGIO GERMONT	*Giuseppe Campanari*
FLORA BERVOIX	*Maud Roudez*
GASTONE	*Roberto Vanni*
BARON DOUPHOL	*Jacques Bars*
MARQUIS D'OBIGNY	*Lempriere Pringle*
DOCTOR GRENVIL	*Eugène Dufriche*
ANNINA	*Mathilde Bauermeister*

CONDUCTOR   *Emilio Bevignani*

JANUARY 4, 1902

VIOLETTA	*Marcella Sembrich*
ALFREDO	*Thomas Salignac*
GIORGIO GERMONT	*Maurice Declery*
FLORA BERVOIX	*Marie Van Cauteren*
GASTONE	*Roberto Vanni*
BARON DOUPHOL	*Jacques Bars*
MARQUIS D'OBIGNY	*Eugène Dufriche*
DOCTOR GRENVIL	*Charles Gilibert*
ANNINA	*Mathilde Bauermeister*

CONDUCTOR   *Armando Seppilli*

La Traviata

AT THE MET

Premiere of the current production,
March 17, 1981
CONDUCTOR, James Levine
PRODUCTION, Colin Graham
SET AND COSTUME DESIGNER, Tanya Moiseiwitsch
LIGHTING DESIGNER, Gil Wechsler

Photographs of the story of the opera by William Harris
Courtesy of the Education Department, Metropolitan Opera Guild

ACT I

Paris. The house of Violetta Valery, famous courtesan.

One of Violetta's *(Ileana Cotrubas)* gala evenings is about to begin. Her friend Flora *(Ariel Bybee)* has arrived with Baron Douphol *(John Darrenkamp)* and the other guests.

ABOVE LEFT: Another arrival, Gastone, Vicomte de Letorières *(Dana Talley),* has brought his friend Alfredo Germont *(Placido Domingo).* Alfredo has heard a good deal about Violetta's charms and has wanted to meet her. Violetta and Alfredo raise their glasses to toast each other.

LEFT: As most of the others go off to an adjoining room to dance, Violetta is seized with a fit of coughing and stays behind.

ABOVE: Alfredo tries to comfort her, and declares his love for her.

OVERLEAF: As the evening comes to an end, Violetta says good-bye to her guests.

Alone, Violetta ponders Alfredo's declarations. What can they mean for her after the life she has lived? She realizes that it is too late for "true love" — it is only "vain raving." She must be free, always free, always find new delights at new parties with new friends.

ACT II, SCENE ONE

Five months later. The outskirts of Paris.
Violetta's country house.

Alfredo has convinced Violetta to live with him, and they are
staying in her country house. He cannot believe how this
new breath of love makes him feel reborn and rejuvenated.

Annina (*Geraldine Decker*), Violetta's companion, comes in. She confesses to Alfredo that she has been to Paris to sell Violetta's horses and carriages, to sell "everything she owns," in order to support them. Alfredo rushes away, deciding to go to Paris himself to ask his father for help. But soon after Alfredo leaves, his father, Giorgio Germont (*Cornell MacNeil*), arrives and confronts Violetta. Alfredo's father tells Violetta that she must give up his son — not only for Alfredo's sake, but for the sake of his young sister who is about to be married. He is fearful that his future son-in-law's family will never accept Alfredo and Violetta's relationship.

Violetta, aware that she is a victim of her own past, knows that she has no choice. She writes Alfredo a letter telling him that she has gone back to her former way of life and to Baron Douphol. Alfredo returns and sees Violetta writing. She tells him that his father has been there. Fighting back tears, she moves toward Alfredo, promises to love him forever, but bids him farewell. Alfredo has read Violetta's letter and is filled with anguish. His father enters and tries to comfort him — telling him that he feels he has won back his son from a life of shame.

ACT II, SCENE TWO

Paris. Flora's house.

Flora is giving one of her famous gambling parties.

Alfredo arrives, alone and distraught. He sits at the card table. Violetta arrives with the baron. The baron tells her that Alfredo is there.

After winning a large amount of money at cards, Alfredo challenges the baron to a duel, denounces Violetta, and hurls his winnings at her. Alfredo's father enters. He berates Alfredo for his offensive behavior. Alfredo is filled with remorse for what he has done.

ACT III

Paris. Violetta's house.

Violetta, ill and frail, is in her bed. She is dying
of consumption. Annina watches over her.

Dr. Grenvil *(William Fleck)* arrives. He knows the truth, but he encourages Violetta. He tells her she will recover.

Violetta, alone, takes out a letter from Alfredo. He has injured the baron in the duel, but he will return soon. He knows of her sacrifice for him.

Violetta moves to a chair after looking in the mirror. She realizes now that she is about to die, that "all is now finished."

Alfredo returns. Violetta and Alfredo reaffirm their love for each other. Violetta sinks to the floor. Alfredo lifts her.

Violetta has collapsed again. Annina arrives with the doctor.
Alfredo's father enters. Alfredo, bending over Violetta, asks her for
forgiveness. But it is too late. She has died. Alfredo and Germont are
left to face their grief alone.

DECEMBER 23, 1903

VIOLETTA	*Marcella Sembrich*
ALFREDO	*Enrico Caruso*
GIORGIO GERMONT	*Antonio Scotti*
FLORA BERVOIX	*Josephine Jacoby*
GASTONE	*Aristede Masiero*
BARON DOUPHOL	*Jacques Bars*
MARQUIS D'OBIGNY	*Bernard Bégué*
DOCTOR GRENVIL	*Eugène Dufriche*
ANNINA	*Mathilde Bauermeister*

CONDUCTOR	*Arturo Vigna*
STAGE DIRECTOR	*Karl Schroeder*

DECEMBER 1, 1906 (MATINEE)

VIOLETTA	*Marcella Sembrich*
ALFREDO	*Enrico Caruso*
GIORGIO GERMONT	*Riccardo Stracciari*
FLORA BERVOIX	*Josephine Jacoby*
GASTONE	*Giovanni Paroli*
BARON DOUPHOL	*Jacques Bars*
MARQUIS D'OBIGNY	*Bernard Bégué*
DOCTOR GRENVIL	*Eugène Dufriche*
ANNINA	*Marie Mattfeld*

CONDUCTOR	*Arturo Vigna*
STAGE DIRECTOR	*Eugène Dufriche*

FEBRUARY 8, 1908

VIOLETTA	*Marcella Sembrich*
ALFREDO	*Alessandro Bonci*
GIORGIO GERMONT	*Antonio Scotti*
FLORA BERVOIX	*Josephine Jacoby*
GASTONE	*Giuseppe Tecchi*
BARON DOUPHOL	*Vittorio Navarini*
MARQUIS D'OBIGNY	*Bernard Bégué*
DOCTOR GRENVIL	*Eugène Dufriche*
ANNINA	*Anne Girerd*

CONDUCTOR	*Rodolfo Ferrari*
STAGE DIRECTOR	*Eugène Dufriche*

FEBRUARY 28, 1908

VIOLETTA	*Geraldine Farrar*
ALFREDO	*Enrico Caruso*

GIORGIO GERMONT	*Riccardo Stracciari*
FLORA BERVOIX	*Josephine Jacoby*
GASTONE	*Giuseppe Tecchi*
BARON DOUPHOL	*Eugène Dufriche*
MARQUIS D'OBIGNY	*Bernard Bégué*
DOCTOR GRENVIL	*Vittorio Navarini*
ANNINA	*Anne Girerd*

CONDUCTOR	*Rodolfo Ferrari*
STAGE DIRECTOR	*Eugène Dufriche*

NOVEMBER 20, 1908

VIOLETTA	*Marcella Sembrich*
ALFREDO	*Enrico Caruso*
GIORGIO GERMONT	*Pasquale Amato (debut)*
FLORA BERVOIX	*Matja Van Niessen-Stone*
GASTONE	*Angelo Bada*
BARON DOUPHOL	*Concetto Paterna*
MARQUIS D'OBIGNY	*Paul Ananian*
DOCTOR GRENVIL	*Bernard Bégué*
ANNINA	*Marie Mattfield*

CONDUCTOR	*Francesco Spetrino*
BALLET MASTER	*Lodovico Saracco*
STAGE MANAGER	*Jules Speck*

NOVEMBER 29, 1910

VIOLETTA	*Nellie Melba*
ALFREDO	*John McCormack*
GIORGIO GERMONT	*Carlo Galeffi (debut)*
FLORA BERVOIX	*Jeanne Maubourg*
GASTONE	*Pietro Audisio*
BARON DOUPHOL	*Vincenzo Reschiglian*
MARQUIS D'OBIGNY	*Bernard Bégué*
DOCTOR GRENVIL	*Giulio Rossi*
ANNINA	*Marie Mattfeld*

CONDUCTOR	*Vittorio Podesti*
BALLET MASTER	*Lodovico Saracco*
STAGE MANAGER	*Jules Speck*

FEBRUARY 2, 1911

VIOLETTA	*Lydia Lipkowska*
ALFREDO	*Dimitri Smirnoff*

GIORGIO GERMONT	*Pasquale Amato*
FLORA BERVOIX	*Marie Mattfeld*
GASTONE	*Angelo Bada*
BARON DOUPHOL	*Vincenzo Reschiglian*
MARQUIS D'OBIGNY	*Bernard Bégué*
DOCTOR GRENVIL	*Giulio Rossi*
ANNINA	*Marie Mattfeld*

CONDUCTOR	*Vittorio Podesti*
BALLET MASTER	*Lodovico Savacco*
STAGE MANAGER	*Jules Speck*

JANUARY 6, 1912

VIOLETTA	*Luisa Tetrazzini*
ALFREDO	*Dimitri Smirnoff*
GIORGIO GERMONT	*Giovanni Polese*
FLORA BERVOIX	*Marie Mattfeld*
GASTONE	*Angelo Bada*
BARON DOUPHOL	*Vincenzo Reschiglian*
MARQUIS D'OBIGNY	*Bernard Bégué*
DOCTOR GRENVIL	*Paolo Ananian*
ANNINA	*Marie Mattfeld*

CONDUCTOR	*Giuseppe Sturani*
BALLET MASTER	*Lodovico Saracco*
STAGE MANAGER	*Jules Speck*

JANUARY 29, 1913

VIOLETTA	*Frieda Hempel*
ALFREDO	*Umberto Macnez*
GIORGIO GERMONT	*Pasquale Amato*
FLORA BERVOIX	*Jeanne Maubourg*
GASTONE	*Angelo Bada*
BARON DOUPHOL	*Vincenzo Reschiglian*
MARQUIS D'OBIGNY	*Bernard Bégué*
DOCTOR GRENVIL	*Paolo Ananian*
ANNINA	*Marie Mattfeld*

CONDUCTOR	*Giuseppe Sturani*
BALLET MASTER	*Ettore Coppini*
STAGE MANAGER	*Jules Speck*

FEBRUARY 6, 1919

VIOLETTA	*Frieda Hempel*
ALFREDO	*Carlo Hackett*
GIORGIO GERMONT	*Giuseppe de Luca*
FLORA BERVOIX	*Minnie Egener*

GASTONE	*Angelo Bada*
BARON DOUPHOL	*Vincenzo Reschiglian*
MARQUIS D'OBIGNY	*Louis D'Angelo*
DOCTOR GRENVIL	*Giulio Rossi*
ANNINA	*Marie Mattfeld*

CONDUCTOR	*Roberto Moranzoni*
STAGE DIRECTOR	*Richard Ordynski*
STAGE MANAGER	*Armando Agnini*

NOVEMBER 14, 1921

VIOLETTA	*Amelita Galli-Curci (debut)*
ALFREDO	*Beniamino Gigli*
GIORGIO GERMONT	*Giuseppe de Luca*
FLORA BERVOIX	*Minnie Egener*
GASTONE	*Angelo Bada*
BARON DOUPHOL	*Millo Picco*
MARQUIS D'OBIGNY	*Mario Laurenti*
DOCTOR GRENVIL	*Paolo Ananian*
ANNINA	*Louise Berat*

CONDUCTOR	*Roberto Moranzoni*
STAGE DIRECTOR	*Samuel Thewman*
STAGE MANAGER	*Armando Agnini*

NOVEMBER 30, 1922

VIOLETTA	*Lucrezia Bori*
ALFREDO	*Beniamino Gigli*
GIORGIO GERMONT	*Giuseppe Danise*
FLORA BERVOIX	*Minnie Egener*
GASTONE	*Angelo Bada*
BARON DOUPHOL	*Millo Picco*
MARQUIS D'OBIGNY	*Louis D'Angelo*
DOCTOR GRENVIL	*Italo Picchi (debut)*
ANNINA	*Grace Anthony*

CONDUCTOR	*Roberto Moranzoni*
STAGE DIRECTOR	*Samuel Thewman*
STAGE MANAGER	*Armando Agnini*

FEBRUARY 27, 1926

VIOLETTA	*Lucrezia Bori*
ALFREDO	*Armand Tokatyan*
GIORGIO GERMONT	*Giuseppe Danise*
FLORA BERVOIX	*Minnie Egener*

GASTONE — *Giordano Paltrinieri*
BARON DOUPHOL — *Vincenzo Reschiglian*
MARQUIS D'OBIGNY — *Louis D'Angelo*
DOCTOR GRENVIL — *Paolo Ananian*
ANNINA — *Grace Anthony*

CONDUCTOR — *Tullio Serafin*
STAGE DIRECTOR — *Samuel Thewman*
STAGE MANAGER — *Armando Agnini*

APRIL 19, 1930 (MATINEE)

VIOLETTA — *Lucrezia Broi*
ALFREDO — *Beniamino Gigli*
GIORGIO GERMONT — *Lawrence Tibbett*
FLORA BERVOIX — *Minnie Egener*
GASTONE — *Giordano Paltrinieri*
BARON DOUPHOL — *Alfredo Gandolfi*
MARQUIS D'OBIGNY — *Millo Picco*
DOCTOR GRENVIL — *Paolo Ananian*
ANNINA — *Philine Falco*

CONDUCTOR — *Vincenzo Bellezza*
STAGE MANAGER — *Armando Agnini.*

JANUARY 16, 1931 (MATINEE)

VIOLETTA — *Rosa Ponselle*
ALFREDO — *Giacomo Lauri-Volpi*
GIORGIO GERMONT — *Giuseppe de Luca*
FLORA BERVOIX — *Minnie Egener*
GASTONE — *Giordano Paltrinieri*
BARON DOUPHOL — *Alfredo Gandolfi*
MARQUIS D'OBIGNY — *Millo Picco*
DOCTOR GRENVIL — *Paolo Ananian*
ANNINA — *Philine Falco*

CONDUCTOR — *Tullio Serafin*
STAGE DIRECTOR — *Armando Agnini*

JANUARY 1, 1934

VIOLETTA — *Claudia Muzio*
ALFREDO — *Tito Schipa*
GIORGIO GERMONT — *Richard Bonelli*
FLORA BERVOIX — *Elda Vettori*
GASTONE — *Angelo Bada*
BARON DOUPHOL — *Alfredo Gandolfi*

MARQUIS D'OBIGNY	Millo Picco
DOCTOR GRENVIL	Paolo Ananian
ANNINA	Philine Falco

CONDUCTOR	Tullio Serafin
STAGE DIRECTOR	Armando Agnini

FEBRUARY 2, 1934 (MATINEE)

VIOLETTA	Rosa Ponselle
ALFREDO	Tito Schipa
GIORGIO GERMONT	John Charles Thomas (debut)
FLORA BERVOIX	Elda Vettori
GASTONE	Giordano Paltrinieri
BARON DOUPHOL	Alfredo Gandolfi
MARQUIS D'OBIGNY	Millo Picco
DOCTOR GRENVIL	Paolo Ananian
ANNINA	Philine Falco

CONDUCTOR	Tullio Serafin
STAGE DIRECTOR	Armando Agnini

DECEMBER 16, 1935

VIOLETTA	Lucrezia Bori
ALFREDO	Richard Crooks
GIORGIO GERMONT	Lawrence Tibbett
FLORA BERVOIX	Thelma Votipka (debut)
GASTONE	Angelo Bada
BARON DOUPHOL	Alfredo Gandolfi
MARQUIS D'OBIGNY	George Cehanovsky
DOCTOR GRENVIL	James Wolfe
ANNINA	Pearl Besuner

CONDUCTOR	Ettore Panizza
STAGE DIRECTOR	Désiré Defrère

MAY 30, 1936

VIOLETTA	Edith Mason
ALFREDO	Armand Tokatyan
GIORGIO GERMONT	Carlo Morelli
FLORA BERVOIX	Charlotte Symons
GASTONE	Lodovico Oliviero
BARON DOUPHOL	Norman Cordon
MARQUIS D'OBIGNY	George Cehanovsky
DOCTOR GRENVIL	Wilfred Engelman
ANNINA	Jarna Paull

CONDUCTOR   *Gennaro Papi*
STAGE DIRECTOR *Désiré Defrère*

MARCH 6, 1937 (MATINEE)

VIOLETTA	*Bidù Sayão*
ALFREDO	*Charles Kullman*
GIORGIO GERMONT	*John Brownlee*
FLORA BERVOIX	*Thelma Votipka*
GASTONE	*Angelo Bada*
BARON DOUPHOL	*Wilfred Engelman*
MARQUIS D'OBIGNY	*George Cehanovsky*
DOCTOR GRENVIL	*Norman Cordon*
ANNINA	*Lucielle Browning*

CONDUCTOR   *Ettore Panizza*
STAGE DIRECTOR *Désiré Defrère*

FEBRUARY 7, 1940

VIOLETTA	*Jarmila Novotna*
ALFREDO	*Charles Kullman*
GIORGIO GERMONT	*Giuseppe de Luca*
FLORA BERVOIX	*Thelma Votipka*
GASTONE	*Alessio De Paolis*
BARON DOUPHOL	*Wilfred Engelman*
MARQUIS D'OBIGNY	*George Cehanovsky*
DOCTOR GRENVIL	*Louis D'Angelo*
ANNINA	*Lucielle Browning*

CONDUCTOR   *Ettore Panizza*
STAGE DIRECTOR *Désiré Defrère*

NOVEMBER 29, 1941 (MATINEE)

VIOLETTA	*Jarmila Novotna*
ALFREDO	*Jan Peerce (debut)*
GIORGIO GERMONT	*Lawrence Tibbett*
FLORA BERVOIX	*Thelma Votipka*
GASTONE	*Alessio De Paolis*
BARON DOUPHOL	*Arthur Kent*
MARQUIS D'OBIGNY	*George Cehanovsky*
DOCTOR GRENVIL	*Louis D'Angelo*
ANNINA	*Helen Olheim*

CONDUCTOR   *Ettore Panizza*
STAGE DIRECTOR *Désiré Defrère*

JANUARY 14, 1942

VIOLETTA	Jarmila Novotna
ALFREDO	Charles Kullman
GIORGIO GERMONT	Leonard Warren
FLORA BERVOIX	Thelma Votipka
GASTONE	Alessio De Paolis
BARON DOUPHOL	Arthur Kent
MARQUIS D'OBIGNY	George Cehanovsky
DOCTOR GRENVIL	Louis D'Angelo
ANNINA	Helen Olheim

CONDUCTOR	Ettore Panizza
STAGE DIRECTOR	Désiré Defrère

DECEMBER 15, 1945

VIOLETTA	Licia Albanese
ALFREDO	Richard Tucker
GIORGIO GERMONT	Robert Merrill (debut)
FLORA BERVOIX	Thelma Votipka
GASTONE	Alessio De Paolis
BARON DOUPHOL	George Cehanovsky
MARQUIS D'OBIGNY	John Baker
DOCTOR GRENVIL	Louis D'Angelo
ANNINA	Thelma Altman

CONDUCTOR	Cesare Sodero
STAGE DIRECTOR	Désiré Defrère

FEBRUARY 14, 1947 (MATINEE)

VIOLETTA	Dorothy Kirsten
ALFREDO	Ferruccio Tagliavini
GIORGIO GERMONT	Francesco Valentino
FLORA BERVOIX	Thelma Votipka
GASTONE	Alessio De Paolis
BARON DOUPHOL	George Cehanovsky
MARQUIS D'OBIGNY	John Baker
DOCTOR GRENVIL	Lorenzo Alvary
ANNINA	Thelma Altman

CONDUCTOR	Cesare Sodero
STAGE DIRECTOR	Désiré Defrère

JANUARY 22, 1949 (MATINEE)

VIOLETTA	Eleanor Steber
ALFREDO	Giuseppe Di Stefano

GIORGIO GERMONT	*Robert Merrill*
FLORA BERVOIX	*Thelma Votipka*
GASTONE	*Alessio De Paolis*
BARON DOUPHOL	*George Cehanovsky*
MARQUIS D'OBIGNY	*Lawrence Davidson*
DOCTOR GRENVIL	*Osie Hawkins*
ANNINA	*Thelma Altman*

CONDUCTOR   *Giuseppe Antonicelli*
STAGE DIRECTOR   *Désiré Defrère*

FEBRUARY 17, 1951

VIOLETTA	*Nadine Conner*
ALFREDO	*Richard Tucker*
GIORGIO GERMONT	*Leonard Warren*
FLORA BERVOIX	*Lucielle Browning*
GASTONE	*Alessio De Paolis*
BARON DOUPHOL	*George Cehanovsky*
MARQUIS D'OBIGNY	*Lawrence Davidson*
DOCTOR GRENVIL	*Osie Hawkins*
ANNINA	*Margaret Roggero*

CONDUCTOR   *Alberto Erede*
STAGE DIRECTOR   *Désiré Defrère*

FEBRUARY 21, 1957

VIOLETTA	*Renata Tebaldi*
ALFREDO	*Giuseppe Campora*
GIORGIO GERMONT	*Leonard Warren*
FLORA BERVOIX	*Helen Vanni*
GASTONE	*Charles Anthony*
BARON DOUPHOL	*Calvin March*
MARQUIS D'OBIGNY	*George Cehanovsky*
DOCTOR GRENVIL	*Clifford Harvuot*
ANNINA	*Emilia Cundari*
GIUSEPPE	*James McCracken*
COMMISSIONER	*Osie Hawkins*

CONDUCTOR   *Fausto Cleva*
STAGE DIRECTOR   *Tyrone Guthrie*

NOVEMBER 2, 1957

VIOLETTA	*Victoria de los Angeles*
ALFREDO	*Daniele Barioni*
GIORGIO GERMONT	*Leonard Warren*
FLORA BERVOIX	*Helen Vanni*

GASTONE	*Gabor Carelli*
BARON DOUPHOL	*Calvin Marsh*
MARQUIS D'OBIGNY	*George Cehanovsky*
DOCTOR GRENVIL	*Clifford Harvuot*
ANNINA	*Mildred Allen*
GIUSEPPE	*Robert Nagy (debut)*
A GARDENER	*Osie Hawkins*

CONDUCTOR	*Fausto Cleva*
PRODUCTION BY	*Tyrone Guthrie*
STAGE DIRECTOR	*Hans Busch*

NOVEMBER 20, 1957

VIOLETTA	*Antonietta Stella*
ALFREDO	*Daniele Barioni*
GIORGIO GERMONT	*Robert Merrill*
FLORA BERVOIX	*Helen Vanni*
GASTONE	*Gabor Carelli*
BARON DOUPHOL	*Calvin Marsh*
MARQUIS D'OBIGNY	*George Cehanovsky*
DOCTOR GRENVIL	*Louis Sgarro*
ANNINA	*Mildred Allen*
GIUSEPPE	*Robert Nagy*
A GARDENER	*Osie Hawkins*

CONDUCTOR	*Fausto Cleva*
PRODUCTION BY	*Tyrone Guthrie*
STAGE DIRECTOR	*Hans Busch*

FEBRUARY 6, 1958

VIOLETTA	*Maria Meneghini Callas*
ALFREDO	*Daniele Barioni*
GIORGIO GERMONT	*Mario Zanasi (debut)*
FLORA BERVOIX	*Helen Vanni*
GASTONE	*Charles Anthony*
BARON DOUPHOL	*Calvin Marsh*
MARQUIS D'OBIGNY	*George Cehanovsky*
DOCTOR GRENVIL	*Louis Sgarro*
ANNINA	*Mildred Allen*
GIUSEPPE	*Robert Nagy*
A GARDENER	*Osie Hawkins*

CONDUCTOR	*Fausto Cleva*
PRODUCTION BY	*Tyrone Guthrie*
STAGE DIRECTOR	*Hans Busch*

November 14, 1959 (Matinee)

VIOLETTA	*Anna Moffo (debut)*
ALFREDO	*Cesare Valletti*
GIORGIO GERMONT	*Cornell MacNeil*
FLORA BERVOIX	*Helen Vanni*
GASTONE	*Gabor Carelli*
BARON DOUPHOL	*Calvin Marsh*
MARQUIS D'OBIGNY	*George Cehanovsky*
DOCTOR GRENVIL	*Louis Sgarro*
ANNINA	*Teresa Stratas*
GIUSEPPE	*Lou Marcella*
A GARDENER	*John Trehy*

CONDUCTOR	*Nino Verchi*
PRODUCTION BY	*Tyrone Guthrie*
STAGE DIRECTOR	*Hans Busch*

February 10, 1962

VIOLETTA	*Gabriella Tucci*
ALFREDO	*Dino Formichini*
GIORGIO GERMONT	*Frank Guarrera*
FLORA BERVOIX	*Joan Wall*
GASTONE	*Gabor Carelli*
BARON DOUPHOL	*Calvin Marsh*
MARQUIS D'OBIGNY	*George Cehanovsky*
DOCTOR GRENVIL	*Louis Sgarro*
ANNINA	*Mary Ellen Pracht*
GIUSEPPE	*William Zakariasen*
A GARDENER	*Vladimir Christiakov*

CONDUCTOR	*Ignace Strasfogel*
PRODUCTION BY	*Tyrone Guthrie*
STAGE DIRECTOR	*Michael Manuel*

December 14, 1963

VIOLETTA	*Joan Sutherland*
ALFREDO	*Sándor Kónya*
GIORGIO GERMONT	*Mario Sereni*
FLORA BERVOIX	*Janis Martin*
GASTONE	*Gabor Carelli*
BARON DOUPHOL	*William Walker*
MARQUIS D'OBIGNY	*Russell Christopher (debut)*
DOCTOR GRENVIL	*Justino Díaz*
ANNINA	*Lynn Blair*
GIUSEPPE	*Lou Marcella*
A GARDENER	*Paul De Paola*

CONDUCTOR   *George Schick*
PRODUCTION BY *Tyrone Guthrie*
STAGE DIRECTOR *Patrick Tavernia*

MARCH 30, 1967

VIOLETTA	*Renata Scotto*
ALFREDO	*Barry Morell*
GIORGIO GERMONT	*Mario Sereni*
FLORA BERVOIX	*Marcia Baldwin*
GASTONE	*Charles Anthony*
BARON DOUPHOL	*Ron Bottcher*
MARQUIS D'OBIGNY	*Gene Boucher*
DOCTOR GRENVIL	*Louis Sgarro*
ANNINA	*Loretta Di Franco*
GIUSEPPE	*Lou Marcella*
A GARDENER	*Peter Sliker*

CONDUCTOR   *Jan Behr*
STAGE DIRECTOR *Alfred Lunt*

SEPTEMBER 18, 1967

VIOLETTA	*Montserrat Caballé*
ALFREDO	*Richard Tucker*
GIORGIO GERMONT	*Cornell MacNeil*
FLORA BERVOIX	*Nancy Williams*
GASTONE	*Charles Anthony*
BARON DOUPHOL	*Robert Goodloe*
MARQUIS D'OBIGNY	*Gene Boucher*
DOCTOR GRENVIL	*Louis Sgarro*
ANNINA	*Loretta Di Franco*
GIUSEPPE	*Lou Marcella*
A GARDENER	*Peter Sliker*

CONDUCTOR   *Fausto Cleva*
PRODUCTION BY *Alfred Lunt*
STAGE DIRECTOR *Bodo Igesz*

OCTOBER 13, 1967

VIOLETTA	*Pilar Lorengar*
ALFREDO	*Bruno Prevedi*
GIORGIO GERMONT	*Cornell MacNeil*
FLORA BERVOIX	*Nancy Williams*
GASTONE	*Charles Anthony*
BARON DOUPHOL	*Robert Goodloe*
MARQUIS D'OBIGNY	*Gene Boucher*
DOCTOR GRENVIL	*Louis Sgarro*

ANNINA	*Karan Armstrong*
GIUSEPPE	*Lou Marcella*
A GARDENER	*Peter Sliker*

CONDUCTOR	*Fausto Cleva*
PRODUCTION BY	*Alfred Lunt*
STAGE DIRECTOR	*Bodo Igesz*

SEPTEMBER 18, 1970

VIOLETTA	*Teresa Zylis-Gara*
ALFREDO	*Giacomo Aragall*
GIORGIO GERMONT	*Robert Merrill*
FLORA BERVOIX	*Frederica von Stade*
GASTONE	*Leo Goeke*
BARON DOUPHOL	*Robert Goodloe*
MARQUIS D'OBIGNY	*Gene Boucher*
DOCTOR GRENVIL	*Louis Sgarro*
ANNINA	*Carol Wilcox (debut)*
GIUSEPPE	*Luigi Marcella*
A GARDENER	*John Trehy*

CONDUCTOR	*Richard Bonynge*
PRODUCTION BY	*Alfred Lunt*
STAGE DIRECTOR	*Bodo Igesz*

OCTOBER 22, 1970

VIOLETTA	*Joan Sutherland*
ALFREDO	*Luciano Pavarotti*
GIORGIO GERMONT	*Sherrill Milnes*
FLORA BERVOIX	*Frederica von Stade*
GASTONE	*Leo Goeke*
BARON DOUPHOL	*Raymond Gibbs*
MARQUIS D'OBIGNY	*Gene Boucher*
DOCTOR GRENVIL	*Louis Sgarro*
ANNINA	*Loretta Di Franco*
GIUSEPPE	*Luigi Marcella*
A GARDENER	*John Trehy*

CONDUCTOR	*Richard Bonynge*
PRODUCTION BY	*Alfred Lunt*
STAGE DIRECTOR	*Bodo Igesz*

DECEMBER 5, 1970

VIOLETTA	*Joan Sutherland*
ALFREDO	*Placido Domingo*
GIORGIO GERMONT	*Mario Sereni*

FLORA BERVOIX	*Jean Kraft*
GASTONE	*Charles Anthony*
BARON DOUPHOL	*Robert Goodloe*
MARQUIS D'OBIGNY	*Richard Best*
DOCTOR GRENVIL	*Louis Sgarro*
ANNINA	*Loretta Di Franco*
GIUSEPPE	*Luigi Marcella*
A GARDENER	*John Trehy*

CONDUCTOR	*Richard Bonynge*
PRODUCTION BY	*Alfred Lunt*
STAGE DIRECTOR	*Bodo Igesz*

APRIL 23, 1975

VIOLETTA	*Adriana Maliponte*
ALFREDO	*José Carreras*
GIORGIO GERMONT	*Robert Merrill*
FLORA BERVOIX	*Cynthia Munzer*
GASTONE	*Douglas Ahlstedt*
BARON DOUPHOL	*Arthur Thompson*
MARQUIS D'OBIGNY	*Gene Boucher*
DOCTOR GRENVIL	*Edmond Karlsrud*
ANNINA	*Ann Florio*
GIUSEPPE	*Luigi Marcella*
A GARDENER	*Peter Sliker*

CONDUCTOR	*Peter Maag*
PRODUCTION BY	*Alfred Lunt*
STAGE DIRECTOR	*Fabrizio Melano*

JANUARY 13, 1976

VIOLETTA	*Beverly Sills*
ALFREDO	*Stuart Burrows*
GIORGIO GERMONT	*William Walker*
FLORA BERVOIX	*Cynthia Munzer*
GASTONE	*Charles Anthony*
BARON DOUPHOL	*Robert Goodloe*
MARQUIS D'OBIGNY	*Gene Boucher*
DOCTOR GRENVIL	*Edmund Karlsrud*
ANNINA	*Constance Webber*
GIUSEPPE	*Abram Morales*
A GARDENER	*Glen Bater*

CONDUCTOR	*Sarah Caldwell (debut)*
PRODUCTION BY	*Alfred Lunt*
STAGE DIRECTOR	*Fabrizio Melano*

MARCH 17, 1981

VIOLETTA	*Ileana Cotrubas*
ALFREDO	*Placido Domingo*
GIORGIO GERMONT	*Cornell MacNeil*
FLORA BERVOIX	*Ariel Bybee*
GASTONE	*Dana Talley*
BARON DOUPHOL	*John Darrenkamp*
MARQUIS D'OBIGNY	*Julien Robbins*
DOCTOR GRENVIL	*William Fleck*
ANNINA	*Geraldine Decker*
GIUSEPPE	*John Hanriot*
A MESSENGER	*Donald Peck*

CONDUCTOR	*James Levine*
STAGE DIRECTOR	*Colin Graham*

[EDITOR'S NOTE: The statistical data on *La Traviata* which follows was compiled from records kept in the Archives of the Metropolitan Opera. Included is a complete listing of the year of the first performance of every artist in the three principal roles, a complete listing of all conductors, and a complete listing of seasons, from the premiere in 1883 through the season of 1981–1982, in which *La Traviata* has been performed at the Met.]

VIOLETTA

Marcella Sembrich (1883); Lillian Nordica (1894); Frances Saville (1895); Nellie Melba (1896); Clementine DeVere (1897); Bessie Abott (1907); Geraldine Farrar (1908); Bernice di Pasquali (1909); Lydia Lipkowska (1909); Luisa Tetrazzini (1912); Frieda Hempel (1913); Amelita Galli-Curci (1921); Lucrezia Bori (1922); Queena Mario (1928); Rosa Ponselle (1931); Claudia Muzio (1934); Eide Norena (1935); Edith Mason (1936); Vina Bovy (1936); Bidù Sayão (1937); Helen Jepson (1938); Jarmila Novotna (1940); Licia Albanese (1942); Eleanor Steber (1945); Nadine Conner (1946); Dorothy Kirsten (1946); Florence Quartararo (1947); Delia Rigal (1950); Jean Fenn (1954); Renata Tebaldi (1957); Victoria de los Angeles (1957); Antonietta Stella (1957); Maria Callas (1958); Anna Moffo (1959); Mary Curtis Verna (1960); Gabriella Tucci (1962); Laurel Hurley (1962); Frances Yeend (1962); Dorothy Coulter (1962); Joan Sutherland (1963); Mary Costa (1964); Virginia Zeani (1966); Phyllis Curtin (1966); Renata Scotto (1967); Montserrat Caballé (1967); Pilar Lorengar (1967); Jeannette Pilou (1967); Colette Boky (1969); Maralin Niska (1970); Clarice Carson (1970); Lillian Sukis (1970); Teresa Zylis-Gara (1970); Gilda Cruz-Romo (1973); Adriana Maliponte (1973); Beverly Sills (1976); Rita Shane (1976); Elena Mauti Nunziata (1977); Maria Chiara (1977); Eugenia Moldoveanu (1978); Mariana Niculescu (1978); Ileana Cotrubas (1981); Catherine Malfitano (1981)

ALFREDO

Victor Capoul (1883); Fernando de Lucia (1894); Giuseppe Russitano (1894); Giuseppe Cremonini (1895); Thomas Salignac (1897); Andreas Dippel (1901); Emilio de Marchi (1902); Carlo Dani (1902); Enrico Caruso (1903); Alessandro Bonci (1908); John McCormack (1910); Dimitri Smirnoff

(1911); Umberto Macnez (1913); Italo Cristalli (1914); Luca Botta (1914); Giacomo Damacco (1915); Fernando Carpi (1916); Giulio Crimi (1918); Charles Hackett (1919); Beniamino Gigli (1921); Giacomo Lauri-Volpi (1923); Mario Chamlee (1923); Armand Tokatyan (1926); Frederick Jagel (1929); Alfio Tedesco (1931); Tito Schipa (1932); Richard Crooks (1934); Nino Martini (1934); Charles Kullman (1936); Bruno Landi (1938); Jan Peerce (1941); James Melton (1942); Richard Tucker (1945); Ferruccio Tagliavini (1947); Giuseppe Di Stefano (1949); Eugene Conley (1950); Giacinto Prandelli (1951); Thomas Hayward (1955); Giuseppe Campora (1957); Gianni Poggi (1957); Daniele Barioni (1957); Giulio Gari (1958); Flaviano Labò (1958); Cesare Valletti (1958); Barry Morell (1958); Eugenio Fernandi (1959); Nicolai Gedda (1960); Dino Formichini (1961); George Shirley (1961); Charles Anthony (1962); Gabor Carelli (1962); John Alexander (1963); Sándor Kónya (1963); Bruno Prevedi (1966); Luigi Alva (1967); Enrico Di Giuseppe (1969); Carlo Bergonzi (1970); Octaviano Naghiu (1970); Ion Buzea (1970); Giacomo Aragall (1970); Luciano Pavarotti (1970); Alfredo Kraus (1970); Placido Domingo (1970); Franco Bonisolli (1972); Leo Goeke (1973); José Carreras (1975); William Lewis (1975); Stuart Burrows (1976); Raymond Gibbs (1976); Misha Raitzin (1976); Luis Lima (1977); Peter Dvorsky (1977); Giuliano Ciannella (1979); Dano Raffanti (1981); David Rendall (1981); Miguel Cortez (1981)

GERMONT

Giuseppe Del Puente (1883); Eugène Dufriche (1894); Mario Ancona (1895); Giuseppe Campanari (1898); Maurice Declery (1902); Antonio Scotti (1902); Taurino Parvis (1905); Riccardo Stracciari (1906); Pasquale Amato (1908); John Forsell (1909); Carlo Galeffi (1910); Giovanni Polese (1912); Giuseppe de Luca (1915); Giuseppe Danise (1921); Millo Picco (1923); Mario Basiola (1927); Lawrence Tibbett (1930); Richard Bonelli (1932); John Charles Thomas (1934); Carlo Morelli (1936); Carlo Tagliabue (1937); John Brownlee (1937); Leonard Warren (1942); Francesco Valentino (1944); Robert Merrill (1945); Giuseppe Valdengo (1948); Enzo Mascherini (1949); Frank Guarrera (1950); Paolo Silveri (1950); Renato Capecchi (1951); Ettore Bastianini (1953); Mario Sereni (1957); Mario Zanasi (1958); Cornell MacNeil (1959); Piero Cappuccilli (1960); Calvin Marsh (1962); Roald Reitan (1962); Vladimir Ruzdak (1963); Anselmo Colzani (1963); Igor Gorin (1964); Sherrill Milnes (1967); William Walker (1969); Dominic Cossa (1970); Russell Christopher (1970); Robert Goodloe (1970); Louis Quilico (1973); Matteo Manuguerra (1975); Ingvar Wixell (1976); Richard Fredericks (1976); Yuri Mazurok (1978); Brent Ellis (1981); Renato Bruson (1981)

CONDUCTOR

Augusto Vianesi (1883); Enrico Bevignani (1894); Luigi Mancinelli (1900); Philippe Flon (1901); Armando Seppilli (1902); Arturo Vigna (1903); Gustav Hinrichs (1904); Rodolfo Ferrari (1908); Francesco Spetrino (1908); Vittorio Podesti (1909); Giuseppe Sturani (1912); Giorgio Polacco (1914); Gaetano Bavagnoli (1915); Gennaro Papi (1916); Roberto Moranzoni (1917); Giuseppe Bamboschek (1922); Tullio Serafin (1925); Vincenzo Bellezza (1929); Ettore Panizza (1935); Pietro Cimara (1939); Cesare Sodero (1942); Giuseppe Antonicelli (1947); Jonel Perlea (1949); Alberto Erede (1950); Fausto Cleva (1951); Kurt Adler (1959); Nino Verchi (1959); Georges Prêtre (1960); Ignace Strasfogel (1961); Jan Behr (1962); Victor Trucco (1962); Nello Santi (1962); George Schick (1963); Francesco Molinari-Pradelli (1970); Richard Bonynge (1970); Martin Rich (1970); Peter Maag (1973); James Levine (1975); Walter Taussig (1975); Sarah Caldwell (1976); Richard Woitach (1977); James Conlon (1978); Thomas Fulton (1981); Nicola Rescigno (1981)

Performances by Season

1883–84 (4); 93–94 (1); 95–96 (4); 96–97 (3); 97–98 (1); 98–99 (3); 99–1900 (2); 1900–01 (1); 02–03 (5); 03–04 (3); 04–05 (4); 05–06 (2); 06–07 (3); 07–08 (6); 08–09 (6); 09–10 (3); 10–11 (3); 11–12 (2); 12–13 (3); 13–14 (5); 14–15 (6); 15–16 (2); 16–17 (2); 17–18 (3); 18–19 (3); 21–22 (3); 22–23 (7); 23–24 (6); 24–25 (4); 25–26 (6); 26–27 (4); 27–28 (4); 28–29 (6); 29–30 (6); 30–31 (5); 31–32 (5); 32–33 (5); 33–34 (5); 34–35 (4); 35–36 (4); 36–37 (5); 37–38 (5); 38–39 (2); 39–40 (6); 41–42 (5); 42–43 (7); 43–44 (6); 44–45 (6); 45–46 (6); 46–47 (9); 47–48 (7); 48–49 (7); 49–50 (6); 50–51 (14); 51–52 (10); 52–53 (4); 53–54 (9); 54–55 (7); 56–57 (9); 57–58 (10); 58–59 (7); 59–60 (9); 61–62 (16); 62–63 (10); 63–64 (10); 66–67 (20); 67–68 (16); 69–70 (14); 70–71 (12); 71–72 (4); 72–73 (8); 73–74 (10); 75–76 (14); 77–78 (13); 80–81 (9); 81–82 (15) — 482 performances in 76 seasons.

SELECTED DISCOGRAPHY

[EDITOR'S NOTE: * indicates recordings not currently available; (I) indicates recordings available as imports from Europe.]

COMPLETE RECORDINGS

[Most recordings make the conventional cuts mentioned in the text above; the Pritchard, Muti, Ceccato, and Prêtre recordings are absolutely complete, and the Kleiber and Bonynge sets restore most of the usual omissions.]

Lorenzo Molajoli, cond.; La Scala Chorus and Orchestra (1928)
    Mercedes Capsir (Violetta), Lionello Cecil (Alfredo), Carlo Galeffi (Germont)
    EMI/Italy 3C-165-18029/30 (I)
Carlo Sabajno, cond.; La Scala Chorus and Orchestra (1930)
    Anna Rosza (Violetta), Alessandro Ziliani (Alfredo), Luigi Borgonovo (Germont)
    RCA Camden CAL-287/289*
Arturo Toscanini, cond.; chorus and NBC Symphony Orchestra (1946)
    Licia Albanese (Violetta), Jan Peerce (Alfredo), Robert Merrill (Germont)
    RCA Victor LM-6003
Vincenzo Bellezza, cond.; Rome Opera House Chorus and Orchestra (1946)
    Adriana Guerrini (Violetta), Luigi Infantino (Alfredo), Paolo Silveri (Germont)
    EMI/Italy 3C-153-17079/80 (I)
Umberto Berrettoni, cond.; Rome Opera House Chorus and Orchestra (1952)
    Rosetta Noli (Violetta), Giuseppe Campora (Alfredo), Carlo Tagliabue (Germont)
    Remington R-199-77*
Luigi Ricci, cond.; Rome Opera House Chorus and Orchestra (1952)
    Frances Schimenti (Violetta), Arrigo Pola (Alfredo), Walter Monachesi (Germont)
    Remington R-199-98*
Gabriele Santini, cond.; Radio Italiana (Torino) Chorus and Orchestra (1953)
    Maria Callas (Violetta), Francesco Albanese (Alfredo), Ugo Savarese (Germont)
    Turnabout THS-65047/8
Francesco Molinari-Pradelli, cond.; Chorus and Orchestra of the Accademia di Santa Cecilia, Rome (1954)
    Renata Tebaldi (Violetta), Gianni Poggi (Alfredo), Aldo Protti (Germont)
    Decca/England ECS-227/229 (I)
Tullio Serafin, cond.; La Scala Chorus and Orchestra (1955)
    Antonietta Stella (Violetta), Giuseppe Di Stefano (Alfredo), Tito Gobbi (Germont)
    EMI/Italy 3C-163-00972/3 (I)
Pierre Monteux, cond.; Rome Opera House Chorus & Orchestra (1956)
    Rosanna Carteri (Violetta), Cesare Valletti (Alfredo), Leonard Warren (Germont)
    RCA Victrola VIC-6004*

Franco Ghione, cond.; Chorus and Orchestra of the San Carlos Opera House, Lisbon (1958)
  Maria Callas (Violetta), Alfredo Kraus (Alfredo), Mario Sereni (Germont)
  Angel ZBX-3910
Tullio Serafin, cond.; Rome Opera House Chorus and Orchestra (1959)
  Victoria de los Angeles (Violetta), Carlo del Monte (Alfredo), Mario Sereni (Germont)
  Angel SCL-3623
  Highlights: Angel S-35822
Fernando Previtali, cond.; Rome Opera House Chorus and Orchestra (1960)
  Anna Moffo (Violetta), Richard Tucker (Alfredo), Robert Merrill (Germont)
  RCA Gold Seal AGL2-4144
  Highlights: RCA Red Seal LSC-2561
Antonino Votto, cond.; La Scala Chorus and Orchestra (1962)
  Renata Scotto (Violetta), Gianni Raimondi (Alfredo), Ettore Bastianini (Germont)
  Deutsche Grammophon 2726-049
John Pritchard, cond.; Florence May Festival Chorus and Orchestra (1962)
  Joan Sutherland (Violetta), Carlo Bergonzi (Alfredo), Robert Merrill (Germont)
  Decca/England SET-249/51 (I)
Georges Prêtre, cond.; RCA Italiana Chorus and Orchestra (1967)
  Montserrat Caballé (Violetta), Carlo Bergonzi (Alfredo), Sherrill Milnes (Germont)
  RCA Red Seal LSC-6180
Lorin Maazel, cond.; Chorus and Orchestra of the German Opera House, Berlin (1968)
  Pilar Lorengar (Violetta), Giacomo Aragall (Alfredo), Dietrich Fischer-Dieskau (Germont)
  London OSA-1279
Aldo Ceccato, cond.; John Alldis Choir, Royal Philharmonic Orchestra (1971)
  Beverly Sills (Violetta), Nicolai Gedda (Alfredo), Rolando Panerai (Germont)
  Angel SCLX-3780
  Highlights: Angel S-36925
Lamberto Gardelli, cond.; Berlin State Opera Chorus and Orchestra (1973)
  Mirella Freni (Violetta), Franco Bonisolli (Alfredo), Sesto Bruscantini (Germont)
  Acanta JB-21644 (I)
Carlos Kleiber, cond.; Bavarian State Opera Chorus and Orchestra (1976)
  Ileana Cotrubas (Violetta), Placido Domingo (Alfredo), Sherrill Milnes (Germont)
  Deutsche Grammophon 2707-103
  Highlights: Deutsche Grammophon 2531-170
Richard Bonynge, cond.; London Opera Chorus, National Philharmonic Orchestra (1979)
  Joan Sutherland (Violetta), Luciano Pavarotti (Alfredo), Matteo Manuguerra (Germont)
  London LDR-73002
  Highlights: London LDR-71062
Riccardo Muti, cond.; Ambrosian Opera Chorus, Philharmonia Orchestra (1980)
  Renata Scotto (Violetta), Alfredo Kraus (Alfredo), Renato Bruson (Germont)
  Angel DSX-3920

(*sung in English*) Charles Mackerras, cond.; English National Opera Chorus and
    Orchestra (1980)
    Valerie Masterson (Violetta), John Brecknock (Alfredo), Christian du Plessis
    (Germont)
    EMI/HMV SLS-5216 (I)
James Levine, cond.; Metropolitan Opera Chorus and Orchestra (film sound
    track, 1982)
    Teresa Stratas (Violetta), Placido Domingo (Alfredo), Cornell MacNeil (Ger-
    mont)
    Electra 60267

Highlights

(Brindisi; Un dì felice; Ah, fors'è lui . . . Sempre libera; Madamigella Valery
    . . . Dite alla giovine . . . Imponete; Addio del passato) Unidentified conduc-
    tor; La Scala Chorus and orchestra (192-?)
    Gilda dalla Rizza (Violetta), Giovanni Manuritta (Alfredo), Giulio Fregosi
    (Germont)
    EMI/Italy MOBQ-9008 *
(Brindisi; Un dì felice; Ah, fors'è lui . . . Sempre libera; De' miei bollenti spiriti;
    Dite alla giovine . . . Imponete; Di provenza il mar; Addio del passato; Parigi,
    o cara) Frieder Weissmann, Victor Trucco, cond.; RCA Victor Chorus and
    Orchestra (1945/50)
    Licia Albanese (Violetta), Jan Peerce (Alfredo), Robert Merrill (Germont)
    RCA Victor LM-1115 *

Individual Excerpts

Act I: Prelude

Fausto Cleva, Metropolitan Opera Orchestra (1953)	Columbia ML-4886 *
Victor de Sabata, Santa Cecilia Orchestra (1947)	EMI/HMV XLP-30118 *
Carlo Maria Giulini, Philharmonia Orchestra (196-?)	Seraphim S-60138
Herbert von Karajan, Berlin Philharmonic Orchestra (1975)	Deutsche Grammophon 2707-090; 2531-145
Tullio Serafin, Royal Philharmonic Orchestra (1959)	EMI/Germany 2C-037-00867 (I)
Arturo Toscanini, Philharmonic-Symphony Orchestra of New York (1929)	RCA Red Seal CRM1-2494
Arturo Toscanini, NBC Symphony Orchestra (1941)	RCA Victrola VIC-1248
Arturo Toscanini, La Scala Orchestra (1951)	Victor/Brazil 886-5000 * (78 rpm)

Act I: Brindisi (Libiamo, libiamo ne' lieti calici: Violetta, Alfredo, chorus)

Mirella Freni, Luciano Pavarotti (197-?)	London JL-41009
Nina Garelli, Tito Schipa (1913)	Rubini GV-29 (I)

Maria Gentile, Alessandro Granda   OASI-601
  (192-?)
Alma Gluck, Enrico Caruso   Olympus ORL-312*
  (1914)
Joan Sutherland, Luciano   London OS-26449
  Pavarotti (1976)

ACT I: Violetta-Alfredo duet (Un dì felice)
Maria Caniglia, Beniamino Gigli   EMI/Italy 3C-153-03480/6 (I)
  (1939)
Fernando de Lucia (tenor solo   Rubini RS-305 (I)
  only) (1904)
Amelita Galli-Curci, Tito Schipa   Lebendige Vergangenheit LV-185
  (1928)   (I)
Nina Garelli, Tito Schipa (1913)   Rubini GV-29 (I)
Giannina Russ, Elvino Ventura   Heritage XIG-8017*
  (1903)
Joan Sutherland, Luciano   London OS-26449
  Pavarotti (1976)

ACT I: Violetta's scene (È strano! . . . Ah, fors'è lui . . . Follie! . . . Sempre libera)
Maria Barrientos (1916)   Rubini GV-515 (I)
Erna Berger (1948)   EMI/Electrola 2C-137-46104/5 (I)
Lucrezia Bori (1928)   Lebendige Vergangenheit LV-298
                                          (I)
Margherita Carosio (1951)   HMV DB-21306* (78 rpm)
Mirella Freni (196–?)   Angel S-37446
Amelita Galli-Curci (1919)   Rubini GV-578 (I)
Hilde Gueden (1952)   London LD-9165*
Dorothy Kirsten (1952)   Columbia ML-4730*
Lilli Lehmann (1906)   Court Opera Classics CO-384/5
                                          (I)
Lilli Lehmann (1907)   Court Opera Classics CO-384/5
                                          (I)
Nellie Melba (1904)   EMI/HMV RLS-719*
Nellie Melba (1907)   RCA/Australia VRL5-0365 (I)
Nellie Melba (1910)   RCA/Australia VRL5-0365 (I)
Magda Olivero (1940)   Cetra LPC-2008 (I)
Graziella Pareto (1920)   Court Opera Classics CO-376 (I)
Lily Pons (1946)   Columbia D3M-34294
Leontyne Price (1971)   RCA Red Seal LSC-3218*
Sylvia Sass (1978)   London OS-26609*
Bidù Sayão (1942)   Odyssey 32-16-0377
Renata Scotto (1958)   EMI/HMV ASD-4022 (I)
Marcella Sembrich (1904)   Sunday Opera MSC-1 (I)
Marcella Sembrich (1906)   Olympus ORL-215*
Marcella Sembrich (1906)   IRCC L-7037*
Eleanor Steber (1950)   Odyssey Y-31149*
Joan Sutherland (1960)   London OSA-1214
Luisa Tetrazzini (1908)   Pearl GEMM-220/7 (I)
Luisa Tetrazzini (1911, London)   Pearl GEMM-220/7 (I)

Luisa Tetrazzini (1911, N. Y.)   Pearl GEMM-220/7 (I)
(Ah, fors'è lui only)
Sigrid Arnoldson (1906)   Court Opera Classics CO-401 (I)
Gemma Bellincioni (1903)   Rubini GV-568 (I)
Gemma Bellincioni (1904/5)   Rubini GV-568 (I)
Toti dal Monte (1933)   EMI/Italy QALP-10089*
Helen Jepson (1940)   Victor 14184* (78 rpm)
Maria Kouznetsova (1916)   Rubini GV-3 (I)
Marcella Sembrich (1903)   Odyssey Y2-35232
(Sempre libera only)
Geraldine Farrar (1906)   Court Opera Classics CO-315 (I)
Maria Galvany (1908)   Belcantodisc BC-208*
Frieda Hempel (1911)   EMI/HMV COLH-135*
Nellie Melba (1904)   EMI/HMV RLS-719*

ACT II: Alfredo's aria (De' miei bollenti spiriti)
Carlo Bergonzi (1974)   Phillips 6747-193*
Alessandro Bonci (1906)   Rubini RDA-002 (I)
Dino Borgioli (1924)   Rubini GV-538 (I)
Roberto d'Alessio (192–?)   Club 99 CL-99-116
Mario del Monaco (1950)   London LL-1244*
Fernando de Lucia (1906)   Rubini RS-305 (I)
Fernando de Lucia (1916?)   Rubini GV-502 (I)
Giuseppe Di Stefano (1947)   EMI/HMV RLS-756 (I)
Placido Domingo (1972)   RCA Red Seal CRL2-4199
Beniamino Gigli (1928)   Pearl GEMM-146 (I)
Aristodemo Giorgini (1908)   EMI/Electrola C-049-03005 (I)
Robert Ilosfalvy (196–?)   EMI/Electrola SME-81032 (I)
Giovanni Martinelli (1917)   OASI-596
John McCormack (1910)   Pearl GEMM-155/60; Court
                                          Opera Classics CO-382 (I)

Luciano Pavarotti (1976)   Cime/Ars Nova ANC-25001*
Aureliano Pertile (192–?)   Bongiovanni GB-1019 (I)
Tito Schipa (1924)   Scala 805*
Richard Tucker (1952)   Columbia ML-4750*
Giovanni Zenatello (1906)   Heritage XIG-8017*

ACT II: Violetta-Germont duet (Madamigella Valery? . . . Pura siccome un
angelo . . . Dite alla giovine . . . Imponete!)
Margherita Carosio, Gino Bechi   EMI/Italy QALP-5342*
(1949)
(Madamigella Valery? . . . Pura
siccome un angelo only)
Fernanda Chiesa, Riccardo   Court Opera Classics CO-375 (I)
Stracciari (1914)
Maria Moscisca, Mattia Battistini   Court Opera Classics CO-325 (I)
(1912)
Giannina Russ, Francesco Maria   Heritage XIG-8017*
Bonini (1906)
(Dite alla giovine . . . Imponete!
only)

Hedwig von Debicka, Umberto Urbano (192-?)	Club 99 CL-99-17
Amelita Galli-Curci, Giuseppe de Luca (1927)	Lebendige Vergangenheit LV-280 (I)
Frieda Hempel, Pasquale Amato (1914) (Dite all giovine *only*)	Belcantodisc BC-207*
Maria Galvany, Titta Ruffo (1907)	Court Opera Classics CO-321 (I)
Nellie Melba, John Brownlee (1926)	EMI/HMV RLS-719*
Graziella Pareto, Matteo Dragoni (1918)	Court Opera Classics CO-376 (I)
Anna Rozsa, Apollo Granforte (1930)	EMI/Italy QALP-5338*

Act II: Violetta's scene (Amami, Alfredo)

Claudia Muzio (1911)	OASI-526
Magda Olivero (1953)	Cetra LPO-2008 (I)
Renata Scotto (1954)	Cetra AT-0389* (78 rpm)

Act II: Germont's aria (Di Provenza il mar)

Pasquale Amato (1907)	Rubini GV-544 (I)
Pasquale Amato (1909)	Court Opera Classics CO-389 (I)
Mario Ancona (1907)	Discophilia KG-A-3 (I)
Mattia Battistini (1911)	Court Opera Classics CO-327 (I)
Giuseppe de Luca (1907)	Court Opera Classics CO-391 (I)
Giuseppe de Luca (1929)	Lebendige Vergangenheit LV-280 (I)
Dietrich Fischer-Dieskau (196-?)	Deutsche Grammophon SLPM-138700*
Cesare Formichi (1920)	Lebendige Vergangenheit LV-229 (I)
Tito Gobbi (1950)	EMI/HMV HLM-7018 (I)
Giovanni Inghilleri (1930)	Lebendige Vergangenheit LV-169 (I)
Yuri Mazurok (197-?)	Columbia M-33120*
Titta Ruffo (1906)	Court Opera Classics CO-321 (I)
Paolo Silveri (1948)	EMI/Italy 3C-053-03769 (I)
Riccardo Stracciari (1905)	Rubini GV-501 (I)
Riccardo Stracciari (1909)	Court Opera Classics CO-375 (I)
Carlo Tagliabue (1947)	Lebendige Vergangenheit LV-270 (I)
John Charles Thomas (193-?)	RCA Camden CAL-199*
Umberto Urbano (1925)	Lebendige Vergangenheit LV-35 (I)
Leonard Warren (1950)	RCA Victrola VIC-1595*
Robert Weede (1952)	Capitol P-8290*
Bernd Weikl (197-?)	Acanta DC-23327 (I)

Act II: Chorus of Gypsies (Noi siamo zingarelle); Chorus of Spanish Matadors (Di Madride siam mattadori)

Giulio Setti, cond.; Metropolitan   Victor 4103 * (78 rpm)
  Opera Chorus and Orchestra
  (192–?)

ACT II: Alfredo's denunciation (Ogni suo aver tal femmina)
  Aureliano Pertile (192–?)   Bongiovanni GB-1019 (I)
  Giovanni Zenatello (1906)   Heritage XIG-8017 *

ACT II: Finale (Alfredo, Alfredo, di questo core)
  Lilli Lehmann (Violetta's part   Court Opera Classics CO-384/5
    only) (1907)   (I)

ACT III: Prelude
  Fausto Cleva, Metropolitan Opera   Columbia ML-4886 *
    Orchestra (1953)
  Victor de Sabata, Santa Cecilia   EMI/HMV XLP-30118 *
    Orchestra (1947)
  Carlo Maria Giulini,   Seraphim 60138
    Philharmonia Orchestra (196–?)
  Herbert von Karajan,   Angel 35207 *
    Philharmonia Orchestra (1954)
  Herbert von Karajan,   EMI/Electrola C-037-00422 (I)
    Philharmonia Orchestra (1959)
  Herbert von Karajan, Berlin   Deutsche Grammophon 139-031
    Philharmonic Orchestra (1967)
  Tullio Serafin, Royal Philharmonic   EMI/Electrola 2C-037-00867 (I)
    Orchestra (1959)
  Arturo Toscanini, Philharmonic-   RCA Camden CAL-309 *
    Symphony Orchestra of New
    York (1929)
  Arturo Toscanini, NBC Symphony   RCA Victrola VIC-1248
    Orchestra (1941)
  Arturo Toscanini, La Scala   Victor/Brazil 886-5000 * (78 rpm)
    Orchestra (1951)

ACT III: Violetta's aria (Addio del passato)
  Sigrid Arnoldson   Court Opera Classics CO-401 (I)
  Lucrezia Bori (1914)   Rococo 5321 *
  Margherita Carosio (1947)   EMI/Italy QALP-5342 *
  Nadine Conner (194–?)   Columbia 73072-D * (78 rpm)
  Amelita Galli-Curci (1920)   RCA Camden CAL-410 *
  Dorothy Kirsten (1952)   Columbia ML-4730 *
  Selma Kurz (1908)   Pearl GEMM-121/2 (I)
  Selma Kurz (1923)   Pearl GEMM-121/2 (I)
  Claudia Muzio (1935)   Seraphim 60111
  Augusta Oltrabella (193–?)   OASI-569
  Leontyne Price (1965)   RCA Victor LSC-2898
  Katia Ricciarelli (1977)   Cime/Ars Nova ANC-25003 *
  Delia Rigal (195–?)   Decca DL-4060 *
  Giannina Russ (1908)   Heritage XIG-8017 *
  Elisabeth Schwarzkopf (1950)   Angel ZX-3915
  Renata Scotto (1953)   Cetra PE-205 * (78 rpm)

Renata Scotto (1974)	Columbia M-33516
Renata Tebaldi (1950)	Cetra LPO-2043 (I)
Luisa Tetrazzini (1913)	Pearl GEMM-220/7 (I)

ACT III: Violetta-Alfredo duet (Parigi, o cara . . . Gran Dio! morir si giovane)

Linda Cannetti, Giovanni Zenatello (1911) (Parigi, o cara *only*)	Rubini GV-27 (I)
Anna de Angelis, Fernando de Lucia (1916?)	Rubini GV-502 (I)
Lucrezia Bori, John McCormack (1914)	Pearl GEMM-155/60; EMI/HMV RLS-743; Court Opera Classics CO-382 (I)
Maria Caniglia, Beniamino Gigli (1939)	EMI/Italy 3C-153-03480/6 (I)
Mirella Freni, Luciano Pavarotti (197–?)	London JL-41009
Amelita Galli-Curci, Tito Schipa (1928)	Lebendige Vergangenheit LV-219 (I)
Josefina Huguet, Fernando de Lucia (1906)	Rubini RS-305 (I)
Joan Sutherland, Luciano Pavarotti (1976)	London OS-26449
Pia Tassinari, Ferruccio Tagliavini (194–?)	Everest 3275 *

Notes on the Contributors

MARY McCARTHY is one of America's most distinguished writers. She is the author of numerous novels, nonfiction books, and essays. Among her most heralded works are *Memories of a Catholic Girlhood, The Groves of Academe, A Charmed Life, The Stones of Florence, Venice Observed, The Group, The Company She Keeps, Birds of America, Hanoi, Vietnam* and *Cannibals and Missionaries.*

GARY SCHMIDGALL, currently teaching at the University of Pennsylvania, is the author of *Literature as Opera* (Oxford University Press) and *Shakespeare and the Courtly Aesthetic* (University of California Press). He has for several years served as correspondent and contributor for *Opera Canada, Opera News,* and other opera magazines.

DAVID HAMILTON, music critic of *The Nation,* is a frequent contributor to musical publications, including *High Fidelity, Opera News, Musical Newsletter,* and *Perspectives of New Music.* Educated at Princeton and Harvard, he has taught at the Aspen Music School and the Juilliard School, and served as consultant to the New World Records bicentennial collection of American music. With Mrs. Dorle Soria, Mr. Hamilton is currently co-producer of The Metropolitan Opera Historic Broadcast Recordings. His book *The Listener's Guide to Great Instrumentalists* was published in 1982.

WILLIAM WEAVER, who was born in America and graduated from Princeton University, has lived most of his life in Italy. He is the Arts correspondent for the *Financial Times* in London and a regular contributor to numerous magazines. He has published *Seven Verdi Librettos, Verdi: A Documentary Study, Puccini, The Golden Century of Italian Opera,* and, in 1981, *Seven Puccini Librettos.* His translations have won National Book Awards on two occasions. Since 1965 he has lived on his farm in Tuscany.

In Violetta's suite of reception rooms, one opening into another, the atmosphere is unusually fevered and hectic, even for this milieu. This is a sign, surely, of her disease, like the doctor's presence at her side, an omen, as in the big mirror over the dainty marble fireplace on the left of the principal room, furnished with sofas, *faces-à-faces,* love seats, footstools, small tables and tabourets, rosewood and buhl cabinets full of Sèvres and Meissen. This is a room designed for moments of intimacy and suggestive of a boudoir. The mirror is Violetta's eternal, warning companion, like the mirror in the fairy tale ("Mirror, mirror, on the wall"), a necessity of her profession of kept woman, who must constantly know the truth about the fluctuating bank account constituted by her beauty. As the saying goes, her face is her fortune, or has been up to now, but it is also her misfortune.

Now, as her guests pour in from Flora's (significant that they should be late, indicating that to them one kept woman's house is the same as another's), Violetta promises an evening of riotous pleasure, to the point where Flora and her new "protector" wonder aloud whether the hostess is allowed to stay up late drinking champagne with so much abandon. "I want it," Violetta says with a little air of obstinacy, glancing at the doctor, who says nothing. "I have the habit. The life of pleasure agrees with me. It's the best medicine I know."

At that very moment, at the entry to the drawing room someone appears who will be her fatal drug: Alfredo. He has hardly been presented to her, as a great admirer, when Flora's marquis speaks to him, tapping him on the shoulder, and the two shake hands. He is a young fellow from the provinces, of middle-class background, and most of the others are titled playboys, but in this house equality reigns; he is greeted by his first name — "Alfredo!" "Marquis!" he replies. Meanwhile Violetta's baron has showed his face among the latecomers who had stayed gambling at Flora's. This seems to be Violetta's signal to summon a servant: "Is everything ready?" At the servant's nod, she calls the company to table as champagne still makes the rounds.

Violetta has put herself between Alfredo and his sponsor, the viscount, who tells her in an undertone about the new young man. Opposite are Flora, with her marquis on one side and Violetta's baron — Douphol — on the other. This is the key group; the rest find places where they can. "He's always thinking of you," Gaston says softly to the hostess. "You're not serious?" she answers, laughing. "When you were ill," Gaston persists, "he came running to ask after you every day." "Oh, stop it!" she decrees, but with a touch of archness. "I'm nothing to him." When she tries to ward off flattery, she is half-serious, half a trained coquette. "I'm not fooling," Gaston retorts, looking toward Alfredo, as if to draw him into the exchange. "Is it true, then?" No longer laughing, she turns to Alfredo. "But why? I don't understand." With her look fixed on him, he speaks to her, shyly, for the first time, to confirm what his friend is reporting. "Yes, it's true." He sighs. Sweetly and seriously, she thanks him for his concern. Then, across the table, to the baron: "But you, baron, how is it you didn't do likewise?" "I've known you only a year," says the baron, harshly. "But this one has known me only a few minutes," she points out.

Alfredo, with his seriousness and shyness, is getting on the baron's nerves. He does not like the change the young provincial is effecting in Violetta. Flora notices this, and, sotto voce, out of the corner of her mouth, chides the baron for his manners. *She* finds Alfredo charming, she adds.

Meanwhile, across the table, Gaston is chiding Alfredo, who is *his* responsibility. "Aren't you going to open your mouth?" he inquires. Flora's protector, the marquis, knows Alfredo well enough to put the burden on the hostess. "It's up to you, my lady," he tells Violetta, "to wake the young fellow up." "I'll be Hebe, your cupbearer, and pour you a glass," she announces to the still dumbstruck Alfredo. "And may you be immortal, like her," he answers, gallantly; he is schoolboy enough for a classical allusion to have loosened his tongue. Then the others join their voices to the wish, raising their glasses. This inspires the viscount to try to jolly up the moody baron. Can't he find some verses — a song — to suit the festive occasion? Without a word, the baron refuses. "All right, it's up to you, then," Gaston tells Alfredo. The others loudly second the suggestion. "A drinking song! Let's have a drinking song!" He, too, declines. "I'm not in the proper mood." "But aren't you a master of the art?" teases his friend Gaston. "Would it please *you* if I sang?" Alfredo turns to Violetta, abruptly altering the tone. "Yes," she tells him, simply. That is all he needs. "Yes? In that case I'll sing. I have the song here in my heart." He rises. "Everybody listen!" cries the marquis. "Attention for the singer," they chorus, the baron excepted.

Alfredo, on his feet, sings in praise of wine — a fairly standard paean. As he goes on, however, more and more carried away, he is singing directly to her, and words and music take on, as it were, an undertone of deeper meaning. Through wine, it is love he is hymning — the hotter kisses that lie at the bottom of the cup. "Love . . . love . . . love" — the word repeats itself like an incantation, as though he were compelled. At one moment, intoxicated by the song, he has pointed straight to Violetta, and now, as his young voice ceases, she, too, rises to her feet as if compelled also, and sings her own paean. Not to wine nor to love but simply to pleasure. Anything but pleasure is folly. The flower of love is born and dies in a day. Take it, joy in it. Seize the alluring occasion, revel in every pleasure, laugh and make merry till dawn.

It is her creed she is pronouncing, of feverish enjoyment, without distinction between sensuous delight and sensual pleasure, a creed, at bottom, of forgetfulness. She has addressed herself to the whole like-minded company and, when she has finished, all but Alfredo join in. Then, in quite another voice, she speaks to Alfredo: "Life is jubilation." Is it an apology for herself or an instruction to him? "Do you hear me, life is having fun," she seems to be telling him, ignoring everyone else. And he replies in the same tone, as though they were alone in a room: "For those who haven't yet loved." This is a mild reprimand or gentle correction. Each of these young people — for all her amorous history, she is not yet twenty-three — is playing teacher. Surrounded by her guests, by a veritable chorus of inane worldlings, they are all by themselves in a schoolroom, as it were, each reciting a lesson, solo. "Don't tell it to somebody who isn't in the know." (To somebody, she is admitting, who has never loved.) "It's my destiny," he says grandly, as if embracing the fate of loving. It is a kind of quarrel — their first falling-out, based on assertions and counter-assertions of principle. Then the mindless chorus breaks in, supporting her side of the argument ("Wine, jesting, and song, All the night long"), but without her desperate dependence on pleasure as oblivion.

At this appropriate moment a band strikes up in the next room. The guests show surprise. "Wouldn't a dance be nice now?" inquires Violetta, who of course has planned it. There is a cry of general delight ("What a lovely thought!"), and Violetta, once more the hostess, leads the way to the center door. "Let's go in, then."

She urges them ahead, to the ballroom. "Oh, my!" She has turned deathly white. "What's the matter?" the choir of guests tunes up. "Nothing, nothing," she replies. "What in the world *is* it?" other voices exclaim, some almost irritable. "Let's go," she repeats. "Oh, God!" She takes a step or two and is obliged to sit down. "Again!" they all cry out. "You're in pain," says Alfredo. "Heavens, what is it?" the others chime. "Just a trembling that comes over me." She makes a gesture toward the inner room, where the band is still playing a waltz. "Please! Do go in! I'll be with you soon." "As you wish," they tell her. And amazingly all of them, except the mute, motionless Alfredo, pass into the next room, drawn by the music like children by a Pied Piper of Hamelin. They leave the drawing room (as Violetta thinks) empty. She goes up to the great mirror over the fireplace — her truth-teller. "Oh, how pale I am." She looks at herself a long time; then a warning instinct makes her turn, and she becomes aware of Alfredo, behind her. "You here?"

He timidly approaches her. "Has your indisposition passed off?" "I'm better," she says curtly. The reserve of her tone tells him that she is trying to put him off, and almost angrily he bursts out. "This way of life will kill you." He moves a little closer so that he can study her still pallid face. "You must take care of your health." "And how am I to do that?" she teases, opposing her experienced lightness to his youthful solemnity. He ignores the levity, and his answer is like a vow. "If you were mine, I'd take *such* care of you. I'd be the faithful guardian of every one of your precious days."

Violetta is startled. "What are you saying? Am I in someone's charge, perhaps?" "No," he replies promptly, flaring up as though a fire in him had suddenly been fanned. "That is because no one in all this world loves you." "No one?" she rallies him. "No one but me." "Is that so?" she gives a trill of laughter, deciding to be amused by him. "Oh, yes, I'd forgotten that grand passion of yours." He is hurt. "You laugh. Is there a heart in your bosom?" "A heart? Well, yes, maybe. And what do you want with it?" He shakes his head sorrowfully. "Ah, if you had one, you couldn't jest."

Up to this point, the dialogue between them in the deserted room has been earnest preaching on his side and on hers a light, practiced fencing, a quasi-professional scoring of points. In other words, she has been firmly treating the interlude as a flirtation, disturbed only by the gravity of his insistent reference to her health, more